Gunkholing*
in the
Gulf Islands

*Gunkholing, the boatman's term for cruising in sheltered waters and anchoring every night, may have originated among the shallow estuaries of Chesapeake Bay, where the anchor usually sinks into soft mud, or 'gunk'—thus gunkholing for those who engage in this low-key, relaxed sort of cruising.

ISBN-0-931923-02-6

Gunkholing*
in the
Gulf Islands

by
Al Cummings
and
Jo Bailey-Cummings

**Photos by the authors.
Aerial photographs by the Canadian Government.
Cover photo by Doug Buxton.
Illustrations by Earl V. Dewald.**

Other books by these authors: *Gunkholing in the San Juans.*

Published by Nor'westing, Inc.
Edmonds, Washington

The delightful and hospitable

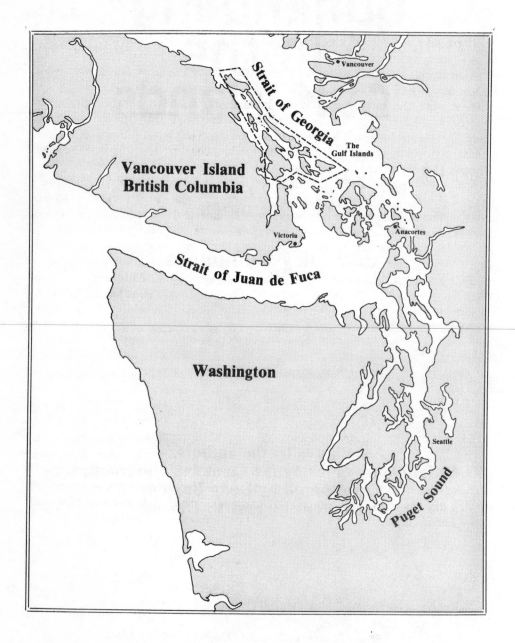

Gulf Islands archipelago

DEDICATION

The purpose of this book, aside from providing useful information to make your cruising more enjoyable, is to salute the early inhabitants of the Gulf Islands. And we want to call attention to the wonderful and exotic threads which make up the human tapestry of this beautiful area.

There were the early Anglo-Saxon immigrants, followed by their European counterparts. Later, the Hawaiians and the Japanese and the American Negroes. All of them came, looking for a place to set down and put down roots; a land where human muscle and sweat could create security in a country where freedom was not dependent on inheritance or religion.

But they found there a people with a civilization that we are only beginning to appreciate: the Salish and the Cowichans and the Samish, the Kulleets, the Penelakuts.

Most of the Indian bands were gentle and gregarious. They made room for the newcomers, they intermarried, they learned the white man's arts of agriculture.

Some of the bands were more independent, they did not want to live the White Man's life nor be governed by his prejudices. Some fought small, hopeless skirmishes. Some slowly and reluctantly came to terms with the newcomers.

But, to some degree, all of the Indians must have felt the pain of loss of their life-ways. Listen to this Salish shaman:

"Another death . . . but there is no one left to properly mourn the passage. I have done all I can, propping the body up to speed his journey to the spirit world. I wish I was able to provide a proper burial. So many of our people die by the white man's diseases and my medicine has been powerless. The old ways are dying and with them our people, too. Last year a headman died and his family was forbidden to potlatch by the white man's government. The winter spirit dances have also been outlawed. How can we survive if we cannot keep our ancestors' ways and customs? Ever since the white man arrived our lives have been changed. We became their trading part-ners and came to depend on their goods. We worked in the mines and were stricken by their diseases. Now they take over our land and forbid us the old ways. I do not know what is to become of our people." (from "Ghosts of Newcastle Island.")

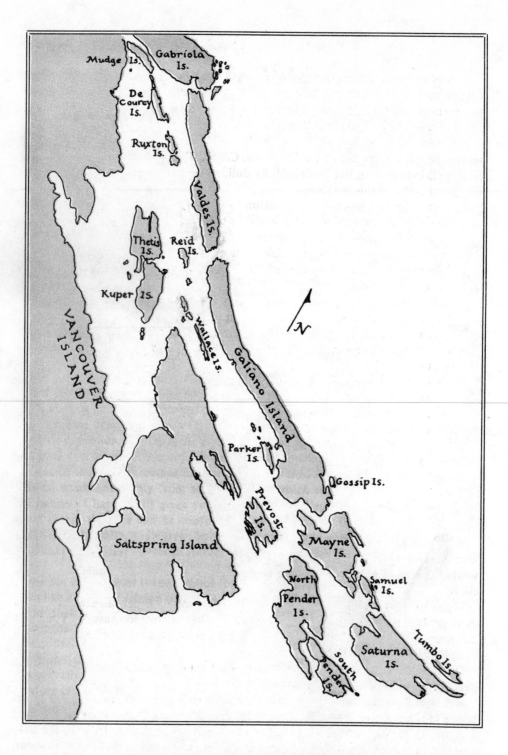

Gulf Islands archipelago

YE OLDE PREFACE

A preface in a non-fiction book (and this is non-fiction, we assure you) is something like a "Bread and Butter Letter." Polite folks who write for a living feel the need to acknowledge the people who offered help and encouragement in the form of a public "Thank You" message. And we try to be polite.

However, dear reader, we know that a list of the friends, acquaintances and service-people we met during our labours in Canada (kindly note the English spelling of labor!) cannot help but be dreadfully dull, so we will postpone that duty to the last paragraphs of this overture.

Up front, we want to call your attention to a few things which we think will make your not inconsiderable investment in this tome worth while.

To begin with, you will find at the end of Chapter Two, a section on how to convert your little rug-rats into happy cockpit-clams. We have discovered that there is at least a whimpering, if not crying, need for shared information on integrating the little cat-maulers into the boating life.

A confession might be salutary here. We are a bit disappointed with the skimpiness of good suggestions we had to offer on this subject. All we can say is that we canvassed our friends who cruise with tads on board, and we gathered up what few pearls of wisdom we found. Mostly, they said "How to keep kids amused on a boat? You tell us!"

We got some government-printed pamphlets of the "Kids and the Great Outdoors" type and they were filled with good suggestions for things for kids to do outdoors, but not too much on what they might do while cruising around on a boat. What snippets we found useful, we included.

So, on this subject, let us echo our friends who are beleaguered parents: you tell us! If you have any workable tips, get them to us somehow and we will include them in the next edition of this book—or maybe even get up a handy pamphlet on the subject.

On to a second matter: we want to turn you on to the use of kayaks as shore-boats.

We have decided that rowing a dinghy is about as much fun as pushing a wheelbarrow. Until someone invents a system for going forward in a rowboat—or a workable rear-view mirror—getting somewhere in a flat-hulled tender is a joyless chore.

When we first toyed with the idea of using kayaks, our pals all scoffed. "You can't get into a kayak from a cruising boat," "They tip over too easy," "You can't carry any gear in one," "You can't take passengers ashore in one." These are samples of the scoffs we got.

Only the last one makes sense. You can't take passengers back and forth from the beach—except small kids, of course.

But as for getting into a kayak from the deck of a ship—no sweat! You have to have a ladder, of course—and a sense of balance. They don't tip over any easier than a canoe, Tyler. We've been out in 8-foot waves and we've never rolled one. The only times we ever got a ducking from our kayaks were when we climbed out of them on the beach. That is tricky. We **have** sent hundreds of curious people out in our kayaks and not one has ever tipped over. A well-designed kayak is very roll-resistant.

As for carrying gear: you can load almost your own weight in supplies and not notice the drag. We've heard stories about Eskimo families who load up a one-hole kayak with dad, mom and two small kids and supplies for a week. Of course, mom and the kids can't be claustrophobic because they are stuffed into the bow and stern with the gear.

A great thing about kayaks is the fact that they tow so easily behind your boat at modest speeds. Two of them, filled with gear, knife through the water at the end of 20-foot painters with less than 5 pounds of drag each, believe it or don't.

And you can paddle a kayak for six hours with very little fatigue, once you've mastered the stroke. Try that in your Livingston, Stanley!

Now for credits and kudos: We've gone over this roll-call dozens of times, trying to be sure we don't forget someone who contributed to our work or comfort up in the Gulf Islands. It's not that we're worried we'll overlook some casual contributor, what we're concerned about is the possibility that we will forget to mention those who aren't included in the book and who helped us so much we got to thinking of them as part of the team.

You Canadian boaters will probably recognize quite a few of them. Yankee cruisers who love the Gulf Islands as much as we do may find familiar names.

These are the folks who spun stories, who drew diagrams of coves and reefs on the back of napkins, who called friends on other islands on our behalf, who helped us repair our boats when they acted up, who loaned us their cars so we could explore inland, who trusted us with their treasured books and pictures.

So a tip of the hat, first of all, to folks at the Canadian Consulate in Seattle: Harold Tomsett and "Skip" Young; Joyce Brookbank, of the Tourism Association of Vancouver Island; Tish Loiselle from Saltspring; Marj Green of Tourism B.C.; Tony and Alice Richards, of the Gulf Islands Driftwood; Lloyd Bingham of the Nanaimo Harbour Commission; Rocky Bevans of Aquapod Flotations in Ladysmith; Peter and Pat Lazenby of Telegraph Harbour Marina; Ann and Bill Phillips of Gabriola, who love the Malaspina Galleries; Joan and Bruce Cavens, our friends in Princess Harbour; the Cliffes of Degnen Bay; Edward Seymour, a Kulleet who is the unofficial custodian of the Shaman's Pool; Ann Williams of the Driftwood; Dave Lane of Malaspina College in Nanaimo; Steve and Susie Barendrick, who started us hunting for suggestions for parents of little ankle-biters; Judge Storey Birdseye, of Seattle, who turned us on to petroglyphs; Bill Bastendorf, who turned Pender Island into a cornucopia for us; and John Dempster, who is a magician at welding, on that same island.

Our heartfelt thanks to Peter and Barbara Kauput of the Easy Rider Corporation who launched us into kayaking.

And a deep curtsey and bow to Friday Harbor's Barbara Marrett, and world traveller, John Neal, who helped us with ideas and artistry in getting the book ready for the process cameras. They, in turn, would want us to salute the skilled graphics team: Cecily Murphy, Louise Dustrude, Marta Anderson, Lunnette Higdon-Hertel and Earl V. Dewald. They would also have many kind words for Smitty and Mary of King Typesetting, who coped with the hundreds of booboos we made.

One final bouquet should go to you who bought this book—and it should come from our legion of creditors!

A TABLE OF CONTENTS

A WORD WITH YOUR NAVIGATOR, PLEASE.

These are the charts you will find useful in your exploration of the Gulf Islands. They are all issued by the Canadian Hydrographic Service, Department of Fisheries and Oceans, Ottawa.

#3450 — "EAST POINT TO SAND HEADS." An overview of the Gulf Islands from Boundary Pass to Dodd Narrows.

#3310 — "THE GULF ISLANDS." Consists of four sheets covering most of the Gulf Island Area.

#3441 — "HARO STRAIT, BOUNDARY PASS, SATELLITE CHANNEL."

#3442 — "NORTH PENDER ISLAND TO THETIS ISLAND."

#3456 — "APPROACHES TO NANAIMO HARBOUR."

#3470 — "PLANS — SALTSPRING ISLAND." Has Ganges Harbour, Prevost Island, Sansum Narrows, Genoa Bay and Fulford Harbour.

#3473 — "ACTIVE PASS, PORLIER PASS & MONTAGUE HARBOUR."

#3475 — "PLANS IN STUART CHANNEL." Has Ladysmith Harbour, Chemainus Bay, Dodd Narrows and False Narrows, and Pirates Cove.

#3477 — "PLANS IN THE GULF ISLANDS." Has Telegraph Harbour, Preedy Harbour, Pender Canal, and Bedwell Harbour to Georgeson Passage.

About the Aerial Photographs—

These high-altitude shots are taken by the Canadian Government and are available to everyone from an office in Victoria. We have used them as "bird's eye" views. They will give you a good picture of the land masses, and in some cases, even submerged rocks and reefs. They are to be used for reference purposes only. Since many of the underwater hazards do not appear in the photos, they are unreliable for navigation purposes. The "North" indication is only approximate. We trust you will always use a chart when setting courses or making entrances into harbours.

1. . . . "And so to Bedwell:" The Pender Islands.

Having taken care of the preliminaries, we will now set out on our visit to the beautiful Gulf Islands. It is a journey, not of 'a thousand miles,' as the saying goes—it's more like 41, from the south end of Pender Island to Nanaimo. And the trip starts with one giant step (for Americans, anyhow) across the International Boundary in **Boundary Pass.** No matter how carefully you scan the waters of this body, you will not be able to spot the dotted line that separates the two countries on the chart. On either side, the water looks no different; Canadian sea gulls are just as irresponsible as Yankee ones. The symbolic American bald eagle has nests in Canadian trees (which seems unpatriotic). No, you can't tell just when you are in a 'foreign country.' The only ones who ever really know are Coastguardsmen and smugglers.

One thing you will discover is that this pass can be ornery on both sides. For example, if you venture out into it when the current is running high, in a slow boat, you may get the feeling you have somehow stumbled onto a moving saltwater sidewalk, travelling as much as 3.5 knots. In other words, on a flood tide you get to Tilly Point, the entrance to Bedwell Harbour, by aiming at the east shore of Moresby Island and making a big arc.

Tilly Point: Your first view of the Canadian Islands may convince you that all Canadians are wealthy. There are posh summer residences on the bluffs above this point on South Pender Island.

It was originally dubbed 'Bilk Point' by two pioneers, Arthur Spalding and Leonard Higgs. They told people they were 'green' and got 'bilked' into rushing out in a boat after dark to rescue someone who was not in any danger, merely showing a light. Later they crept back, hoping they had not been seen. How it finally got to be named 'Tilly' is not clear.

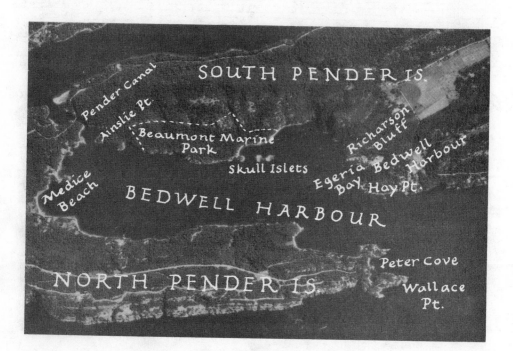

Hay Point is marked with a red-topped tower on a rock. It is a quick-flashing red light. The land behind it is a very small Indian Reserve. (It might be well at this point to acquaint you with the fact that what we call 'Indian Reservations' in the States are called 'Indian Reserves' in Canada.)

Just before you get to Hay Point you will see a small islet with a twisted tree. The islet looks as though it had been sliced from the headland with a giant meat cleaver.

Egeria Bay is the name of the body of water which houses the Bedwell Marina and the Customs dock. This is your first stop. And why are you heading for Bedwell? To go through Customs. The office in Bedwell is one of two convenient points of entry. The other is in Sidney, on Vancouver Island. If you choose that course, we will pick you up in this book on page 75, and take you up Sansum Narrows.

Canny skippers will tell you that you should check recent Canadian Customs regulations before pulling into the dock.

Bedwell Harbour. (Time for an 'aside' conversation as they say in Shakespeare. Note the 'u' in the title. That's Canadian. So in proper names, we will use the Canadian spelling. In text, we will revert to good old U.S. spelling. For example, the harbor we are discussing is Bedwell Harbour.) (Neat, eh?) This harbor was named, you are undoubtedly dying to know, after Edward Parker Bedwell, who served as Second Master aboard the British Survey vessel 'H.M.S. Plumper' in 1857.

In the first cove to the north after you enter the harbor, you see the distinctive red railings of a government wharf. That is the location of the Customs office. There is not a lot of space at the dock, 165 ft. (50 M.), and you can't tie up elsewhere before you clear, so you may have to hover offshore for a bit while waiting for your turn.

Bedwell Harbour Resort is right next to the Customs area. It is a rather elaborate complex, with newly-expanded marina facilities and a lot of moorage for transient

Egeria Bay offers a customs dock, marina and a resort.

boats. A breakwater extends out from the base of **Richardson Bluff.** The store carries groceries, ice, bait, gifts, books and fishing licenses. (Another Anglicism: it's always spelled 'licence' in Canada.

Other facilities at the resort include a waterfront pub, 'licenced premises' dining room, swimming pool, housekeeping cottages, a laundromat and showers. There is also a mailbox.

Beaumont Marine Park: Just northwest of the resort is this popular moorage; the first Provincial Marine Park you will encounter in the Gulf Islands. There are at least eight mooring buoys (no charge) off the park, which extends over 80 acres (34 hectares) along the shore and includes Skull Islet.

Skull Islet consists of a rock and a reef and a red-topped tower. It is a daymarker—no light.

Often during the summer the anchorage is so full that boats must overflow to near **Ainslie Point** or over into the northwest corner of the harbor.

Here you may first come to discover that some places in the Gulf Islands have their very own resident freaky winds. They are swirly and squirrely. This means that the hook should be set well, with enough scope to allow for swinging in all directions. (You will read this warning in many places in the chapters to come. Take our advice. Don't count on what you might see at the moment—or the official weather forecast!)

There are pleasant trails within the park, they lead to campsites and views of the bay. There are picnic tables along the shore trail. The beach at Beaumont has contiguous areas of sandstone and gravel, but the water seldom warms up enough for swimming. There is drinking water from a pump at the 11-campsite area.

For serious hikers, there is a sort-of trail to the top of Mount Norman, which at 890 feet (260 M.) is the highest spot on the Pender Islands. It's a steep climb, but the reward is a magnificent view, from the San Juans to Swartz Bay. To find the trail, go past the men's outhouse at the top of a stairway at the park's east beach. Then you go up a narrow ravine surrounded by arbutus trees. (In the San Juans, they are called 'madronas.') From there on, follow the orange survey tapes all the way to the top.

For history buffs: Mount Norman was named after William Henry Norman, who was the paymaster (and therefore a very important man) on the 'H.M.S. Ganges'. Sidenote: the mountain was named after him by the crew of the 'Plumper' which you have already met. The reason they honored him from the second boat was that he was the paymaster for the 'Plumper' also. Makes sense.

The waters adjacent to the park have been busy places for centuries. The first boaters were Salish Indians. They were followed by the 18th and 19th century explorers. This group was succeeded by rumrunners and wool-smugglers, hauling their illegal goods into the United States via the San Juans.

Beaumont Park land was donated by a B.C. philanthropist, Captain Ernest Godfrey Beaumont, in 1962. Adjoining lands were donated by the Crown Zellerbach logging company.

Now that you're prepared to do your doctoral dissertation on the Captain's park, let us proceed.

Bedwell Harbour, northwest corner: Drew Rock, which has about 7 feet (2.1 M.) of water over it at lower tides, is marked by kelp. There are several other rocks, also kelp-marked, between Drew Rock and the head of the harbor, a swampy spot called 'Medicine Beach'. About midway between Ainslie Point and Medicine Beach, there is a dock. Go up the ramp and you will find a thrift shop called the 'Nu-to-Yu' store. If you like browsing, you'll love it. It has raised thousands of dollars for the Pender Island Medical Centre, to which the folks point with pride.

At the top of the wharf, you will also see the P.J. General Store. It carries a full line of staple foods and other necessities. It is easily accessible to boaters.

Pender Canal: This is a 'parting of the ways' spot for two kinds of boaters. The narrow canal has a low bridge, 26 feet (8 M.) at high tide, which turns back most sailboats. Powerboats, even very large ones, can negotiate it.

"Low Bridge" on the Pender Canal.

It wasn't always 'North and South Pender,' of course. During the Nineteenth Century, the Penderites could walk from one end of the island to the other, crossing a low spit between the islands. Boaters, on the other hand, had to drag their boats across a few hundred yards of sand in order to avoid having to row all the way around the island. This resulted in one of the early splits in the Pender society—it was boaters vs. walkers. In 1903, the boaters won out and a channel was dug separating the two islands.

Old timers on the islands say that a predictable thing happened: a rivalry grew between the halves. To this day, the North Penderites consider the southerners as stodgy old hayseeds. The "Rebel" faction sneers at the Northerners as a bunch of subdividing parvenus.

And—as you see in the cruising directions, the canal is still creating schisms: between sailboaters and stinkpotters.

Going through this man-made canal can be a little tricky. If you have Strip Chart #3310, Sheet #3, it will come in handy. You can also use Plans Chart #3477. You will get a blow-up view, 1:12,000. You will see the symbol for a black buoy (actually, all of those markers have been replaced with green ones) to port, leaving Bedwell Harbour and a red buoy to starboard. (You are supposedly returning to Port Browning, 'red, right, returning,' remember.) If you study the chart carefully, you will notice that there is a rock that dries at 4 feet (1.3 M.) (average low water) close to the center of the cut. It indicates that the safest course is to hug the green buoy. But that has its drawbacks, too. See the rock that peeks out at 1 foot? A tad nerve-wracking, isn't it? Now to further complicate the matter, both of these markers are buoys which means that they are chained to the bottom and when the tide is low, they can move around quite a bit. You may ask yourself, "Why don't they just put in fixed markers there on the rocks?" A good question, one that island residents have long wondered about and complained about—to no avail.

One poor skipper, the owner of a beautifully restored, wooden, 33-foot power boat, the 'Bytown Lady', hit that submerged rock at low speed, capsized and sank. Fortunately, the crew escaped. The operator told our friend, who salvaged the boat, "But I was in the main channel!"

Our advice here is: put somebody on the bow, go on slow bell and keep to the right of center in the channel.

Poor old 'Bytown Lady!'

Standing on the edge of history.

The Pender Dig: Just before you pass under the bridge, you will see a sign announcing an archeological dig—'visitors welcome'. You can anchor your boat off **Mortimer Spit** in **Shark Cove** and dinghy back to visit. You can watch the archeology students excavating Indian middens which date back more than 6,000 years. (See: 'The Millennia Pit', page 30.)

This spit is a delightful spot to beachcomb and swim. It was named after John Mortimer, owner of a stone-yard in Victoria, who had quarried an especially hard sandstone at Browning Harbour in the isthmus in the late 1900's.

Port Browning: The next half-mile or so of shoreline between **Aldridge Point** and **Hamilton Beach** ... (they don't manufacture food-mixers there). It was named for Alexander Hamilton, who worked for John Mortimer. Not *our* Alexander Hamilton, you understand. (This is getting complicated!) *This* Alexander Hamilton was a quarry worker and he squatted a quarter-section of land in 1885, built a log cabin, dug a well, cleared a few acres to put in crops. Then, in 1888, he took time off from his job to travel back to Scotland and get his bride-to-be, Jeannie Leiper.

Port Browning Marina: We have tried, in this book, to be objective about the commercial establishments we report. But in some cases, we just flat out can't help but jettison our detachment. Like in the case of this marina. We love it. We felt 'at home' there. The owner, Lou Henshaw, is warm and outgoing. Although the floats are often apparently full during the summer, one of her friendly dock attendants can always manage to find space to squeeze in 'one more'. The pub is a favorite spot for

locals and visitors alike. The food is good and not expensive. There is often live music. Over the bar, you see the Indian word 'Sh-qu-ala' which means, in Salish, 'watering place'. You will also see a totem pole carved by a famous Indian carver, Simon Charlie, of the Cowichans.

It has a store, laundromat, showers, pool, tennis courts, scuba air and a playground for kids. It's about a half mile from the Driftwood Centre, which is a mini-shopping mall, where you will find the post office and liquor store, also a deli and restaurant. The hike is made more pleasant by the roadside beds of wild sweet peas.

There is a privately-owned marine railway in **Brackett Cove** adjacent to the marina. The cove is lined with homes. There is a reef that extends out quite a ways from the point at this cove. It is marked with a pole, on top of which is a cone, sort of a dunce's cap, you might say.

Farmers' Market

Island-grown fruits and vegetables are the offerings of the day at the famous Pender Islands' Farmers' Market each Saturday morning during the summer. Flowers, baked goods, eggs, craft items and just about anything else produced on the islands are for sale at the market.

Tables are set up and vendors arrive with their goods about 9 o'clock. As they arrange their items in the yard at the Driftwood Centre, the area is roped off so that prospective buyers can only watch eagerly and decide what they will want to purchase.

Just before l0 a.m., as a hundred or so islanders and visitors mill about, anxiously waiting to buy, one of the local suppliers is handed a giant triangle. At 10 a.m. exactly, he clangs the triangle, the ropes are dropped and the crowd rushes in. It's like a race. But there's lots of laughing and talking, no pushing or shoving. Within 10 minutes all but a handful of items are sold and the rest of the morning is spent comparing purchases and chatting. It's wonderful.

The Farmers' Market was started in 1978 by Joyce and Frank Jones with help from the Pender Island branch of the Farmer's Institute in Canada. It's a co-op dedicated to helping farmers, and a service to the community.

Vendors rent their spaces for $5 for the whole season, or about $1 a week.

Boaters particularly love the market as it's a wonderful opportunity to have garden fresh fruits and vegies and home-baked goods, and mingle with the islanders.

Port Browning Marina pool.

Port Browning Government Wharf has a haulout grid.

Port Browning Government Wharf: On the north shore, just beyond Brackett Cove, there is a dock with bright red rails and a float of about 300 feet (90 M.). It is listed in the official records as '50 M.' but a couple of new floats have just recently been installed. It is usually filled, but a newcomer can almost always raft up. On the west side of the float is a grid, one of a series of facilities originally intended for fishboat operators, but open to the general public.

There is good anchoring ground off the floats in 3 to 5 fathoms (6 - 10 M.) Many boats drop the hook at the head of the bay, also.

You will spot a fair number of crab-trap buoys as you leave Port Browning.

Razor Point: It's well-named. At low tide, you will see a long series of sharp-edged rocks trending out to a marker. Don't go inside the red 'U 56' buoy, or you might be on 'the razor's edge'. Behind the reef is a house and a private breakwater.

Say Again?

You may have noticed that the Coast Guard and many knowledgeable skippers use the phrase "Say again" on the air when they want to repeat information.

If you were a radioman in the Second World War, you will smile at this anachronism.

You were warned, with dire consequences involved, never, never to say 'repeat' in a functional radio communication. The reason was that the Artillery had taken dibs on that word. It was used by an observation post to order the firing of another salvo with the same pattern as the previous. You were told that, in the heat of battle, some gunnery sergeant might hear you say 'repeat' and fire a flock of shells on friendly forces.

The prohibition stuck, apparently. Here we are, 40 years later, afraid of uttering the fatal word in our peacetime exchanges on the VHF radio.

Brackett's Bell

In the wonderful book 'A Gulf Islands Patchwork,' there is a story about a thundering gong known as 'Brackett's Bell.'

The original Brackett home in Port Browning was built in 1896 by J.A. and Margaret Brackett. If you are fond of occasionally 'sleeping in' you can be glad you weren't living in the cove then.

"The gong consisted of an 'I-Beam' about three feet long and 18 inches high. It was hung on chains between two fir trees in the front yard at a height of about 25 feet. An eight-pound sledge was the striker. It was so rigged that a person standing on the ground could operate it by pulling on a long pole which was hinged to the hammer handle. The result was a not unmusical note which could be heard for some miles. Every day at noon, Mrs. Brackett struck 12 strokes, calling the menfolk of the valley from the fields or woods or bay to their respective lunches. Other signals consisting of a certain number of strokes called individual family members. There was also one signal calling to the Hamilton Family across the bay into shouted conversations."

Of course, on New Year's Eve, the bell welcomed in the new year.

Plumper Sound, Port Browning to Tilly Point: As we said, most powerboaters head northwest from Port Browning up to the middle and upper Gulf Islands. So, for the sake of completeness, let's check out the shore line of South Pender down to Boundary Pass and over to the entrance to Bedwell Harbour.

This three-mile stretch of shoreline does not have much to interest the passing boater, except for some choice scenery. There are no real anchorages until you come to the eastern extremity of the island.

Chart #3477, which is a large scale one, deserts you just before you reach the end of Plumper Sound. On #3441, you can see the tip of the island.

Teece Point: (It's not in the history books, it must have been named after a latter-day resident.) This is a pleasant park-like blunt headland which hosts a long trailing bed of kelp that apparently doesn't hide any rocks to worry you.

You may want to swing around the kelp in the passage between this point and Blunden Islet. There is plenty of water here.

Blunden Islet: Looks to be about 7 acres (3 hectares) with a few trees on the ridge facing Teece Point. There is no beach or shelf for landing a small boat. It was named after Edward Raynor Blunden in 1861. He was a 'master's assistant' (whatever that was?) on board the 'H.M.S. Hecate'. We doubt he was very much thrilled by the honor.

Just off the end of Blunden Islet, you will see some wavy lines on the chart in Boundary Pass. They signify tide rips—and they can be ornery. At an average current run, they made us spin the wheel of the 20-ton 'Roanoake'.

Camp Bay: There was a fishing camp there at one time. It would have been a fine place for one. There is a beach at the head which is split in half by a rocky reef, and a home in a cove. Along flanks of the entrance are steep bluffs. It has good depths for anchorage and would be ideal except in a southeast wind.

Higgs Point has some ugly dried rocks off shore.

Canned Cod Bay: We couldn't find anybody on the Penders who knew the origin of the name, but it's got to be an interesting story. It consists of three small coves with beaches and two reefs that divide them. There are houses adjacent to the beaches. It's a shallow bay and might make an interesting lunch-hook spot on a calm day.

Gowlland Point: John Thomas Gowlland got his name hooked onto a lot of real estate in British Columbia in the 1860's when he was 'second master' of the 'H.M.S. Plumper'. The point has a green-topped tower with a white flashing light and a solar panel. In front of this tower you will see a concrete monument or bench-mark, although the charts do not indicate it.

Incidentally, it beats us why they put this marker on a relatively unimportant spot when they could have used it nicely on Blunden Island to signal the entrance to Plumper Sound!

Drummond Bay has all sorts of barriers in front of it. There is a good beach for combing, though, all piled with drift logs.

Just east of Tilly Point is a small islet, which you can call 'Tilly Point Islet', for convenience sake. It is 17 feet (5 M.) high at low water and has some interesting wave-carved rocks.

Now, since we have back-tracked to Bedwell Harbour, let's leap-frog up to Razor Point and catch up with the stinkpotters who are headed up Plumper Sound.

Plumper Sound, Port Browning to Hope Bay: By now, you can guess at the reason for the name of this body of water. We think 'Plumper' is a goofy name for a royal survey ship! 'Plumper' sounds like a quote from an ad for roasting hotdogs. It was quite an imposing ship, apparently. It was one of the earliest 'auxiliary steam sloops' on the West Coast.

The eastern shoreline of North Pender Island is steep and hilly. It is capped by Mount Menzies which rises to 615 feet (186 M.). Just offshore from this peak is **Perry Rock**, which is at about 7 feet (2.1 M.) at low tides and shouldn't trouble you deeply. We couldn't see any kelp near it, incidentally.

The next peak is Bald Cone. (It's not totally 'bald.') After that, the hills taper down to about 100 feet at the shoreline and houses begin to reappear. They continue

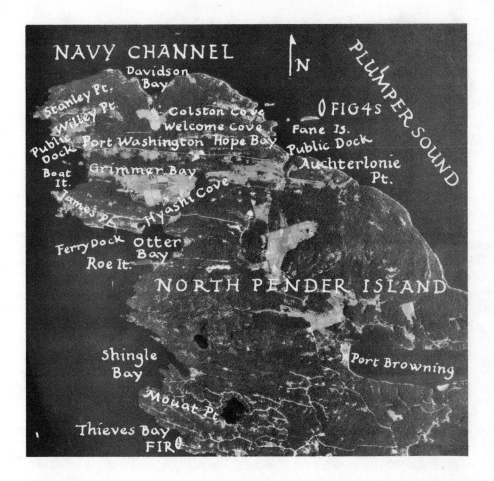

to **Auchterlonie Point** which fronts Hope Bay. James Auchterlonie was the first postmaster at Hope Bay and doubled as Justice of the Peace. He died in 1912.

Hope Bay: This is a tiny community in a tiny bay, almost hidden behind Fane Island. There is government wharf with 465 feet (141 M.) of moorage. There is a closed-down general store, a real estate office and several post-boxes and nothing much else at the landing.

But within walking distance up the hill is an art center, featuring local potters, sculptors and painters. Nearby are two bed-and-breakfast establishments: Corbett House on Corbett Road and Cliffside Bed and Breakfast off Clam Bay Road. The United Community Church is a bit up the road.

The wharf was built in 1901. The store was established in 1905 by R.S.W. Corbett and Son. It has been only since 1984 that the store closed its doors, and the beautiful old building with its stained glass doors stands empty. Nearby, a modern building houses a yoga center.

Fane Island: It's an intriguing spot. There is an elaborate series of walkways and ramps and a fine dock. On shore is a very attractive little house. At one time, there was a high wind-charger tower to provide electricity, but it's pretty dilapidated now.

Fane Island

We thought we could make out 'For Sale' signs on the property. It would make a neat summer home. On the eastern end of the island, you will find a navigation marker, a white tower with a green top. It has a flashing green light every 4 seconds. Don't be surprised if you don't see it on your charts. It is apparently a well-kept secret. When we were confused by its non-appearance on a recently-revised new chart, we called the Coast Guard on the radio. The man on duty told us he had never heard of it. When we persisted, he said he would check with other sources. About 15 minutes later he called back, somewhat abashed, and said that it had been installed in January, 1985, but the word hadn't gotten around.

More on this phantom (apparently) light. A Pender Island boater who plies those waters frequently asked the captain of a ferryboat which passed the point every day if he knew anything about it. The skipper said he had never noticed it!

Make a note of it on your chart!

Welcome Cove and **Colston Cove** on the north side of Hope Bay could provide temporary anchorage, but they are both exposed to southeast winds coming up Plumper Sound. The water is shallow, also.

Navy Channel, Hope Bay to Stanley Point: There isn't much to see along the Pender Island side of this channel, except for homes, trees and scenery. The currents run fairly strong in here and there is a lot of wash from large boats and ferries. It was the site of many pioneer picnics and clambakes.

Davidson Bay, locally called 'Clam Bay,' offers only marginal anchorage and is quite shoal.

Hope Bay Government Wharf.

Rutherford Hope

Rutherford lived as a bachelor in a tiny log cabin on the original Hope farms near the center of Pender Island. (There was only one Pender Island in those days.) His may have actually been the first house on the island. It was built in 1878. The log cabin was about 12 by 16 feet, its fir logs were chinked with clay and dry grass.

Hope was an important pioneer who owned much land and whose name ap-pears frequently in island history. For a time, he was assistant postmaster at the office in Hope Bay. There were no letter boxes back then and patrons stood in front of the little counter. As each item came out of the bag, the owner's name was called out and his mail was handed to him, just like the army's 'mail call.'

Hope married in 1895.

Now aren't you glad we turned you on to all that fascinating information?

Currents in Plumper Sound and Navy Channel

Currents in the Gulf Islands don't always do what you might expect. You might find it interesting to take a chart and follow some of these vagaries.

For instance, the tidal streams flood northwest and north through Swanson Channel and northwest through Plumper Sound. But a branch flows east into Navy Channel, meeting that flowing through Plumper Sound off Hope Bay, where tide rips are formed.

From this position, the combined stream flows north, through the narrow channels at either end of Samuel Island, into the Strait of Georgia. The ebb tidal stream is from 2 to 3 knots at the east end of Navy Channel; the maximum rate of the ebb tidal stream is from 2 to 3 knots off Croker Point; and from 1 to 2 knots in Navy Channel. Even little Blunden Island usually has strong rips in its vicinity.

This rundown comes from personal experience, sloshing around in strange currents, the B.C. Small Craft Guide, and the Current Atlas.

'Plumper'

We mentioned above that the 'H.M.S. Plumper' was an unique ship. Here is some more information. She was 'barque-rigged,' which means she was a 3-master, with a square rig on the fore- and main-masts and a mizzenmast which was fore-and-afted. She weighed 484 tons. The steam engine delivered 60 HP and would push the craft 6 knots. She was designed by an architect named Fincham and launched at Portsmouth, England in 1848. She was armed with two long 32-pounders and ten short cannon. She arrived in these waters in 1857 and was on station until relieved by the 'H.M.S. Hecate' in 1861.

How Come 'Gulf' Islands?

The islands were named after the wide expanse of water that separated the mainland from Vancouver Island. The early explorers probably thought they were exploring a 'Gulf', that somewhere up yonder the body had an end. When somebody discovered that you could actually go through the channels at the west and circumnavigate Vancouver Island, they rectified the error, it was the 'Strait of Georgia'. But by this time, too much had been written about the 'Gulf Islands'. So the name stuck for the islands. But, the official title of the body of water is 'The Strait of Georgia'.

Peter Cove

Corbett Store

We get a charming glimpse into early island living when we read the annual stocktaking book for 1909. Among the items are "20 sacks rice bran; 25 sacks coconut oil cake; 3 sacks rice shorts; 15 yards black skirt lining; 15 yards red sateen; 9 bathing suits at 30 cents each; 8 pairs ladies' side combs; 19 pairs ladies' high button boots; 7 lbs. gun powder; 15 lbs. shot; 1 keg cooking molasses; 9 pkgs GERMEA; 11 pkgs. FORCE; 1 caddy plug tobacco; 3 doz. hat pins; 2 school slates; ¼ gross slate pencils."

The coves on each side of **Stanley Point** also offer no incentive to more than lunch-hook anchorage.

And now, mes amis and sailboat skipperpersons , let's return to the 'parting-of-the-ways' spot and pick up our windpowered friends whom we left languishing in Bedwell Harbour, back on page 4.

Your course will probably be west up Swanson Channel. So you might want to take note of **Peter Cove:** this finger on the southwest Bedwell Harbour shore terminating at Wallace Point is made up of lichen-covered rock. At the head of the cove are two beaches with houses adjacent to them. A drying rock sits in the center of the entrance.

This cove was well known in the last century because it was the last hideout spot before crossing Boundary Pass to the U.S. On shore, there was nothing but sheep corrals. It became the favorite rendezvous of rumrunners who would transfer their contraband from Canadian boats to fast American launches for ports in the San Juans. Legend has it that there were frequent hijackings among the smugglers.

Wild and Woolly Scofflaws

Something even more lucrative than booze that was clandestinely carted across the border, was, of all things, wool. Consequently, sheep-napping and wool-running became a lively occupation in the old days of Pender Island.

In a delightful, tape-recorded conversation between two grand old ladies of Pender Island history, as heard on the CBC:

Beatrice Freeman: .."I can remember very well that somebody was stealing sheep. We were never allowed to walk back over the hill into Camp Bay and up in the valley, because it was rather lonely and there were sheep there and sometimes people did come and steal them. If it was getting dark we had to go around the other way. On one occasion I was late. I used to milk the cows and help with everything. I was late so I thought: ' Well, I'll just chance it and I'll go home by Camp Bay.' I just froze when I suddenly heard a whistle from one side of the field, it was getting quite dark, and then another whistle from the other side and I was about half way up this field. It was very lonely and nobody was near. So I didn't know what to do, so I walked as quickly as I could to the top of the field and dashed over the fence and up to the other side of the valley with nothing but sheep trails and deer trails. It was quite dark by then and I could still hear these awful whistles going on behind me. However, I got home and I got into an awful lot of trouble for having done it. But there were sheep taken afterwards, they'd disappeared. It was undoubtedly a sheep stealer.

"The sheep would be taken to the American side. There was an awful lot of it went on in the early days..

"We had a lovely old smuggler, though, that used to come–Old Burke. He was a tiny little man, always wore a very, very high hat and had a very big boat, a big dark-grey boat. You'd see him with just his hat above the gunwale and these huge oars. He used to come over from the United States and always brought some horrible cheap candies, but we loved them."

Mrs. Fred Smith: "The wool was taken over by Mr. Burke, a smuggler from the States who came once a year with his little dark boat and his padded oars and oarlocks. He would take all the wool people would let him have and row it back. The authorities got a little suspicious because his little island on the other side had the biggest wool crop in Washington, and it was just a rock! So they had their suspicions. They came to South Pender and they put some markers in some bales of wool that I think were waiting in the wharf shed for him, and, of course, he was traced then. It was a great pity; he was a very nice little man."

Beatrice Freeman: "He bought wool and took it back and then they caught him and he was taken into court over on the American side. We all loved Old Burke, you see, so my cousin, Leonard Higgs, went over to defend him and got him off by showing that it was impossible for him to be at a certain place at a certain time owing to the tide. So Old Burke got off."

Wallace Point to Grimmer Bay: Rounding **Wallace Point,** you will see a tiny cove behind it. There are extensive kelp beds extending out into Boundary Pass.

It was named after a medical officer, Peter William Wallace, an M.D. in the R.N.

who served on board the survey vessel 'H.M.S. Satellite' when it was on surveying duty in the islands in 1860. You'll be introduced to this ship a little later on. This point was the site of a logging camp in 1903.

Proceeding now along the western face of North Pender Island, you will see **Smugglers Nook**, so named for obvious reasons. It has steep cliffs with homes perched high atop them. There is a small beach (in case you want to go ashore and 'stash' something). There is also a nasty rock guarding the place.

The rocky cliffs beyond are called 'Oaks Bluffs'. Alexander Hamilton, who brought his lassie from Scotland to be his bride, used to raise sheep in this rugged terrain. The area made the headlines during WW I when a visiting Italian warship used the bluffs for target practice. Gunners lobbed a number of shells at the 300 foot cliffs. Unfortunately, the Italians' marksmanship left something to be desired and several shots went high, landing uncomfortably near the homes of residents. There were some hurried consultations with the authorities and the target practice was not resumed. A number of the non-explosive shells were later unearthed from among the rocks. You might want to see if you can spot any holes made by the shelling.

You may also encounter a string of fishboats when the season is open. There is nothing much to attract the passing sailor until you get to the first niche:

Boat Nook: And that is just about what it is, a 'nook'. It might look good if you were caught in a nor'wester, but it would be marginal at best. There are several mooring buoys for the small fishing boats belonging to the residents nearby, but when winds threaten, they are all taken ashore. There is no public upland space and the beach is in the front yard of quite a few homes.

Beddis Rock, in the opening to Boat Nook, does nothing to break up the waves. It is really a string of rocks.

Smugglers Nook

Thieves Bay. Magic Estates sports fishermen moor here.

Do not try to steer a direct course from off Beddis Rock to the light on the point outside Thieves Bay because there is a kelp-covered reef between them. The light is powered by a solar panel, incidentally.

Thieves Bay is tucked in behind a breakwater. It has a marina which is primarily dedicated to the residents of a local community called Magic Lake but there is occasional transient moorage. There is a public launching ramp and a nice little public park at the head of the bay. As you enter Thieves Bay, beware of a rock a short distance from the end of the breakwater. The marina locals have installed a square styrofoam marker over the rock. It is painted green. Keep it to the left, of course.

Mouat Point is next along this shore. This is your first encounter with a famous Gulf Islands sea captain. William Alexander Mouat worked for the Hudson's Bay Company most of his life, skippering their steamers during the middle 1800's. Something to look for: on the cliff just south of this point, you will see that someone has climbed up the steep rock face and drawn some figures which are either monograms or cattle-brands. Rounding this point, you will find a shallow, unnamed bight which could be good refuge. It has good depths.

Shingle Bay has a nice little protected cove at its head. The water is not very deep, unfortunately, in the half of the cove nearest that end. There is an abandoned wharf, pilings and footings on the east side. Notice the reef that intrudes into the opening of this inlet. There is space for possibly three boats to anchor. The rest of this bay is quite deep, 65 to 90 feet (20 - 27M.) and offers no refuge from waves and winds. There is a rather dramatic reef flanking the northeast shore of the bay. It might be fun to explore behind it in a shore-boat.

A small bight between Otter Bay and Shingle Bay is usually filled with log booms, but if it is empty, it could offer anchorage.

Otter Bay: It's the location of the Pender Islands' ferry terminal. The landing is in the outer portion of the bay. Farther in, in **Hyashi Cove**, there is a good mud bottom for anchoring. It is exposed to the ferry wash, though. Tucked back inside this cove, out of the turbulence, is Otter Bay Marina, a facility with moorage, power, water, laundry, showers, a store, a launching ramp and even a moped and bike rental.

The well-known 'M/V Queen of Storm' is based at this marina.

Otter Bay has two coves. One is occupied by the marina, and has a long reef acting as a natural breakwater. The south cove has a fine sandy beach.

Roe Islet separates Otter Bay from **Ella Bay.** It is the site of Roesland Resort. The little island is covered with arbutus. The cottages overlook Swanson Channel and Otter Bay. The family resort offers boats for the use of guests. It has been a popular place for decades.

Between **James Point** and the ferry landing is Pender Lodge. It has housekeeping cottages, sleeping units, a licenced lounge and dining room, a swimming pool and tennis courts, all in an idyllic setting.

Southwest of **Grimmer Bay** is **James Point,** with an attractive small islet to its south. It is interesting to explore.

Port Washington: It is a delight! There is a government wharf of 370 feet (112 M.). The bay is open to wash from those huge B.C. ferries, as they go back and forth through Swanson Channel between Swartz Bay and Vancouver.

Government Wharf at Port Washington.

'Queen of Storm'

There is a guy in the Gulf Islands who loves storms, people say. When the wind is smoking across the Georgia Strait at 40 knots and is blowing spume off the 8-foot whitecaps, this dude stays close to his VHF radio every waking hour, listening for distress calls. At night, he has a pager beside his bed that can get him on his feet. His 'thing' is — saving boaters.

The battle to pluck people out of the water or off wallowing boats in a gale is more than a hobby to this member of the Canadian Lifeboat Society. He's never really said it, we doubt he would admit it to anyone, but we believe he absolutely loves fighting the seas to rescue hapless sailors.

His name is Horst Klein. He and his wife, Joyce, live aboard an 80-foot ex-halibut schooner turned salvage tug. Down in the engine room, which is cavernous, is a massive 12-cylinder Detroit diesel engine the size of a small car. It can push the big 100-ton ship through heavy seas at 15 knots.

But when Horst gets 'scrambled' to a rescue mission, the big tug stays secure at the dock, Joyce acting as communications link in the radio room. Horst drops into a rescue boat, an 18-foot Boston Whaler. He fires up the 200 h.p. Mercury outboard, throws off the lines and is under way in less than a minute. The 'Queen of Storm Whaler' has been clocked at 50 knots, so he can be on scene anywhere in the Gulf Islands area in less than a half hour.

Once at the distress spot, he goes into action with efficiency born of 8 years and over a thousand distress incidents. Horst's first concern is saving human life. When he is on a rescue mission, the threatened boat is strictly of secondary importance. However, many times the safest way to protect boaters is by keeping the craft afloat and off the rocks. It is dangerous to try to transfer people from a

"Queen of Storm" whaler to the rescue.

pitching boat into a whaler in stormy seas, so often he gets a heavy line aboard the disabled craft and tows it to the nearest safe anchorage. Horst knows every nook and bay in the Gulf Island chain. He has been able to tow boats that are large enough to hoist his whaler up on davits.

When Klein is on a rescue mission, he is not 'commercial assistance'. He answers distress calls in all weather and all hours without a single question about money. Once the emergency is over, he asks for a voluntary donation to cover the costs of fuel for the run. The 200-horse Mercury burns about $50 an hour worth of gasoline, and that is considered the minimum proper donation for his services. This does not cover the high cost of maintenance of that engine and the loss of gear — that runs about another $20 per hour of operation. But, over the years, grateful boaters have often been generous in their contributions. On the other hand, many times, the owner of a boat demurs at even a minumum repayment. In those cases, Horst shrugs, wishes them well and heads home, hoping his next contact

The Mother Ship—"Queen of Storm"—at Otter Bay.

will be generous enough to keep him from having to pay for the fuel costs out of his own pocket.

Once the passengers and crew of a boat are safe, if repair or salvage is needed, Horst offers his services at rates less than or comparable to other salvors. That's when the big 'Queen of Storm', with her professional crew, goes into action. Because he is not an aggressive business man, Klein barely manages to keep his operation afloat financially. In re-cent years, he and the other members of the Canadian Lifeboat Society have been able to draw upon the contributions made to the little collection bottles on pub and grocery store counters.

If you find one of those colorful reminders at hand when you have some spare change, you might be as generous as you can. If you are a boater in the Gulf Islands, you might very well be getting your contribution back in life-saving service.

Old Percival's General Store

Above the Port Washington Government Wharf is 'The General Store', established in 1910 by S. Percival. It has gone through a series of owners since then: J.B. Bridge, 1921; W. Cunliffe, 1956; S. Kent, 1965; D.W. Shultz, 1974; D.A. Nance, 1977; and since 1984, Russ and Shirley Searle.

The latest owners could hardly be more charming. In 1985, they held a '75th Anniversary' celebration, and everyone dressed in elegant turn-of-the-century costumes for the occasion.

The store, true to the 'general store' tradition, carries groceries, fresh meat, deli meats, produce, cheeses, fresh eggs, frozen foods and meats. It has the largest book supply on the island, hardware, housewares, clothing for kids, fishing gear, various sundries, ice and gas for cars. Boaters can fill gas cans there. Store hours are 9:30 a.m. to 5:30 p.m. Tuesdays through Saturdays; and noon to 4 p.m. on Sunday and Monday, all year long. Mail can be dropped off there.

Port Washington is on **Grimmer Bay** and the government wharf often has space available at two floats which offer 370 feet (112 M.) of moorage. The bay is open to wash from those huge B.C. ferries, as they go back and forth through Swanson Channel between Swartz Bay and Vancouver City.

In the middle of Grimmer Bay is **Boat Islet,** an attractive little spot with a beacon. Do not attempt to go behind the marker except in a shallow draft boat. Interestingly, there is a light fixture on top of this beacon, but it has never been turned on, apparently.

Now that we are ready to continue our upward course into the Gulf Islands, we will be able to forget the distinctions between the rag sailors' course and that of the stinkpotters. From here on, there are no limitations imposed by bridges.

Let us, then, cross Swanson Channel and poke our noses into the many interesting spots on Prevost Island.

The Pender Islands--Now and Then

As with all the islands, the first inhabitants were the native Indians, but they were gradually displaced as pioneer farmers and loggers moved to the island in the middle and late 1800's. There are many fascinating books written which cover the early history of the settling of the Islands. We won't try to do more than a kind of thumbnail history here, because some of the pioneer names appear on charts and road maps. So we'll try to give you at least a nodding acquaintance with a few of the most well-known persons.

The Penders were named for Lt. Daniel Pender of the Royal Navy who was second master of the surveying vessel, 'H.M.S. Plumper'. He arrived in the area in November, 1857, and worked with great enthusiasm at the hydrographical surveying task until the survey terminated in November, 1870.

Sheep farmers arrived on Pender Island in the mid-1870's. Washington Grimmer was one of those who bought about 1400 acres in 1882. Three years later he married Elizabeth Auchterlonie. Her family and the Hope family owned the northern half of Pender Island from Otter Bay to Browning Harbour. Port Washington, on Grimmer Bay, on the northeast side of the island got both of his names.

Grimmer was the first postmaster for Pender. He rowed to Mayne Island to pick up the mail bag because the mailboat did not stop at Pender until 1891 when a wharf was finally built there.

Grimmer, James Auchterlonie and Andrew Davidson arranged for the first schoolteacher to come to the island in 1893 to teach the 8 school-age children. In 1894 a small school building was constructed.

There is a small cemetery in the center of North Pender, and the first recorded burial was that of little Albert Menzies, the 16-month-old son of Mr. and Mrs. A.H. Menzies. He was buried December, 1894.

Pender Islands' Cemetery.

25

Navy Neptune Grimmer

The early settlers were a hardy lot. Many lived well into their 80's and 90's. Coming into this world was often the most difficult part of their existence.

Ann Robson and Elsie Bennett of Mayne Island were well-known for their midwifery skills, and women from other islands often boarded with them during their confinements. Nevertheless, the safe delivery of a healthy baby was always at risk.

It was a winter day in 1896 when Elizabeth Auchterlonie Grimmer, wife of Washington Grimmer of Pender Island, set out in a rowboat to go from Pender to Mayne to await the birth of her first child. She waited longer than she should have to depart, however. 'Navy Neptune Grimmer' put in his appearance in a rowboat in the middle of Navy Channel — hence the name. 'Nep' was spry and alert and well-loved until his death recently at 98. It's safe to assume he never had to worry about being seasick.

Let's Come to Terms

(NOTE: The word 'shallow' in a previous item refers to the profile of the cove, not the depths of the water. We could not find a workable synonym for a relatively flat arc. So, throughout, we will give water soundings in 'shallow' bights and coves.)

Please Observe the 'Left-of-Way'

From the time the first horseless carriage appeared in British Columbia until 1922, drivers observed the British custom of keeping to the left. In that year, Parliament decided to join the U.S. in driving in the right lane. The changeover didn't cause a lot of fuss — there were very few cars in B.C. Only the rural mailmen were dismayed.

So there is an Auchterlonie Point, Hope Bay, Plumper Sound and so on. We recommend 'A Gulf Islands Patchwork', to find out more fascinating stories of these early settlers, but we'll be tossing in anecdotes about them every now and then.

The Penders now have a population of about 1,200 folks, most of them on North Pender, about 720 households, we were told.

There is one school on the islands for kids from Kindergarten through Grade 8. From then on they go by water taxi to Saltspring Island daily for their education.

Although Port Washington is the oldest settlement and still has a wonderful general store, the present hub of the island is the Driftwood Centre, near Port Browning. Here are the necessities for islanders: a post office, liquor store, real estate office, service station, restaurant, deli and car and moped rentals. This is the scene of the famous weekly farmers' market during the summer. It is also the stopping place of a couple of travelling tool-sharpeners, known as The Tinkerers . They tell people they live a life of 'voluntary simplicity'.

A grass air-strip is near the centre. It is, incidentally, the only landing field in the entire Gulf Islands.

Ferries are the lifeline to Vancouver Island, the mainland and the other islands. The Pender Islands' terminal is at Otter Bay.

The only airstrip in the Gulf Islands.

About two thirds of the residents of the Penders live in Magic Lakes Estates, a subdivision on the southwest side of North Pender. The huge development of the late '60's and early '70's attracted many residents from Alberta. It also helped bring about the formation of the Islands' Trust in 1974. This group of 26 islanders were to help research the special needs of the Gulf Islands and to 'protect and preserve' these islands through responsible growth and planning. Many islanders saw the Magic Lakes Estates development as a harbinger of the future and felt zoning regulations and bylaws were necessary to prevent similar developments on other islands.

North Pender Island has a beautiful 9-hole golf course in the center of the island. It is accessible for boaters because of the island taxi service. The course is about 6 miles from Port Browning, and one mile from Otter Bay. Green fees are $8, payable in an honor box. Clubs may be rented for $2. Every Wednesday is Ladies' Day from 10 a.m. to 3 p.m., Thursday is Men's Day—same hours. There is no bar, but soft drinks are served downstairs in an attractive clubhouse.

Some Pender residents classify their islands as 'basically a retirement community'. But there is a growing construction business and a number of service businesses offer employment to the younger residents. Two doctors share a practice on the island at a clinic, there is a volunteer fire department, three RCMP officers are located on the Penders—they look after all the outer islands except Saltspring—a dentist comes to the island once a week. There is also a physiotherapist, a library and community hall. There is an arts group and a crafts group which spins and dyes yarns from islands' sheep.

There are two charming churches on the island, the United Community Church in the Hope Bay Area, and St. Peter's Anglican Church in Port Washington. Set in the trees above the road, deer often wander through the churchyard, perhaps listening to the organist who practices for Sunday services.

A roadside store. There's no one in attendance, just leave your money. You're on the honor system on Pender.

St. Peter's Anglican Church.

Dam Good Tinkerers

A friend of ours, who is a word buff, is adamant: "There is no such thing as a 'tinkerer'. Tradesmen, who traveled from town to town in the 'old days' repairing pots and pans, were called 'tinkers'." Our friend is right—but he would have a hard time convincing some folks we met in the Gulf Islands. The proudly announce they are 'tinkerers'.

Their names are Jurgen and Judith Engelhardt. They don't often mend pots (although they undoubtedly can). They sharpen tools. They travel from island to island. They must do quite well, financially, because they spend their winters in Mexico.

If you decide to bring your tools: scissors, chisels, carving knives, plane blades and the like, try to allow enough time to stay and watch them work and chat with them. They will tell you that they love their life because it gives them a chance to meet new people with whom they can discuss their philosophy.

Their consuming interest is the mostly unexplored world of human potential. Their brochure reads, in part: "We're using today's materials and information to live our tinkerers' life. We participate in the ongoing evolution of humankind by living and working in public. In this expression of social responsibility we show our discipline and skills, explain and demonstrate what we are doing, answer questions, and encourage others to pursue their personal potentials."

If philosophy is not your thing, you will find they have a world of information about the care and handling of hand tools.

You might come across their neat little shop/house/truck on North or South Pender. If you want to find them, just ask any resident on those islands.

The Millennia Pit

On the canal that separates South from North Pender, archeologists from Simon Fraser University are stripping away centuries with small trowels. For the past couple of years, they have been inching their way downward in several pit areas. In some places they have reached bedrock, which they call 'The Glacial Till'. Traces of organic compounds that lie on top of the solid stone have been dated for radioactive carbon.

The two students in charge of the dig told us without a trace of awe in their voices that the specimens tested are probably 6,000 years old. And that, mixed with the carbon-bearing substances, they found items that had been held in the hands of human beings. They had also found human bones—the remains of North Americans who lived there 3,000 years before Cheops commanded that his burial pyramid be built in Egypt!

People were living and hunting and dying here a full 4,000 years before the tribes of Celts built the Stonehenges in the land Anglo-Saxons spring from.

And the crude cutting-stones of flint could still be used to skin an animal. The spear heads, fixed to staves, could still kill prey.

How deep are the pits? Ten or twelve feet, at most. When you look down the sides of the excavation you realize you are reading the history of centuries in every paper-thin layer.

Then you become aware of the fact that this creek and these shores must have been very much like they are today. Indians gathered shellfish here. Not a hundred yards away, on the other side of the creek, there is a sandbar where you could dig clams. The firs and pines that tower over the spot are hundreds of years old, but they must be the grandchildren, hundreds of times removed, of the trees that sheltered the tribe that camped here.

Visitors often find themselves speaking in hushed tones, as if they were in a hallowed spot. They look into the trays of relics of ancient people and shake their heads.

The students point to a box made of flat stones that protrudes from the side of the pit. It is about two feet square. It is in the debris dated only 2,000 years old. It was a burial box, we are told.

But what kind of a coffin was that? we ask. They tell us that these people didn't bury bodies in these boxes. They allowed the dead to decay or be eaten by vultures, then they reverently gathered up the bones and interred them in a box. We do something similar in today's culture, except we do it 'high tech'. We reduce a human body to ashes under extreme temperatures and then put the traces into a jar.

But you cannot reconstruct a human body from ashes. You can put together the collected bones of a woman of middle age who died twenty centuries ago and you can picture her carrying children, stooping to dig clams, placing herself in the arms of her mate.

You ask yourself, what is civilization? Is it the sum total of our toolmaking? If so, how far have we come from an arrowhead that killed a deer in the centuries before Christ to a modern lead slug from a 30-30?

It makes you a little careful about how you use words like 'primitive', and 'savage'.

And what about things that are not functional? For instance, only a few days before we visited the dig, the workers had unearthed two black sandstone figures. They were almost identical, about a foot long and several inches across. They were recognizable. No one who had ever seen a killer whale, or even a picture of one, could have been uncertain about them.

How old were they? The students thought they were relatively recent, probably not more than 600 years old, judging from the level at which they were found. You realize that at the time Chaucer was writing the scandalous 'Canterbury Tales' in England, a sculptor, sitting on the banks of a creek in a land that had not yet been discovered by Columbus, carved two killer whales out of solid rock with an artistry that any medieval sculptor would have admired.

You wonder: why did he do it? They have no practical value. You couldn't dig in the earth with them very well. They are not sharp enough to flay a skin. They are not designed to grind corn. Unquestionably, the man was inspired to create a thing of art.

Hovering around the dig was a representative of the Cowichan Tribe. He was the 'Historical Interpreter', a representative of a consortium of many tribes that visited the area in centuries past. His chief job was to ensure that the bones of their ancestors were treated with dignity and respect. It was a duty that everyone took very seriously. Each human remain was turned over to a tribe for proper reburial.

He is a delightful, roguish, ageless man. His seamed face is often caught up in a grin. His eyes sparkle. The young white students were teasing him about the fact that he had danced with every available woman at the Port Browning Pub. Modesty is not a virtue with Indians — he admitted it readily.

We were introduced to him. His name was Abel Joe. How old was he? 70. Did he speak any Indian dialects? Cowichan, of course, also some Salish and Lummi. Did he know any of the tribal songs and chants? Oh, yes. Would we like to hear some of them? He took an ornate deerskin drum out of a canvas bag. He began to thump it with rhythms that we have always associated with Indians. He sang some of them. He sang Salish and Kwakiutl and Saanich and Haida songs. The words were mostly long vowel sounds, so we guessed that they were not actual lyrics that could be translated. He saved his own tribe's song for the last.

"This is the Cowichan song," he told us. He began to beat out a somewhat faster rhythm on the tomtom. Then he paused for a couple of beats and continued solemnly:

"Oh, Lucky Lager. We lo-o-o-ve Lucky La-a-a-ger!"

He grinned mischievously. We applauded.

We hope that when you get to Pender, the dig is still in progress. We can't guarantee that Abel Joe will still be there, or that he will sing the Cowichan Chant.

But, if he isn't there, you might drift up to the Port Browning Pub and wait until the music starts.

Pender Sea Story

Cruising the Gulf Islands, especially in the winter, has always been tricky, as the early settlers well knew. The first steamboat brought to Pender arrived in 1902. This 30-foot boat, complete with canvas curtains that could be unrolled along the sides for protection against rain or salt-spray, belonged to brothers Howard and Stanley Harris. To the islanders, the 'Pearl' was a wondrous ship.

The brothers volunteered to take a group from Hope Bay on North Pender to Miners Bay on Mayne Island for a Christmas Concert. After they deposited their passengers, Stanley loaded two bales of hay on board to take back home to their cow.

They had more passengers on their homeward run. There was a student minister, Clara and Victor Menzies and several members of the Hamilton Family. They started out after dark.

"They felt the wind but did not meet any sizeable waves until after they were outside the harbor. Now, Stanley, always confident, didn't think of turning back. Having been born and brought up in Ontario, he knew nothing of the sea and its treachery. He was unfamiliar with tidal currents and hidden shoals and reefs. He did have trust in 'Pearl'. He possessed the strength and optimism of youth. Besides he was a 'good sailor', he never got seasick.

"In spite of the storm, Stanley managed to navigate through Active Pass. He avoided Enterprise Reef and all the dangerous rocks in Navy Channel. All went well until he started to cut in to Hope Bay. Nobody saw Fane Island until the boat was almost on it. The student minister yelled "Reverse!" Stanley reversed the engine, thus avoiding crashing on the rocky shore. But the wind and waves had washed a rope off the deck. When the engine was reversed, the rope fouled the propeller, bringing the boat to a standstill. It was impossible to disentangle it in the stormy darkness. All the men could do was drop the anchor and hope and pray that it would hold.

"They broke open the bales of hay and made the girls as comfortable as possible. Too seasick to care about their best frocks becoming rumpled and their coats stuck full of hayseeds, the young women rolled and moaned all night.

"The men were much relieved to find that the anchor was holding. Stanley did his best to keep the canvas curtains tight and the passengers as dry and warm as possible. The preacher went from one person to another trying to comfort and encourage.

"When daylight finally came, Stanley got into the dinghy and with some help from the others, freed the propeller. The Menzies were put off on Hope Bay wharf, whence they hurried home to milk their cows, very thankful to have their feet on firm ground. Stanley ran the Hamiltons around to their home in Browning Harbour.

"For many weeks the Harris boys' cows found hairpins in the hay." (From 'Gulf Islands Patchwork')

2. Prevost Island: Watching the Ferries Go By.

This is an anomalous bit of water-locked real estate. Right in the middle of the southern Gulf Islands, it is the only one of any size that is not served by the ferries. That means it is dependent upon private boats for communication and transportation with the other islands. There are a few roads, according to Strip Chart #3310, Sheet 1. Strangely, the roads are not indicated on the larger charts. It would appear that they begin with a sort of subdivision at the east end of the island near the head of Glenthorne Passage and wind up into the hills. Another road seems to lead from Ellen Bay over to Diver Bay. Since there were 'no trespassing' signs all over, we couldn't explore in person. There are no cable crossings, so it would appear there is no power or telephone for the island's few permanent residents.

It was named after Capt. James Charles Prevost, the master of the 'H.M.S. Satellite' in 1859. Prevost was appointed the first British Commissioner whose duty was to help settle the dispute over the ownership of San Juan Island, which had been involved in the so-called 'Pig War.'

In addition to Strip Chart #3310, Sheet 1 or 2, Plans Chart #4370 is good for all but the northeastern section of Prevost Island. The whole island is shown on Chart #3442.

The western profile of Prevost Island resembles the fingers of your right hand. **Peile Point** is the thumb; **Selby Point**, the index finger; **Annette Point**, is the middle finger; the peninsula of **Glenthorne Passage** is the ring finger. The little finger looks skeletal, with an unnamed islet in line with **Secret Island** and **Glenthorne Point**.

The shoreline of Prevost from Peile Point eastward in Trincomali Channel is rocky and seems to be uninhabited.

Charles Rocks, less than one mile from Peile Point, are visible at all times, but there are some rocks that bare at 10-13 feet (3-4 M.) in line with the point of Hawkins Island.

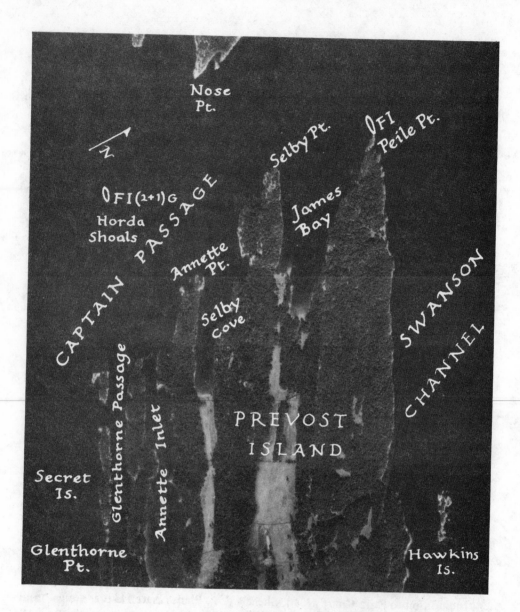

Hawkins Island, east of Charles Rocks, looks like a camel's hump. The beach on Prevost Island at this point is gravelly and quite inviting—a good spot for kayakers. It would be a nice place to build a summer cabin. There are extensive beds of kelp off the eastern end of Hawkins Island. If you run with your fathometer on, you may get a little uneasy about the depths between Hawkins and the Prevost shore, but there are no perils. It shouldn't get below 17 feet (5 M.).

Portlock Point has a light that is quite picturesque. At one time it must have had a keeper. The tower is covered with white shingles and has a couple of windows. A windcharger behind it provides the power for it.

Portlock Point Light has a windcharger.

The point was named after Capt. Nathaniel Portlock and his son, Joseph, who became a major general. Capt. Portlock served with Captain Vancouver on the 'Discovery.' He commanded a fur-trading expedition to this coast in 1785. He also commanded a ship which went to the South Pacific accompanying one skippered by the notorious Capt. Bligh of mutiny fame.

Richardson Bay, behind the lighthouse, is narrow. It ends in a mossy shell beach. There is room for possibly one boat to anchor, but it would be rough with the passing traffic in Swanson Channel. We didn't try it.

Although the bays at the eastern end of Prevost Island look like tempting anchorages, they are all exposed to heavy ferry wash and southeasterlies that often spring up without any warning. A good indication of an anchorage is the number of boats you see anchored in it. The many times we passed Prevost, we saw very few boats taking advantage of what otherwise might look like good moorage. The route through Swanson Channel is used by the big super ferries as well as the smaller boats of the B.C. System, also freighters and tugs.

Diver Bay (no 's', notice) is flanked at its entrance by two sets of islets, **Bright** and **Red Islets.** Red Islets are indeed, red colored—at least they are golden. They are covered with bright mosses. It looks like a better anchorage on the chart than it does in person, so to speak. There is plenty of room, good depths and only one bugaboo-rock. But it is open to the ferry wash in Swanson Channel. There are three beaches at the head of the bay. The shoreline on the northeast beach has some beautiful park-like areas. We didn't see any 'no trespassing' signs. Another beach is piled high with drift logs, driven there by the wash down the bay, mute testimony to the kind of wave action that could be encountered in this bay. The shallow coves at the northern entrance are fronted by rocks and offer no attraction for big boats.

Weather Reporting In The Gulf Islands

From time to time, we find ourselves tempted to say, in suggestions about winds and anchoring, to listen for the radio weather forecasts. Normally, a boater would expect to get the information he or she needs from the Environment Canada weather station in Victoria. Unfortunately, such is not the case. Not that the continuous weather reporting isn't valid. It just doesn't allow itself to get involved in the capricious weather that stirs around this archipelago.

You can be bucking into 4-foot waves, generated by 30-knot winds from the southeast in Stuart Channel. The tomfool barometer can be blithely high. The weather station can be predicting gentle zephyrs from the NW. They will recite the conditions reported at a number of stations in B.C. Coastal Waters, all veritable mill-ponds. You wonder where in Hell this wind is coming from. Is there a movie company somewhere up ahead filming 'Typhoon'?

The fact is, mes amis, the weather in the Gulf Islands is kinky! It shuns all correlation with the weather in the Straits of Georgia and Juan de Fuca. It is as doggedly independent as the humans who inhabit the lands below.

So, it "don't mean a thing" as the song says, to know what the conditions are at East Point. The lighthouse crew on Saturna that makes that contribution can be looking at a mirror in the Strait while a few miles away, in Bedwell Harbour, you will have snarling whitecaps.

Ye who are addicted to the motive power of flying canvas will be delighted. Ah-h-h, a great wind for sailing! You hoist the proper gennies and away you go—two miles or so. And then...you find nary a ripple and you disconsolately bag your yard-goods.

The moral to this story is that the winds in the Gulf are unprincipled. And so, when you put down your hook for the night in some small cove, be ye not deceived by the flat calm or the prospects for some predictable wind. Make sure you have holding power and swinging room in every direction. Otherwise you can have a bummer of a night!

Although **Ellen Bay** is also exposed to ferries and southeastern winds, if you can get far enough into the head of it, anchorage is fair with a mud bottom. There usually aren't any ferries running after 11 at night or before 6 a.m.

Passing the **Point Liddell** beacon, your first sight is the **Acland Islands,** two little islands just off the south shore of Prevost. If you use Chart #3470, you can see how to navigate your way through the pass between Prevost and the Aclands. But beware of the mid-channel rock which dries at 2 feet (0.6 M.) off the eastern island. Watch for reefs and rocks. There is foul ground—kelp covered—off the western island. Southwest of the islands is the Acland Islands Light Buoy, 'U 60', flashing red with a radar reflector.

Just beyond the Aclands is **Glenthorne Point** which is separated from **Secret Island** by a very narrow passage—only 3 feet deep (0.9 M.) with lots of rocks in it. It's a great passage to kayak or canoe or row through, but not suitable for larger craft.

Secret Island is certainly not a secret. It is fully developed and bristles with docks and summer cabins. It reminds Puget Sound area boaters of Bainbridge Island. The cabins are on both the Captain Passage side and the Glenthorne Passage shore.

You can easily pass between Secret Island and the unnamed island off its western end. Just stay in the middle and beware the kelp-covered shoals on either island. This isle off the entrance to Glenthorne is a pleasant-looking spot. There does not seem to be any habitation. It has a very attractive beach. It might be a good place to visit by small boat from one of the anchorages.

Glenthorne Passage is as popular with boaters as with realtors. It has good depths for anchoring throughout. Where it widens after passing the Secret Island shore, there is room for at least 30 boats to swing on the relatively short scopes needed. It would be well to creep into this bay at night, because boats will be riding all along the passage. As you can see from chart #3470, the neck of land that separates Glenthorne from Annette Inlet becomes very narrow near the east end. It is probably only 165 feet (50 M.) wide at its narrowest and you can see the masts of sailboats in Glenthorne from the shallows in Annette Inlet. It's a short walk from the head of one inlet to the other.

There are not many places to land a shore boat in Glenthorne Passage. We found only one small shell beach across from the Glenthorne Point opening—in case poor old Fido has to be taken ashore. The narrow peninsula between the two inlets has some goats grazing on it. The land is marked 'Private'. We did not see the booms mentioned on the chart.

Annette Inlet: This is a lovely protected area and good anchorage as long as you check your tide book and depth sounder carefully before dropping the hook. There are few homes and mostly just wooded shores gently coming down the hillside. It's a particularly great spot in the 'off season' when you may well be the only boat in there. The inlet widens out at the head of the bay and goes dry at very low tides.

It has a good holding ground with a mud bottom. The water is that shade of murky green you encounter at the shallows in bays.

This is a wonderful place for bird-watching: herons, eagles and all the others. There is a kelp-covered rock at the entrance to the inlet.

Annette Passage

Selby Cove shoreline.

A sloppy kayaker with loose hatch-ties.

Just around Annette Point is **Selby Cove** which has always been a favorite of ours over the years. We would drop the hook just inside a tiny rocky inlet just off the point. Kids find it a wonderful place to play. The kids would dinghy over and explore the small caves and low cliffs. The islet adjoins the point at low tide with a sand and rock isthmus. The cove itself is a good anchorage with no rocks or shoals, although it is open to northwesterlies. There is a sandy beach at the head of Selby Cove with a farmhouse.

Follow the forested shoreline around Selby Point and into **James Bay**. This is another good moorage. Note that each of these bays has become progressively wider since Glenthorne Passage.

James Bay ought to be a refuge in case of a strong southeast wind, but we found that the wind sweeps up over the low hills on Prevost and stirs it up quite a bit. There appears to be an old orchard near the beach. We saw no signs posted on the shores

Prevost Landscape

For those folks who are intrigued with Prevost Island and find the thought of a summer cabin snuggled into one of the little bays irresistible, we can tell you a bit about what the land is like, thanks to a wonderful map of the landscape given to us by the Forestry Service of Environment Canada.

Much of the island is made of 'shallow till and colluvium'. Did you know that before? Do you know that now? Well, it may help to learn that 'shallow till' is a thin layer of assorted clay, sand, gravel and boulders. 'Colluvium' sounds like something you could be sent to jail for, but it means soil that accumulates at the bottom of a slope. These two surfaces are "veneers over bedrock; shallow, residual loamy soils derived from weathered shales." 'Weathered shales' sounds poetic!

These soils are 1-3 feet deep (30-100 Cm.) on a moderately sloping terrain.

"Douglas fir predominates, but red cedar, arbutus and lodgepole pine may be present." What does that mean—"may be present?" Do they sometimes go visiting?

They sum it up by saying that the land is suitable for open space, recreation and residential development; the latter needs to be "kept low for satisfactory sewage disposal". That makes us wonder about the clusters of homes we saw in spots.

Well, there it is: a readout on the geology and flora of Prevost Island. If that scoots you off to your friendly neighborhood realtor, tell 'em Environment Canada sent you!

Prevost History

The history of the pioneers on Prevost Island is woefully lacking. All we could garner was that one Thomas Caffery was the sole Prevost Islander who was registered to vote in 1886 in the Mayne Island Polling Division, Cowichan District. As far as we can tell, that's all he ever did: register to vote.

From the 'Gulf Islands Patchwork' book we picked up a tidbit about a Mrs. Richardson of the Prevost Island lighthouse. It seems she always spent Christmas Day with John and Margaret Deacon at their home in Village Bay on Mayne Island, along with the Grimmer Family of Pender Island (whom you met earlier). One holiday, as Mrs. Richardson and the Grimmers neared Village Bay in their rowboat, a stiff northwesterly started to blow. And though they had a sturdy seaboat which seemed to ride through anything and everything, they found they needed to keep concentrating on the thought of the roast goose on the spit at the Deacons' home in order to keep up their courage.

The moment they hit the beach, wave after wave came up over the stern of the boat and it pitched over. Like so many drowned rats, they hurried up the slope to the Deacon home.

Mrs. Richardson used to refer to that Christmas party as the 'Goose or Die Dinner'.

of that bay. The rocks indicated on the chart just inside Peile Point are dome-shaped. The finger of land there does not seem to be inhabited.

O'Reilly Beach is beautiful and there is no house near it.

So that's the portrait of Prevost Island. It almost seems that it doesn't deserve a whole chapter to itself. But it resists being lumped in with any of the surrounding islands because it is so uniquely independent and relatively unpopulated.

Summer Weather Averages in the Gulf

We've seldom heard the old buzzword about the Gulf Islands being a 'Banana Belt', like we do in the San Juan Islands. Whether the weather is better than that in the islands to the southeast would be a battle of statistics or subjective notions.

When it comes to getting day-to-day readings of temperatures in Canada, you are confronted by that modern-day nuisance: Celsius readings. When you are practically gasping for air and perspiring like a sinner in a tent meeting and the digital sign on a bank reads 35° you might begin to wonder if you have a fever until you remember — it's 35° Celsius — cotton-pickin' metric!

How do you make the conversion? The quick-and-nasty way is to double the figure and add 32°, since it starts up and down from our customary freezing temperature. If you're picky, you might deduct about 10% from the total. So — altogether, class — twice 35 is 70 + 32 = 102, lop off 10% or 10° = about 92° Fahrenheit. Actually, it's 95°, non-metric — close enough for jazz.

If you're ultra-picky, take the Celsius, multiply by 9, divide by 5 and add 32. Incidentally, don't complain to the Canadians about their metric system — they hate it too! They're just more sensible than we are.

Getting back to average temperatures: On Saltspring Island, May, 16.8 (62); June, 19.3 (66.7); July, 22.3 (72); August, 21.9 (71.5); September, 19.5 (67); October, 13.9 (57).

Anybody know what temperature growing bananas need?

Canada Marine Weather Broadcasts

Weather for the Gulf Islands can be heard on the Weather #2 channel, which is the Victoria Weather Station. Channel #2 is on 162.40 MHz. The forecasts are issued by Environment Canada in Vancouver at 5 a.m., 11 a.m., and 7 p.m. PST. If special warnings are issued, they can be broadcast at any time. 'Small Craft Warnings' are issued for the Georgia Strait and the Strait of Juan de Fuca, but they are only given during the April to October period. 'Small Craft Warning' means expected winds in the range of 20-34 knots. 'Gale Warnings' are issued for winds 35-47 knots, 'Storm Warnings' for winds in excess of 47 knots.

The format for the broadcasts calls for a weather synopsis first. It gives the broad weather picture, tells how the weather is moving, and suggests how fast the weather is changing.

Wind directions from various points are given in 'true', not 'magnetic', directions. Winds less than 12 knots are called 'light'.

A booklet issued by Environment Canada adds a note of interest to mariners in the Gulf Islands area:

"Among islands, winds are usually lighter than on open water. In inlets they may be stronger due to 'funneling' of the air flow by the sides of the inlet." The brochure does not expand on this 'funneling' effect, but sailors in the Gulf area will attest that the blasts of wind are not necessarily confined to inlets and narrow passages. You may find winds from unforecast directions and at speeds exceeding the predicted highs.

You will do a lot better in understanding Gulf Islands' weather by listening to commercial radio stations. You can usually rely on the forecasts and reports from the Nanaimo radio stations: CHUB, 1570 KHz; and CKEG, 1350 KHz.

A number of Victoria radio stations also broadcast weather: On the AM band, CJVI, 900 KHz; CFAX, 1070 KHz; CKDA, 1220 KHz. and CFMS-FM, at 98.30 MHz.

KIDS AND CRUISING AND SANITY
And some tips on how to preserve all three.

Whenever we gather with other boaters during the summer, the conversation usually gets around to KIDS. Information is exchanged on how to keep them from driving themselves and their parents wacky. Adults wail, "Why doesn't Chapman have a chapter that really is important? Not some stuff about how to tie double beckets in a rope—or figure variation in compass courses. Why doesn't he tell us how to keep kids occupied and content on long cruises?"

Ah-h-h, if only Doctor Spock had been a boater!

When they discover that between us we have about 15 grandchildren, they turn on us. "You do it!" they commanded, "write a chapter on kids and boats!"

Well, we'll give it a college (or looney-bin?) try.

All during the summer we were researching the Gulf Islands, we talked to parents and got suggestions. We scribbled notes, we asked questions, we interviewed rug rats. To tell the truth, there weren't as many helpful hints forthcoming as we had hoped.

One of the problems is the very scope of such an inquiry. Kids come in all sizes, ages and capacity for deviltry. Parents come in all sorts of limits of patience and tolerance. Boats come in all sizes. And finally, weather—the most critical of variables—is often unpredictable in the Pacific Northwest.

Given a week of rain with two bubble-gummers on board a small boat, and you have all the necessary elements of a nightmare. The ideal parent-skipper would combine the instincts of a saint, a psychiatrist and a muleskinner. Since that mix hardly ever appears among our acquaintances, we are thrown back on what will look like a list of first-aid recommendations.

To begin with, we recommend that young couples get their pre-toddlers out on boats as often and long as possible. The tads should learn to walk on land and sea at the same time. One couple we know has turned a V-berth area into a big play-pen for their little one. They have it screened in with safety netting to prevent the kid from being chucked out on his head in a roll—and to prevent him from dispersing his toys all over the cabin sole.

For toddlers, a safety net attached to the lifelines is a must. A junior-sized safety harness and line wouldn't be a bad idea just in case the youngster decides to crawl under the net and into the drink.

A life jacket, one that is designed for small tots, is an absolute requisite! There are now compact jackets on the market that are not bulky and look good. You might try decorating these with patches and insignias and the like to make the kid like to wear it. And of course, teach your little one to swim as early as possible.

So much for safety, now for entertainment.

One young couple we know plug the scuppers of the cockpit of their fiberglass sailboat and fill it with a couple of inches of warm sea-water. They have a complete menagerie of rubber duckies and animals, and a whole fleet of tugboats and ferries.

Bubble pipes and sudsing liquids are good for sunny days. Kids can sail bubbles off into the wind. If you don't want to spend 29 cents for a bottle of the commercial stuff, you can use a couple

teaspoons of JOY in a basin of water. For older kids, we recommend quantities of Legos, dominos, checkers, crayons, paper and coloring books.

For pre-teens through high-schoolers those highly portable radio-earphone combinations are ideal. That way the kids can listen to their favorite maniac music while the parents maintain some tranquility.

We had a very successful gimmick on board the Roanoake. It was an adaptation of darts. There was a flannel hanging with a target on it and a half dozen balls with Velcro on them. Matter of fact, when the kids would leave, we would find ourself tossing the balls. Eventually, we—not the visiting kids— lost all of them. But it was a great success while it lasted.

Did you know that a boat is an ideal base from which to fly a kite? Naturally, we'd suggest plastic ones that could be dunked in case they take a dive into the chuck. But if you can get one started up, with a fishing line and reel attached, you'd be amazed how high they can go. Besides, you don't have to worry about power lines and trees.

All of the foregoing is not designed to be comprehensive, of course, but as a starting place for your own creativity and self-preservation. The suggestions are all designed to cope with the problem of keeping kids occupied when at sea.

Now, let's look at what youngsters do and should do when you are in port.

How can we properly impress boating parents with the first rule of safety and courtesy in a moorage: thou shalt not put thy kid in a 12-foot dinghy with a 35-horse outboard and turn him or her free to terrorize the neighboring boaters! This can cause pint-sized kamikazes when they smash their boats or capsize them, or large wakes or overturned dinghies.

Let's discuss what kids find to do on shore. Almost all kids are natural born naturalists. They can be occupied for hours looking at the little critters in the inter-tidal areas. Just remember to tell them they can't take live animals. They are also avid collectors of all manner of treasures: shells, rocks and driftwood. Along with the paper products you stow on board, you should get a good supply of plastic baggies for storing these finds.

Some of these beachcombed items can be made into a collage; kids are usually masters at paste-ups of seashore items. We have a friend who supplies her kids with good stock paper cut into postcard size. She encourages her youngsters to find pretty bits of seaweed. They place these little tendrils on the paper while they are still wet. When they dry they are firmly attached with a remarkably strong natural glue. These pictures are pressed and used as note cards or stationery.

Incidentally, there is a marvelous book by H.A. Rey (who wrote all the "Curious George" books) called "Look at the Stars" which can be used by you and your kids for stargazing and identifying.

As kids get into their teens they can start fishing while you're under way. They don't have to be very big to do that. You might get them started by buying them their own pole, reel and gear.

When you're on a dock, give them a shrimp net. They can spend hours hunting shrimp along the pilings and dock edges—and they can contribute to dinner. We once offered a grandson a penny for every shrimp he caught. After a couple of hours, we owed him $1.87!

Most kids like to be useful. Let your young ones learn to help handle lines and steer the boat as early as possible. Teach them to row a dinghy by the time they are four or five. They can do it and love it. Kids we know—like the grandkids—have begun kayaking at 7 or 8.

Put them at the helm and let them get the feel of the boat. We discovered that one of the 8-year-olds could last about 30 seconds on the tiller of a sailboat; after that he was bored to death. But when he took the wheel of a powerboat or a sailboat, he was a natural. Kids learn to steer toy cars and it becomes natural for them to steer a boat helm.

They can also learn to tie knots, the useful kind and the decorative ones. Tell them they're learning "marlinspike." Start simple, don't criticize, be patient.

Make a heaving line, let them practice throwing it at targets in the water. It's fun and useful.

Tow a toy sailboat at the end of a fishing line. Watching that can keep them occupied for a long time.

Teach your kids to use and respect the VHF and CB radios. They could be very useful in case of emergency. Do not let them turn the radios on when you are not present, however. The temptation to play is often too compelling and they can paralyze the airwaves.

Teach kids to read charts, to use dividers, to figure out the tide tables, read a depth sounder, winch in sheets, help set and hoist anchor, furl sails—in other words, be a real part of running the boat. The earlier you start the better. The more useful a kid becomes, the less you have to try to figure out things for him or her to do to keep them occupied.

One of the favorite pastimes for our kids from the age of about 5-years-old up was to ride in a dinghy which is being towed slowly in calm weather. They loved it. They felt like they were the captains of their own boats. Try it—it's great fun. (They should be wearing life jackets, of course.)

As all parents know, kids love to imitate adults, and often do a good job. If you have a camera, get your child a simple box or Instamatic camera and teach him or her how to use it.

You keep a ship's log, so when your child is old enough to write, let them keep their own log of a trip. It might turn out to be an even better record of the vacation than yours is!

Those are our offerings of some things to do with the kids. You'll undoubtedly have many more, but at least that's a start.

Happy family cruising!

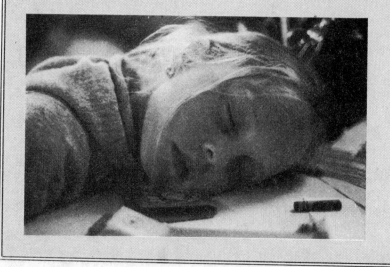

3. Saltspring: the BIG Island.

Just for the sake of contrast, let us now consider the whopping big island with three—count 'em—ferry terminals, a complete business community, several mountains, a newspaper, and even...a sewer system! This latter and recent development, the sewer system, is regarded by many as a godsend and by some as an invitation to downfall. Visiting boaters will eventually benefit by it, as you shall see if you read on.

The island got its name, as you might guess, from springs on shore that had a high content of brine. The engineers working for the Hudsons Bay Company dubbed it thus when they determined that the artesian water contained '3446 grains of salt per Imperial Gallon' in 1856. That, incidentally, is much saltier than sea-water. The Indians had called the island 'Chuan'.

A surveying officer, one Captain Richards, thought that such a magnificent hunk of land ought to have a historic name, so he dubbed it 'Admiral' Island after his superior officer, Rear Admiral Baynes. He probably recognized a military truism: it never hurts to butter up the top brass.

But the residents didn't find 'Admiral Island' a grabber. They continued to call it Saltspring and the mapmakers yielded to the majority.

Where are the salt springs now? They used to abound in the north end of the island between Fernwood, North Beach and North End Road, roughly from St. Mary's Lake to Trincomali Channel. A long-time resident told us that most of them are no longer in existence. The story goes that although they were interesting phenomena, they weren't worth diddley when it came to irrigating crops. Furthermore, they had a considerable sulfur content and they stunk; so, sensibly, the people who owned the land plowed them under. There are a few driblets located on private land, but they are not worth much of a search.

The area of the island is 69 square miles (180 KS.), about a fifth larger than San

The quickie-ferry at Vesuvius.

The Saltwater Springs

Evidently, in the latter 1800's, the water from the salt springs on the north end of Saltspring Island was not as briny as it was in later years.

Islanders in those days were advised by the Governor, to "take a native woman and settle down".

"On their grant of land this would probably be undertaken with the proverbial 'sack of flour' and little else, to start on. Deer were plentiful in the woods however — other game also. Their wives were expert in fishing, and at every low tide the 'butcher shop' was open for clam digging, etc.

"On this part of the island lie mostly the salt springs which have given it its name. During the drought of summer, they leave on some fields a white deposit on which vegetation grows. These springs permeate the soil here and there. Fortunately the saltiness is not too pronounced and it is said that horses reared there have refused any other kind; but in calling at the home on a summer day, one would be in two minds — whether to suffer thirst, or ask for a glass of water. Wells have been sunk on the place from time to time in hopes of finding a normal supply, but so far without success."

Juan Island in the State of Washington. In 1981, it boasted a census of 5,443, but residents say the population has grown considerably since then.

Ferries go from Long Harbour to the mainland terminal at Tsawwassen; from Swartz Bay, near Sidney, to Fulford Harbour; and a third quickie-ferry goes from Vesuvius to Crofton, on Vancouver Island.

This would be a good time to discuss what seems to be a strange situation to

Americans. There are no incorporated communities in the Gulf Islands. Even Ganges, which by all standards looks like a prosperous town, is not a political entity. The whole complex of islands has been governed by an instrumentality called 'The Islands Trust'. You can bone up on this outfit by reading the article on page 73.

Now that you have been properly introduced to Saltspring, let us take you to the southeast corner and usher you up Swanson Channel to the northwest point. This is a main-travelled route to the other Gulf Islands.

Fulford Harbour: This is a fine harbor and we will discuss it after we take you past the doorkeepers, **Cecil Rock** and **Russell Island.**

We haven't any idea how Cecil Rock got its name. We can make a guess, though. These old explorers had a strong sense of destiny and they wanted to be down in the books for all time so they attached their names to every little rock and reef as well as to bodies of water and islands. In so doing, they probably started with the Old Man and gradually worked their way down through the officer staff, then they immortalized the lesser gods. Probably some apprentice seaman said, "Hey Captain, how about naming something after me?" and the Old Man said, "Okay, Cecil, here's a rock just outside Russell Island. It's yours." It is in one and a half fathoms (3 M.) at lower water and has a few strings of kelp attached.

Fulford Harbour from Mt. Maxwell.

Russell Island is somewhat built-up on the northwest side. There is good anchoring depth on that shore, but even at calm times, currents and ferry wakes would make you uncomfortable. We were at the dock in Fulford Harbour one gusty night when, at about 3 a.m., a boat came in quietly and rafted up to us. The skipper told us he had been anchored at Russell Island, but the wind came up and he bounced all night and finally cleared out. Let's call that 'local knowledge'.

Jackson Rock is actually two rocks which are usually exposed. When the tide is out you can see a narrow strip of beautiful white shell beach between them. We saw flocks of gulls and cormorants there, and it is probably a rookery, although it is not posted.

There is a big hill above Jackson Rock, called 'Reginald Hill'. Rumor had it that when the original island Indians saw attacking Indians come into Fulford Harbour they would roll rocks down onto the canoes and kill the attackers. It didn't look like such a tactic would have worked very well because of the sloping terrain. We checked with a lifelong island resident, Bob Akerman, who sort of shook his head. "There's just no way that would have worked," he told us.

Beyond these rocks there is a nasty cluster of sharp ones just below the surface that look like 'Jaws III'. There is a friendly quick-flashing red buoy to keep you away from them.

The shoreline beyond Jackson Rocks is a small Indian reserve.

Fulford Harbour: (The best chart of this area is #3441. It is metric, please take note, this is important! A meter is only about half a fathom; you could be way off in your calculations if you don't make the conversion. The 'quick-'n-dirty' way of making the switch is to multiply meters by 3.3 to get feet. We'll give you English measure as well as metric, however.)

Keep on the alert for an usually-exposed rock just offshore on the northeast side of the harbor about a third of the way in.

The beach at Drummond Park.

BERTHING LIMITED TO 7
DAYS IN ANY ONE MONTH
EXCEPT BY SPECIAL
PERMISSION of WHARFINGER

Fulford Harbour Government Dock.

The public wharf is almost at the head of the bay. It has two float areas with a total of 241 feet (73 M.) of moorage. There is a small tie-up float seaward from the ferry dock and a larger moorage area behind the ferry dock. The B.C. information sheet says that the large area has garbage disposal, power and water. One cruising guide we read says that there is a 'tidal grid' at this port, but we couldn't find it. You can use the men's and women's heads in the ferry terminal during operation hours.

Incidentally, our chart #3452, which was corrected to 1980, shows neither the ferry dock or the public dock for some reason. They have been there for over 30 years. Ferry service to that port began in 1930.

On the dock you will see a small steel shed with a sign saying it is the 'tide gauge'. Inside is a recorder which registers the tides 24 hours a day. Fulford Harbour, you see, is the reference point for all of the tides in the lower Gulf Islands.

Fulford is one of three small settlements besides the village of Ganges; Fernwood and Vesuvius are the others. It was originally a pioneer farming community in the mid-80's. There are still farms in the area, raising both sheep and produce. There is also a brand-new grade school in this community, with over 100 students.

At the top of the wharf you will find the Kingfisher Restaurant, which is a pleasant little place catering to hungry people waiting for the ferry. Next door is a little outdoor craft concession which features beautiful knitted things: sweaters, vests and the like.

Fulford Benchmark

Once a day Bob Patterson, the retired owner of the Fulford General Store, goes down to the shed and reads the record and phones it in to Victoria. The official benchmark is located at this area. The explanation in the Tide and Current book is somewhat vague. It says the mark is located "...85 feet (yes, feet) north of the approach to the ferry dock." If your curiosity overwhelms you, you might want to clamber over the rocks behind the Morningside Gallery and look at it. It's no big deal. It's a three-inch circular brass

plate with a cross in the middle and the words 'Canadian Hydrographic Service' embossed on it.

The Patterson General Store sells groceries and pumps gas for cars. (There must have been gas on the dock at one time because there are fuel lines leading out to it.) The general store was established in 1915 by Roy Patterson who lives across the street from the place. He is in his mid-90's. His grandson, Bruce, runs it now.

An interesting art gallery is across the street from the store. It's called 'Morningside.' There are some fascinating items offered. Some of the cut glass and ceramic pieces are beautiful and strange. There is an artist's studio in the neighborhood, too.

A welcome spot at the Fulford Dock.

St. Paul's Catholic Church.

From the center of the harbor, you can see a picturesque grey church with a red roof and a white spire. It is St. Paul's Catholic Church, built in 1884, and is an historic landmark. It is about a half-mile hike from the wharf to the church. To keep you entertained, there are copious blackberry bushes en route, so take along a bucket. Just before you get to the church, off the road to the right, there is a tiny, ancient graveyard. The church itself is a great photo subject. In the foreground, you will see more old headstones: graves of pioneers.

A short walk takes you across a small bridge and you are at the Fulford Inn. It's a handsome English Tudor building with a pub, licenced premises, a dining room and rooms to rent.

Drummond Park: It's a short distance beyond the Inn, a pleasant little seashore park with parking space, camp sites, picnic tables, outhouses and a launching ramp.

At low tides, you can dig some small clams, but it is not a bountiful area.

The most interesting feature of Drummond Park is the Indian petroglyph that is located there. It can be found near the parking lot and the boat ramp, between two cedar trees.

Despite the fact that Fulford Harbour is one of the largest bays in the Gulf Islands, it does not offer much anchorage. The area at the head of the bay is all tideflat and the water before it is quite shallow. There is no refuge from south winds which can whistle up Shute Passage and stir up the fetch in the harbor.

Some protection might be found in a small nook east of the ferry dock.

The Fulford Harbour
Petroglyph

This rock carving is on the flat surface of a large rock which used to rest farther up the shore, across from the ferry dock. It is described as 'controversial' in some guidebooks, because moving it from its primitive spot to a public park may have seemed like sacrilege to ethos-buffs. In its present spot, it can certainly be enjoyed by more people.

The carving is that of a seal's face. As you stare at it, you wonder if it was the Indian's personal totem, or a magic symbol to bring seals to be caught? It's a sort of round 'smiley-face'. It's quite easy to take a rubbing of this one.

This Indian rock carving was found at Fulford Harbour on the shoreline opposite the ferry wharf.

Fulford Harbour was once inhabited by the Tsawout Indian Tribe and was used by all of the Saanich Indian people for their traditional way of fishing and hunting.

Swanson Channel, Fulford to **Ganges:** Leaving Fulford, there is plenty of water inside Russell Island. Avoid **Louisa Rock**. It is indicated by a thin band of kelp. According to the chart, it is in no less than 9 feet (2.7 M.) but it is prudent to keep away from it. Just north of this rock, you will see a beautiful cove with a tiny islet and on the shore, a fine home complete with a pasture and horses.

Eleanor Point is a rubbled knob of rock. A small exposed rock just off its tip is a good fishing spot for cod. You might pencil on your chart that there is a triangular daybeacon on shore just south of this point.

Beaver Point is a public park. It is accessible by car, primarily, although there is one mooring buoy in the cove just west of the point. This is a very popular place for campers. You can usually see a rich profusion of tents of various colors along the shore. There is a green-banded white tower which houses the flashing light. There are cable crossings both north and south of Beaver Point. The tiny coves at the northern cable crossing would be ideal for cartoppers or kayaks to explore.

Yeo Point has a nice little cove behind it which would be a good spot to visit in an outboard or kayak.

The whole southeastern shore of Saltspring along Swanson Channel is dotted with interesting niches. Some of them have favorable depths for anchorage. But ferries, tugs and tows and large commercial vessels that ply these waters create almost constant wakes. At times, there can be as many as four ferries in view at once. When you are proceeding up the channel, you will find that it is difficult to predict the wakes. Sometimes two ferries passing each other will have wakes that virtually cancel each other. At other times, they will add up to whitecaps.

Beaver Point.

All it takes is a piece of cloth and some crayons and patience.

A legend, anyone?

Opposite Yeo Point is **Deep Ridge.** It extends for almost a half mile in a line leading to the Channel Islands. The eastern end of this system has a recently-installed buoy with flashing green and red lights. The code here is green-red-green.

Channel Islands: They are three in number. The single southern island is about 4 times the size of the others. It is dome-shaped and well forested. There is a clear passage between the south and north islands. There is a white flashing light mounted on a standard on the channel side of the northwest island. At night, our advice would be to stay well away from this light and the red-green one at Deep Ridge.

At this point, Swanson Channel is intercepted by Captain Passage, which leads up to Ganges Harbour.

On chart #3442 (metric, again!) you can find Cusheon Lake up in the hills above the channel. Note **Cusheon Creek** comes down to the passage and has created a delta. A community of summer cabins has grown up there. On a point, you will see an extraordinary house built of fieldstone and cedar. It is three stories high, and it looks like a house meant for history. Is it, perhaps, just a house waiting for its legend? It is off **Batt Rock** named after David Batt of the *Clio* in 1859. Do you suppose he was thrilled at the honor?

You are now about three nautical miles from the settlement at Ganges.

Ganges Shoal ought not cause you much concern, it is about 13 feet (4 M.) at low water.

Ganges

Now, here, bless its little civic heart, is a town that knows it's a seaport! It may not be the biggest community in the Gulf region, but the shopping center is adjacent to the dock. You won't have to hike a mile up hill or call a cab to get your vittles and ice down to the dock. The liquor store is only a couple of blocks away. There are two complete grocery stores and a late-closing 'mom and pop' store. There is a Pharmasave drug store, a library, two bookstores, two banks, an information center, a shopping mall, a hospital, and a combination hardware and dry goods store. You will find a health-food shop and—beware!—an absolutely sinful bakery! If you develop a thirst, there are pubs and licenced premises. And, of course, there are the usual tourist attractions: boutiques, art/craft galleries, (there are more than two dozen craftspeople and shops on Saltspring Island), ice cream parlors and the like. Repair people can work on your boat, your propane system and your electronic gear. There is even a man in the Mouat Mall who can repair cameras and binoculars. You can get ice and propane. The 'Gulf Islands Driftwood', a weekly paper serving residents in all the islands, with special editions for visitors, is based in town.

There are two—count 'em—two, government docks. One has 20 amp power available. There are pleasant and helpful dock-people.

All is not perfect, of course. Although there are plans developed to make the rest of the amenities available, in 1985, there were no nearby showers or laundromat; and there was no water on the public docks. Some of the improvements were already in progress. The nearby park has been upgraded and attractive wooden walkways and a band shell were added.

By the time you visit, the minor inconveniences may be remedied.

Ganges Harbour, Gulf Islands crossroads.

Sometimes a piano-player accompanies films.

Grace Islet is a little tree-covered rock which divides Ganges Harbour into two bays. There is a drying reef between it and a small peninsula which forms the attachment of the breakwater. There is a white tower with a green top and a flashing green light on the seaward end of it.

The most northwesterly head of Ganges Harbour has two government floats, one of them for seaplanes. The one for boat-moorage does not have electricity. It is rather exposed to waves down the harbour and serves as a kind of overflow for the dock behind the breakwater.

There is another small dock in this immediate vicinity. It is used as the moorage for the water taxi boats. They travel all over the lower Gulf Islands, transporting school children to and from Saltspring, in addition to providing taxi service between the islands.

Also nearby is the Ganges Esso Marine Gas Dock which offers gasoline, diesel, ice and some moorage.

The Ganges Main Public Dock

If you decide to moor at the government wharf behind the breakwater, which is the only protected moorage in the harbor, we'll give you some tips.

As you head west toward the head of the harbor, be aware of lots of crab trap floats, they're in a long line.

There are dolphins marking the entrance to the moorage. Stay within these. We saw at least one boat each day go aground while entering outside these dolphins. When you turn the corner and get your first sight of the floats, you may just decide to bag the whole thing and leave for a less crowded spot. It is often packed. But even during the stormiest times there seems to be space for just one more boat. The first dock on the right is for commercial vessels, the other two are for pleasure boats. During the summer, the fishing boats are usually out and they put visitors in the open spaces on these reserved docks. Rafting is often a must.

Take note of the sign that indicates reserved sections on the left hand float. One space at the end of the dock is reserved for the B.C. Hydro boat 'Thunderball'. It has to be free to take emergency crews to repair outages on the other islands. At the head of that dock, there are spaces reserved for the R.C.M.P. and Canadian Coast Guard boats.

Pay attention to the sign on that dock that says you may not raft up on the outside of that float. The water is quite shoal just off the float and many boats get grounded there when trying to turn around.

Water is shoal near the dock in Ganges Government Marina.

Beyond the log dump on the village shore is the Ganges Marina which has available moorage, both leased and transient, at 25, 35 and 45-foot slips. There is power and water available. It has a gas dock which carries diesel as well as gasoline. You can get air for your scuba tanks here, or even rent tanks if you wish. A floating store carries ice, fishing gear, licences and boat supplies. For customers there are restrooms, and they hope to have showers and a laundromat shortly. The marina is open from 8 a.m. to 8 p.m. all summer long, 7 days a week. The dock attendants will take propane tanks up to the shoreside filling station and get them replenished. A mechanic is available.

Which Fishing Licence?

Zo was chatting with Brad Brown, of Ganges Marina, on Saltspring Island. She told him she was doing research for a book about cruising the Gulf Islands and she wanted to include various services to boaters, such as selling fishing licences.

She told him she hoped he sold better licences than the one she had bought. She had been using it for six weeks and hadn't caught a single fish.

"What kind of a licence did you buy?" he asked her.

"You know, a licence to go fishing," she explained.

In a serious tone, he said, "Ah-h-h, that's your trouble. You bought a licence to 'go fishing' and it's worked perfectly, hasn't it? You've been able to 'go fishing' every day. Right? Now, what you should have bought was a licence to catch fish."

Zo was about to ask him if there were really two different kinds of licences, when she saw him begin to grin.

So, her advice is: demand a licence to catch fish!

Meet the owner of the Ganges Marina.

At the very head of this bay is Ross and Ganges Marina. They have transient moorage, with power and water. There is a haulout rig that can handle boats up to 30 feet. There are skilled mechanics who double as underwater repairmen. There is a small tug, the 'Great White', which is available for emergencies. It also offers fishing, diving, and sailing charters. Their motto is, "We service everything".

Approaching this facility, take note of the two reef-bearing rocks which lie directly seaward from the dock.

The south shore of Ganges Harbour is quite shoal. You will see an elaborate complex of moorage floats, just west of Walter Bay. It belongs to the popular Saltspring Sailing Club. It offers no public moorage.

Walter Bay is mostly a tideflat. The outer portion of it has some anchorage in 16 feet (5 M.) and would be a refuge from a southeaster. The low spit would protect you from waves, but would not dampen the fury of the winds. Most of the area dries at 5 feet (1.5 M.). As expected, there are many mooring buoys for small outboard boats here.

The **Chain Islets** are a string of islands of varying size, extending from Second Sister Island at the southeast end of the chain, to a cluster of rocks just shoreward from Goat Island at the northwest end.

Second Sister Island: It stumps everybody why the outermost of these islands got the name 'second.' There is a red-topped tower on the Channel-side of the island; the light flashes red. There are really two islands here. The big one is hilly and forested. It comes down to a notch where it is joined to the smaller by a drying spit. There is a long stairway from the shoulder of the large island down to the beach level and it ends on a dock with a float. Across the spit, on the islet, is another float and dock. Tucked away, almost out of sight, is a little A-frame house. Extending northwest from the islet is a shoal which has a dry rock in its middle.

Second Sister Island has a niche.

All that's left of the castle on First Sister Island.

Third Sister Island is second in line. Does this remind you of the old Abbott and Costello routine, "Who's on First?" It is separated from Sister #2 by a shallow channel, 10 feet (3 M.). There is a rock just off the islet that dries at 1 foot tides (0.3 M.). If you choose to duck between the Sisters for rubbernecking, hug the Third Sister. This island has a veritable marine minefield just northwest of it, consisting of rocks and reefs and who-knows-what. It is called 'Moneymaker Reef' for easily guessed reasons.

The third of this trio is, you've guessed it, **First Sister Island.** Now this island has a good dock and float and a picturesque fieldstone boathouse—and a history. It was once called 'Castle Island'. In the twenties, a wealthy Scot came to the area and fell in love with this island. He decided to build a pint-sized castle on it. He took a reduced scale design of a Scottish castle and built it, complete with battlements, with stone from local quarries.

The legend goes that he was a trifle too fond of the alcoholic beverage which comes from his homeland, and it eventually did him in.

For a while after his death, the shooting-match was on the market but found no takers. Eventually, in the 40's, an American decided to make it his summer place. He bought it and after a few years, discovered that it was a trifle too primitive for modern day occupancy—and too hard to keep warm. So he had it torn down. For some reason, he never got around to building a new house in its place.

Just recently the island got a new owner. He was the holder of a winning ticket in a raffle.

Deadman Island is next. It was so-called because it was a burial ground for an Indian tribe that lived there in the 1800's.

There are three islands in this complex, the center one is wooded and has a ridge 115 feet (35 M.) high. There is a green colored house and a dock on the east side.

The Ganges Massacre

The Chain Islands were the scene of a series of bloody skirmishes between bands of Indians, with at least one horrified white onlooker.

The story was told by historian Wallbran:

"On Wednesday afternoon, 4 July, 1860, a canoe of the Bella Bella Indians from the north, containing nine men, three women and two boys, with a white passenger named McCawley, arrived in Admiralty Bay (Ganges Harbour), on Saltspring Island, and these travellers were invited by half a hundred Cowichan Indians to come on shore and rest. McCawley called on a settler named Thomas Henry Lineker, whose house was close to the beach, when, in a short time, firing being heard at the water's edge, it was found that the Cowichans had deliberately shot and killed all the men among the new-comers. with the exception of one who escaped, badly wounded, into the bush. Taking the women and boys for slaves, they then seized the canoe and decamped. The settlers on Saltspring Island, at that date, did not number more than seventy, and great alarm was expressed by them at the treacherous act, they fearing that when the Bella Bellas heard of it the latter would take a fearful revenge in which white people might be involved.

"A few days after..(the incident)..two Cowichan Indians in a canoe were quietly fishing about two hundred yards from the shore (having had nothing to do with the massacre), near them being a boat in which were two white men similarly engaged, when suddenly appeared, round a point of land a short distance off, several canoes filled with Port Rupert Indians, who, on perceiving the fishermen, made directly for them. The Cowichans got into the white men's boat, evidently seeking protection, deserting their own canoe which went adrift. The Fort Ruperts dashed alongside the boat, and, seizing the unhappy redskins, five or six knives were buried in each, their heads cut off and the bodies thrown to the fishes. No violence was offered to the white men, who were terribly alarmed at the awful sight. Nothing was asked, no explanation given by the Fort Rupert Indians, who continued on their journey, taking the heads with them. The next day one of the heads was found stuck on a tall pole on a small island near Saltspring Island."

Deadman Island, perhaps?

Some of Ted Akerman's most prized Indian artifacts.

The ruined dock at Welbury Bay.

Just off the north shore of the center of Deadman Island, there is a foul area consisting of two rocks which dry at about 2.5 feet (0.7 M.). There is a daybeacon fronting this spot that is set on a third rock. It is a concrete base with a mast and a marker indicating the best course is to the right.

Goat Island is a hilly and wooded island about ½-mile long. Off its northwestern end there is another patch of foul ground which has a daybeacon mounted on a mast set into a concrete pylon. The daybeacon, #2, is red. There is a house, not too visible, on the north end of this island.

All of the islands in Ganges Harbour are privately-owned. However, you may land a shore boat and wander any beaches. All beaches are 'Crown Land' in British Columbia, which means they are open to the public—up to the high tide line.

The shoreline of the Saltspring Island peninsula that ends in Welbury and Scott Points has many beautiful beachfront houses and docks. Moorage is possible in from 16 feet (5 M.) to 18 feet (5.5 M.).

Welbury Point: This sharp peninsula forms the southwest shore of Welbury Bay. There are two very attractive white shell beaches near its tip.

Welbury Bay has space and good depths for anchoring at its head, but the wave action from Captain Passage would make it chancy in south winds. There is a long dock which is in disrepair that comes out from the southern shore. Behind it is a large quonset hut that at one time was a factory that produced potter's clay which was dug near the beach.

Scott Point: During the summer when you pass this point, you may be surprised to see an old salt standing on the point looking out to sea. As you get closer, you might recognize a peg-legged sailor in old British Tar uniform, a dead ringer for Long John Silver. You almost expect to hear his voice ring out over the harbor, "Avast ye! Stand well off the point!" It is an extremely life-like wooden statue, of course. And it is only on display when the owner of the property is in residence, we were told.

Long Harbour is an inlet of about two miles. It is the site of the ferry terminal on the mainland-to-Vancouver Island run. There is a lot of good anchorage in this bay.

On the inside of Nose Point the land is parklike. There is a small cove just northwest of the point which has a nice beach. The area is a little too close to the outside to offer good anchorage except when you can be sure of calm weather.

The little cluster of unnamed islets just beyond this cove are interesting. They are known locally as **Fisherman Islands**. One of them has what looks like an old abandoned house or barn on it. A red conical buoy, 'U 50', marks a rock just beyond these islets. This rock has 6 feet (1.8 M.) over it.

The south shoreline has many private homes and docks on it. On this side of the bay you will come to the Royal Vancouver Yacht Club out-station. A sign notifies all that non-members and those with reciprocity may not apply for moorage at the dock.

At one time, there was a marina here, Scott Point Marina, but it is defunct and the docks are in poor repair.

The RVYC outpost in Long Harbour.

The Seagoing Schoolbus Lady

Youngsters in the 'Outer Gulf Islands', namely, Saturna, Mayne, Galiano and the Penders, all attend grade school on their own islands and then go to the consolidated high school on Saltspring Island. Since ferry service is too slow, a water taxi is used to transport them.

This boat is speedy. It has rows of double seats, just like a regular land bus. In fact, there is a whole fleet of water taxis based in Ganges which are used for emergencies, excursions and the like.

The waterborne school bus driver is a good-looking young woman. She's the independent kind of gal who could have functioned just as well in a pioneer environment if she had lived in those days. Still she's a lively part of this modern day world.

At the age of 17, Sandy (Klein) Tiger was already an accomplished boater. She and her father, Horst Klein, who founded the Canadian Lifeboat Society, patrolled the waters whenever boats were in danger. One day they answered a 'mayday' call that said a fishing boat was on fire. When they reached the scene in their rescue boat, they saw the skipper floating near the burning boat.

Sandy was wearing a wetsuit because it was midwinter. She went over the side into the icy water of the Strait of Georgia. She grabbed the inert body and with her father's help got him in the boat. She immediately began giving the man artificial respiration.

"He wasn't breathing," she remembers, "and I just started giving him A.R. the way I had been taught. After a while, I heard a helicopter. All of a sudden I saw a man in an orange suit coming out of the sky and into the boat. I gave the victim one last breath and they whisked him up into a helicopter."

The fisherman lived. Sandy was given an Award of Valour, which hangs in a prominent spot in the wheelhouse of her liveaboard boat, the 42-foot 'Storm Princess', in Ganges Harbour.

This blonde, blue-eyed young woman has her First Master's ticket, which means she can pilot a 40-ton, 40-passenger vessel. She's had the licence since she was 21. She is also a certified scuba diver and has a private pilot's licence.

"Normally there are 32 high school kids who commute daily by water taxi to and from the outer islands. The kids come aboard, they're relaxed, we joke, we have a good time," Sandy said. "But they know they better follow the rules because they know I mean what I say." Sandy doesn't mince words when she talks with the kids. She speaks their language (that is, their 'away-from-home' language.) "They love it when it's rough. The stormier the better, they say."

Sandy, 26, has been driving the water taxis since she was 21 and is on 24-hour call with the firm, Gulf Islands Water Taxis, Ltd.

"I have to confess that I have an unusual occupation for someone like me who often gets seasick — unless I am at the wheel!"

Farther in, a small island seems to dominate the passage. It is not named on the chart, but when you come abreast of it, you will see a sign telling you it is called **Clamshell Island.** It offers protection from winds out of the channel and down the inlet, so it is ideal moorage.

There is a white tower on a square concrete base. It is red-banded and has a quick-flashing red light on top, just south of Clamshell Island.

Behind this island is a green buoy, 'U 55', which indicates a rock that has 9 feet (2.7 M.) over it.

The B.C. ferry dock has a remarkably large holding area for cars because this run from the mainland to Sidney discharges and picks up a lot of cars on summer weekends. The dock is turned at an angle from the channel because it is so narrow there. The ferry has to go beyond the dock, then turn and back up into the wing walls.

The shoreline from Nose Point to the head of the harbor is lined with homes which belong to a development called 'Maracaibo Estates'.

There is a very inviting beach tucked in behind a reef, just west of Clamshell Island.

Incidentally, the water quality and temperatures during hot days in summer can produce a phenomenal crop of jellyfish in this area. We have seen it so thick that it almost looks like pale gelatin! If you chose to swim in among them, they wouldn't sting you, but it gives a person a queasy feeling when they brush against you. It's like swimming in Jell-O.

Beyond the submarine cable crossing, the harbor widens somewhat and there is a basin for moorage with depths of 21 feet (6.4 M.), almost ideal depth except at unusually low tides. Note the rock that dries at 2 feet (0.6 M.) and locate it before dropping the hook in this area.

The harbor narrows a little toward the head end and you will see a large con-dominium moorage, called 'Maracaibo Marina', behind a log breakwater. It is for the use of the home-owners of the development.

There are many docks and mooring buoys in this small bay. At the far end of the harbor, you will see an entrance to a remarkable inlet. It is only open to small shore boats and kayaks during high tides, but it stretches for almost three quarters of a mile back inland. It ends in a wide marshland. Strangely, the left hand shore has few homes. It is heavily wooded. Notice that passage is restricted at a narrow spot by two rocks that dry at 5 feet (1.6 M.).

Just before entering the marsh, you will see a beautiful house and dock. It looks like a government installation, primarily because of an imposing flagpole and red painted rails, but it is a private residence.

We stopped and chatted with some young people who were vacationing there. The husband had a delightful German dialect. We asked him where they were from, he said 'Geneva, Switzerland'. In the course of the conversation, we found out that he was a professional actor on the legitimate stage in that city. We paddled back out the inlet somewhat dazzled by the romantic idea of meeting a man who might be a famous Swiss actor.

Trincomali Channel, Nose Point to Southey Point: Rounding **Nose Point,** and heading west, we are in a major marine highway in the Gulf Islands, Trincomali Channel. It continues up past the Secretary Islands, along Galiano Island, and half way up Valdes Island, where it splits into Pylades and Stuart Channels at Pylades Island.

Nose Point: It was named in 1865 after Jimmy Durante. (Ha! Caught you, didn't we? Skipping biographical notes! Shame! What will you do when you come to the blue-book quiz at the end of the book?) Frankly, this point didn't show us much to comment on, but we didn't want to cut it off to spite something. There is a nice little cove just beyond it, but you wouldn't anchor there unless you stern-tied. There is a triangular daymarker on shore where the submarine cable exits. It is a fishing boundary marker.

About a quarter mile east of Nose Point, if you look carefully, you will see a fascinating sod house above the beach.

From here to Walker Hook the shoreline doesn't offer any landing possibilities. On the hills above the shore, you will see a line of powerline towers that jar the sen-

The White Renegade

"In the summer of 1863, Ganges Harbour was, as usual, crowded with Cowichan and Saanich Indians. Vague rumors got abroad that a party of Bella Bellas contemplated a trading expedition to the Hudson's Bay post at Victoria. They were solemnly warned that if they passed Ganges Harbour they would be murdered to a man. Trading with the Bella Bellas at that time was a renegade Englishman named Macaulay who came to the coast from the Sandwich Islands. Thinking that he would have a good chance to secure a couple of loads of very valuable furs cheap if the Bella Bellas would venture down and be murdered by their foes, the wretch persuaded them that no harm could come while he was with them. So it happened, that about noon one day, in the summer of 1863, thirty Bella Bella warriors, women, and boys appeared in their canoes off Ganges Harbour. They landed and came up to the white man's cabin (Mr. Lineker's). Macaulay was with them. They were sitting around talking when suddenly the alarm was given. Nine hundred Cowichan-Saanich warriors were coming down the harbour. The Bella Bellas fled to the beach, sprang into their canoes, and prepared to fight it out. Their foes in overwhelming numbers formed on the beaches—about two hundred yards below the cabin—and opened fire with their flintlocks.

"The northern braves returned it in good shape, the squaws loading the guns for the men. Fiendish yells were echoed back by the rocky hills around, and many a bullet lodged in the cabin walls while for three long hours thirty held out against the nine hundred. But at last a boy and girl were taken prisoner by some Cowichans who had taken to a canoe—and only one northern warrior was left alive. Seeing that his sole chance lay in flight, he paddled his canoe to the foot of the ledge that rose almost perpendicularly from the sea at that point. Wounded in the leg and cheek, and followed by a swarm of bullets, the plucky fellow climbed the rocks like a cat, and reached the top in safety. A yell of baffled rage from below, then the whole band made for the side of the mountain to head him off. Now began a race for life. Running a few yards ahead, the warrior hid in a clump of wood. His foes rushed past, so

The scenic inlet in Long Harbour.

close that he could hear their laboured breathing. When they had gone far enough he left his covert, made a detour around the cabin and standing before the door, coolly asked the white man to hide him. This Mr. Lineker dared not do, for the Indians had warned him before the fight, that if he interfered in the least, they would cut the throats of his wife and children. However, he put the warrior on the trail to a settlement of whites in the opposite direction from where his out-witted foes were hunting him. But in a short time they were on his track again, and he had to change his course. Successfully eluding them a second time, he reached a rocky ledge on the shore, and having bound a couple of logs together with pine twigs, tired and wounded, he paddled across to Saanich peninsula, armed with his faithful flintlock.

"Here he was attacked by a couple of Saanich Indians, who seeing his plight, immediately concluded that he had been in a fight with their friends on the island, and it would have gone hard with him, had not two white men from Victoria who were out hunting, come to his rescue.

"When the Indians on the island had given up the chase after their wily prey, they returned to the harbour and carried the bodies of the northern warriors and women to a little island in Ganges Harbour, and piled them up on the shore. (The furs had all been thrown overboard to clear the canoes during the fight.) Then they went back to their camps. By six o'clock that evening not a vestige of evidence remained to show that a deadly struggle had taken place in Ganges Harbour.

"It may be mentioned that Macaulay had stolen a double-barrelled gun, the only firearm Lineker possessed, and fled before the fight began.

"H.M.S. gunboat 'Satellite' came to the harbour shortly after, and Captain Prevost, having learned the particulars, compelled the victorious tribe to release from slavery the boy and girl they had seized, and give up the ringleaders in the fight. Every fortnight after the battle the gunboats 'Forward' and 'Grappler' called in turn at the island to protect the settlers by putting the Indians in wholesome fear of British Law." (Capt. John T. Walbran)

Saltspring—a Haven for Negro Ex-Slaves.

The State of California proclaimed almost from the day of its coming into the Union in September, 1850 that it was a "Free State," slavery was forbidden.

In that same year, the legislature began a series of laws which took away much of the black man's freedom. Acts were decreed which disqualified Negroes from giving evidence against white persons. This meant that a black man could not protect his property from a white man.

In 1852 the state passed the 'Fugitive Slave Act,' which provided for arrest of any slave who might have escaped his master. The law specified that a fugitive could be returned to his master, but that he could not be held in slavery in California. This compounded the blow to the Negro's freedom since he could not even defend himself in court.

In 1856, black people held a convention in Sacramento and denounced these laws, which put them in the same class as criminals. They pointed out that they owned taxable property of an estimated value of $5 million.

The Democratic governor elected in 1858 announced his policy concerning black civil rights. In no uncertain terms he was clearly a-straddle a fence. No slavery in California, he reiterated. But, it was not nice to agitate for abolition since it was an attempt to tell another state how to conduct its affairs.

In that year a milestone case came to light. A Californian who had come from a Mississippi plantation brought with him a Negro boy who was his "body-servant." The boy escaped and was arrested and held for extradition to the plantation, where he was worth $1,500. The master said that although he was residing in Sacramento, he "intended to go back to Mississippi."

A United States commissioner neatly sidestepped the intent of the law. He said that since the boy, named Archy, had not fled to California, but had been brought there, he had no jurisdiction. The verdict was in Archy's favor, but no attempt was made to make the Southerner release the boy.

Fearing that eventually the California law would prohibit him from keeping the boy, the Southerner decided to put him aboard a tramp steamer and smuggle him back to the plantation. The Negro community got wind of this move and managed to swear out a warrant for

sibilities. They sort of march along the heights until they branch off to the spot where they cross Long Harbour to provide power for Ganges.

Walker Hook: By the time you reach this spot, you have passed **Atkins Reef,** which has one rock poking up at most waters, just east of it. The reef is about 0.7 miles long. The beacon is a concrete base set in the submerged part of the reef. A standard with a green daymarker indicates the preferable passage is to the right, but you can pass on either side.

The eastern side of the hook has a very attractive beach and is a popular place for daytime anchorage. It is accessible by land only by going beyond a 'No Trespassing' sign put up by the owner to shoo away some undesirables who used to use the spot for drinking sprees.

Notice the reef that is a few yards off the joint of this dogleg peninsula. Walker Hook is a good overnight anchorage in calm weather.

kidnapping against the master.

The man was arrested and the boy was released. But it was only a minimal victory. The case attracted so much attention the blacks realized it was only a matter of time before the backlash took place. They decided they had to emigrate. They chose British Columbia.

A delegation of 65 went to the British Colony to see if they could purchase land there. A month later the delegation returned with heartening news. There was another meeting, with about 300 in attendance, 50 of whom were well-wishing white people. The delegation told the group they had been received "..most cordially and kindly by His Excellency the Governor, and heartily welcomed to this land of freedom and humanity." They said that land could be obtained at 20 shillings an acre, one quarter in cash, and the remainder in four annual payments with interest at five per cent, but with no tax on the land until full payment; that landowners after a residence of nine months had the right of electoral franchise, of sitting as jurors, and all the protection of the law as civilians of the Colony.

The group raised $2,500 to charter a boat and transport several hundred of them to their new home. Their next act was to prepare a "Declaration of the Sense of the Coloured People."

"Whereas we are fully convinced that the continued aim of the spirit and policy of our Mother Country is to oppress, degrade and entrap us—we have therefore determined to seek an asylum in the land of strangers . . ."

Their Resolution #8 read: "That we now unitedly cast our lots (after the toil and hardships that have wrung our sweat and tears for centuries) in that land where bleeding humanity finds a balm, where philanthropy is crowned with royalty, slavery has laid aside its weapons, and the coloured American is unshackled; there in the lair of the Lion we will repose from the horrors of the past under the genial laws of the Queen of the Christian Isles."

A small group of those Victoria-based black families came to Saltspring Island. They settled in the Fernwood and Ganges areas. One of them became the island's first schoolteacher.

Their history has become completely interwoven with that of the white people on Saltspring. (Early Remembrances)

There is a drying flat inside the west end of the hook and it is filled with private mooring buoys which would discourage anchoring even at high water. It has a good crop of kelp. Most of it dries at low water.

Fernwood Point has a government dock which can be seen from quite a distance because it has such a long red pier leading out to the float. It has about 80 feet (24 M.) moorage space on three sides. There are no amenities on it. It is not recommended for overnight tie-ups because of its vulnerability to the winds in both directions. The public dock is there primarily to serve the people of the nearby Secretary and Wallace Islands as a contact point.

Approaching the dock from the east you will see a long sand and rock beach. The wharf stands on the edge of a shallow shelf. At low tide, it is not advisable to go closer to the beach than the mooring float.

The Fernwood Government Wharf.

The Fernwood Store, owned by Ian and Liz Cornish for the past couple of years, has possibly longer business hours than any other store in the Gulf Islands. They open at 9 a.m. and close at 9 p.m. seven days a week all summer long. In the winter, they shorten their hours to 10 a.m. to 7 p.m. They have fresh fruits and vegetables, frozen meats and staples. You can get bait and ice. They pump gas for cars. They even have stamps. A microwave heats up hand-foods.

It isn't listed on the chart, but there is a great and inviting beach just about a quarter-mile west of the Fernwood Dock. It is called **Hudson's Point,** although there really isn't any noticeable protrusion. This is a popular clam-digging beach. We dug enough clams with our bare hands in a half-hour to make two meals.

Victoria Rock off Fernwood Point, has a red/green buoy just marked 'UE'. It is a marker of the junction of Houstoun Passage and Trincomali Channel. The rock is about 14 feet below the surface (4.3 M.) at lower water, so we wouldn't fret much over it.

Governor Rock is nearer the center of the channel. It has a green buoy with a flashing green light and a radar reflector on a standard. The rock comes into view at 6 feet (1.8 M.) above lower water. Look for the identification 'U45' if you are in doubt.

Victoria Shoal completes this little trio of baddies. It's pretty deep, though—14 feet at the shallowest (4.3 M.) It has a flashing green light like Governor Rock. There is a radar reflector on it. The legend reads 'U43'.

Walker Rock over near Galiano Island is on a drying ledge and it is a leg of a range light system with one on the Saltspring Island shore. It is a route marker for ships which want to go from Trincomali Channel to Houstoun Passage, going safely between Victoria Shoal and Panther Point on Wallace Island. At night, going in either direction, follow the white light. If you see either red or green, you are out of the safe area.

Who's Tending the Store?

Americans, accustomed to layers of local government such as counties, towns and city charters, legislative districts and the like, are often bewildered to discover that there are no incorporated areas in the Gulf Islands. Even Ganges, on Saltspring Island, which looks for all the world like a town, has no mayor, no town council, no town marshalls. There is a school district which covers all of the lower Gulf Islands: Saturna, Galiano, the Penders, Mayne and Saltspring Islands. Almost all children of school age reside on these six islands. The R.C.M.P. takes care of law enforcement. Nearly all public wharves are managed by local people, usually retirees, who collect moorage fees and keep a percentage of it.

The Gulf Islands are administered by an entity called the 'Capital Regional District', which is an authority like a county commission. It is part of a larger body called 'The Islands Trust'.

There was a movement to get local control. In 1873, Saltspring Island incorporated as a municipality. It did not work well, as Tony Richards, of the 'Gulf Islands Driftwood' the weekly newspaper, explains:

"It was a municipality of seething internal hostility. For eight years there was bickering and factional dispute, both on the island and in the Victoria press.

"A Victoria news report in 1882 termed the municipal administration 'a reign of terror,' but the newspaper was eager to trounce the government and may have exaggerated slightly.

"By 1883 the government had thankfully wound up the island township and it was unorganized again.

"It remains so to this day.

"Islanders living in insularity and sometimes in isolation, are an independent group. For every ten voices raised to have a road widened, there are ten shouting to keep it the way it is. Mostly they like things the way they are."

The Island Trust came into being June 5, 1974. It consists of three government-appointed general trustees and two locally elected trustees from each of the thirteen islands involved: Bowen, Denman, Gabriola, Galiano, Gambier, Hornby, Lasqueti, Mayne, North Pender, Salt Spring, Saturna, South Pender and Thetis, 29 trustees in all.

Their job: to make recommendations to the cabinet on general development policy for the islands, make recommendations to the cabinet on the acquisition and use of Crown Land in the area, coordinate and assist in the determination, implementation and carrying out of municipal and provincial government policies for the Islands, and make decisions on specific developments or zoning bylaws.

The history of the Islands Trust has not been one of total approval by the affected island residents, as might be expected from such a rugged and feisty group. Some complain that it is too much influenced by economics and too little by protection of the environment. (Now where have we heard that before!)

A Lasqueti Island oyster farmer voiced this philosophy.

"I am horrified that all our concerns about land, sea or air have to be justified by economics.

"People should not be seen as 'users' and 'abusers' of land. They are 'elements' in a system.

"People view the world as something to be used and not as something to be lived in.

"I became aware that the islands are slowly changing in a pattern inconsistent with the intent of the Trust. It seemed to me to be at variance with what the Trust was all about."

Debating responsibility for the Trust was "like adjusting the deck chairs on the 'Titanic!' " he summed up.

(Gulf Islands Driftwood September 11, 1985)

Almost a rural 7-11 store.

On the shore at the range light tower you will find The Last Resort, a small but popular resort area. They have a small float in front that visitors can use for drop-in visits in calm weather.

This would be a good time to explain why we keep talking about sudden winds springing up.

We tied to this float. We knew it was really a dinghy float and not meant for a heavy boat like a sailboat. The evening was warm and calm and the water was mirror-like. We paddled ashore in the kayaks and spent a pleasant evening with these hospitable folks.

During the night, we noticed a wind coming up. By 4 a.m. we were rolling violently. By 5:30 a.m. the morning was breaking and we decided we had had enough of it. Untying the 'Sea Witch' from the wildly tossing raft was a battle and we got soaked to the waist from the breaking waves before we got loose. Once free, we flew downwind to Montague Harbour under 30 knots of wind. It was an exhilarating although scary way to start a day.

There had been no prediction of winds, the barometer was just as steady as it had been for days, but the wind really whistled in.

In Houstoun Passage, now, with the Trincomali rocks safely behind you, the only other bugbear is a series of islets and shoals off Wallace Island. The eastern terminus of these menaces is a flashing red light buoy. It is marked 'U44'.

We will get around to describing this reef system off Wallace Island in another chapter. Right now, we are going to lead you to the northwest end of Saltspring Island before we head you in another direction.

Southey Point was named after a secretary to a Rear Admiral who commanded the 'Ganges'. It peters out into a drying ledge, at the end of which you will find a pretty white tower.

Southey Cove is a drying inlet that looks attractive until you get close enough to discover that practically every available spot for moorage has been spoken for with private mooring buoys. If you can find a spot, it's pretty good anchorage.

Well! We've led you, safely we hope, to the northwest end of Saltspring Island. We'll tell you all about the southwest side of this island in the chapter on the Sansum Narrows entry to the Gulf Islands.

4. Sansum Narrows: Family Entrance to the Gulf Islands.

Most American visitors to the Islands do not go through customs at Sidney. For one reason, the customs dock at that town is the hairiest moorage in the Pacific Northwest. The wind seems to live right there in the harbor. There is an alternative port of entry in Tsehum Harbor, but not many people know about it. And it is not a convenient spot, either. As we said in the previous chapter, most Americans enter the Gulf Islands through Bedwell Harbour.

So, the folks who cruise up the west side of Saltspring to enjoy the Gulf Islands are mostly the Canadians from the Victoria area. Since we hope that a lot of them will be interested in this guide, we are going to convoy all those who are interested up Sansum Narrows. Incidentally, the Narrows were named for Arthur Sansum, R.N., 1st Lieutenant on the 'Thetis'. He died of apoplexy in the Gulf of California in 1853. (Apparently nobody warned him about life in California!)

As a matter of fact, the path down this scenic channel is a very nice cruise for folks returning to the States.

Shute Passage will take you around the thread-the-needle course in **Colburne Passage** and put you in Satellite Channel. Use Plans Chart #3476 here. We won't even try to describe the best route, but the 1:10,000 scale will help you. Good luck!

Satellite Channel, Isabella Island to Musgrave Landing: This channel was not named in the present age of outer space exploration. It was dubbed after the very terrestrial 'H.M.S. Satellite', described as a 'screw corvette'. It was undoubtedly powered by steam and boasted of 400 H.P. It was built at Devonport, England, in 1856. A year later it made its proud entry into Nanaimo and promptly ran up on an unnamed reef in the harbor, because the marking buoy had taken up residence in another spot nearby. This reef promptly got named 'Satellite Reef', of course. We shall look at it in a further chapter.

Peter, the Cowichan Royalist

In an Indian fishing village on one of the Gulf Islands, lived a Cowichan named Peter. He spoke English, an unusual accomplishment in those days when Chinook was the common language. He had learned it as a child when he worked for the governor in Victoria. His job was to scare crows away from the governor's garden. His pay was fifty cents a week.

Peter was intelligent, and was a devoted subject of Queen Victoria. He called her his 'yas tyee', (Big Chief). He felt personal loyalty to her and thought of her as taking an interest in his race. When her son, Edward VII, came to the throne, he felt rebuffed. "He does not care for us," announced Peter.

His royalist sentiments were reawakened when the Duke of Connaught, who was Governor-General of Canada, visited Vancouver. Peter and some of his tribe went to the city to see his arrival. When the Indians pressed too far forward against the lines to see the Duke, the police pushed them back. The Duke, seeing this, said "You must not treat them like that—they are my very good friends." He then shook hands with Peter.

For the rest of his life, the Cowichan retold the story. In his declining years, he went to live at 'The Gap', which is now called 'Cowichan'. He explained that he came there to live because he had 'come old'.

It got its name appended to the Channel under more auspicious conditions in 1861.

Isabella Island is about 1 acre in size and has a few trees. It has a small islet just west of it. A drying spit connects it to the Saltspring Island shore. There is a white tower with a green band at the top and a quick flashing white light on its southeast tip.

The shoreline along the southwest shore of Saltspring has little to interest the pleasure boater, except for fishing. There are some rather brisk ad-hoc type winds which whip around capriciously in the channel off Saltspring.

You will note a power line comes ashore about a mile southwest of Isabella Island. You might amuse yourself trying to trace the power lines that march on stiff white poles up the side of Hope Hill to feed the radio towers on top.

Along that shoreline, you will see a solitary house in a small clearing on the beach. It is a beautiful spot. The house is an old log cabin which is obviously abandoned. If you are interested in a 'fixer-upper' as they say in real estate ads, you might want to buy it and restore it. You certainly wouldn't be plagued by neighbors or visiting boaters!

Cape Keppel is not one of those unforgettable places. It isn't even a bump on the landscape. The chart indicates there is a road down to it, though. The Chemainus Harbor Limit line is terminated here on Saltspring. That means that ocean-going shipping which anchors in the area beyond is in control of the Chemainus Port Authority.

Isabella Islets

Bill Wolferstan has a beautiful color photograph of this cluster of rocks in his treasure-trove book on the Gulf Islands. He also has an interesting story of the nearby shoreline. He says that the area was settled by several 'Kanaka' families— emigrants from Hawaii. They moved there in the late 1800's after a brief stay in the San Juan Islands. When those islands were turned over to the U.S. by the agreement reached after the 'Pig War', the Polynesians decided that they preferred to live in a land with a monarch rather than a democracy, so they came to Saltspring Island. At the turn of the century, many of the geographical features of this corner of the island had Hawaiian names, but the map-makers decided they were too hard to spell and pronounce, so they replaced all of them with more customary English names and words.

The Isabella Islands are part of a 627-acre ecological preserve. It would be interesting to anchor temporarily off the northeast end of the complex and paddle or row over and look at the plant life.

Patey Rock, a half mile or so offshore, dries at 7 feet (2.1 M.) above lower water. There is a tower set upon the rock. Its color is white and the light is an 'eclipsing group-3 white', which means it glows for ½ second, fades for 2 seconds, glows again for a ½ second, fades for two seconds, lights up for ½ second, then goes dark for 6½ seconds. In other words: a Morse Code 's'. It is a marker indicating the point at which Saanich Inlet joins Satellite Channel.

Now that you are provided with this sterling bit of trivia, would you care to proceed?

Musgrave Rock never gets higher than 7 feet (2.1 M.). It has a red buoy chained to it, which reads 'U 26'. Kelp waves away from it toward the Saltspring shore where it points to a rather stark reef islet which is high and menacing. You wouldn't want to take your boat between this islet and the shore, believe us!

And now we are at **Musgrave Landing,** which we love! We had heard about it for years and never stopped there before, which is a shame, we think. It is a jewel. It's the first stopping place below the Narrows. It was quite popular when that channel

Musgrave Landing—a treasure.

A Simon Charlie carving.

was a favored fishing ground. Usually there were a number of small sports fishing boats tied up there waiting for the right currents to invite the fish. Recently, the runs have been less rewarding and so the Landing may have some space for you.

There is a small Government Dock, about 80 feet (24 M.), total space on both sides of the float. It is considered customary to allow other boats to raft up alongside if you are at the float. The dock leads up to a gravel road, but there are no houses in evidence.

There are actually two coves in Musgrave Landing: the one that the wharf is in and another around a tiny point. The point is very inviting and parklike, with paths leading from one cove to the other.

It is not wise to anchor in the cove with the wharf. There are a number of old logging cables buried in the bottom and local skippers have told stories of fighting to free anchors which get snagged. We took the kayaks and explored the shoreline, and sure enough, there were a number of old rusty 2" cables leading out into the water. If you insist on dropping the hook in this cove, stay as far away from the head as you can.

If you are annoyed by graffiti, you will not appreciate the work of turkeys who had to immortalize themselves in white paint on stones. 'WIMPY' was there once, shame on him. One of the dates is 1971 and the paint is still quite clear. That shows you how long defacement like that lasts.

The cove to the north of this one has space for several boats if they stern-tie. There is not much room for swinging.

Now comes the bad news. By the time you get there, you may find the shore area all posted. The place has been dotted with surveyor's stakes and the lots are offered for sale. On the shore opposite the wharf, there was a posted notice that the developers were applying for a permit to get 'water rights' to the shoreline from Musgrave Point. A local resident said that she had heard there were plans to put in a marina there. She is part of a prominent American family who once owned all of the land thereabouts and had sold off the portions around Musgrave Landing. She said that they never dreamed it would be subdivided. "The folks around here are all up in arms about it," she said. "Why don't you put a chapter in your book entitled 'The Rape of Musgrave Landing'?"

It is a shame that the Provincial government can't come up with enough money to buy the area and convert it to a public park. As boaters, we certainly feel saddened by the prospect of the place becoming commercialized. However, if such an installation would enhance tourism and add to the tax-rolls, maybe it would be a benefit.

Instead of a 'rape', maybe we should think of it as more of a 'shotgun marriage.'

Sansum Narrows currents are only 3 knots at the maximum. While this is not a white-knuckle situation, it is well to try to choose your time to traverse the area.

Northwest of Musgrave Landing there is a cove that is protected by an islet, some submerged rocks and beds of kelp. There is a nice float and a boat-house on shore. A rocky ledge rims the shoreline at this point and at the top of the ledge, you will see a float and a fine rambling Panabode home. High above the ledge, you will see a beautiful house that was once owned by the famous sailor, Miles Smeeton. The story goes that he bought it, sight unseen, when he was in India. When he got back to this continent, he went to see his purchase and fell in love with it and lived there a number of years. The view from this house must be spectacular—down over the busy narrow and out toward the Malahat Range on Vancouver Island.

When Miles' wife and shipmate, Beryl, died, he had a bronze plaque installed on the bench beneath the house, which must have been one of her favorite places. The inscription is a touching quotation from Tennyson's *Ulysses*.

Burial Islet.

The tablet is on private property so the best you might do, if you were so impelled, is to look for it with binoculars from the cove below.

Just beyond this spot, there is a shoal that dries at about 3 feet (0.9 M) and closer to shore there is a rock to avoid if you try to follow the shore closely. The shoal is covered with kelp and should not be too difficult to spot.

Our advice, however, is to follow the 20-fathom contour (40 M.) and stay clear of the problems.

Burial Islet is a reef and a dry rock which sits in the Narrows just beyond a kelp-bed and an unnamed point. It is mostly rock, with a little grass and bracken atop it. It was probably named after the Indian custom of putting their dead, with all of their treasured belongings, in an exposed place until nature reduced it to bones. One can see why this rock, removed from the usual camping spots, was ideal. The light that is built on it is a red-topped tower which has a quick-flashing red pattern. You can safely pass behind it. The kelp will show you where the submerged reef extends to the south of it.

Across the narrows, on the Vancouver Island shore, you will see a reef and a cove (Chart #3470). There are kelp beds flanking this reef. Except now the north side of it is taken up with an aquaculture farm. We poked into the cove and tried to get information from a worker on the dock who was very laconic. He did say that they were breeding salmon there, and it was called 'Sea Farms'. When we tried to get further information, he just shrugged. When we told him we were writing a cruising guide of the islands and weren't just rubberneckers, he called attention to a very impressive old steam-powered cruiser of about 40 feet which was tied to the floats behind the sea pens. We didn't hear the name and we were not invited to stop, so we went on.

Log booms in Burgoyne Bay.

Sansum Point: Just off this point, you will see little curlicues on the chart; these refer to whirlpools; there are also patches of wavy lines which indicate eddies and overfalls. Both can be unsettling, to put it mildly, to a slow boat. Off the point, you will see charted, drying and submerged rocks and beds of kelp, which is nature's way of saying: 'No Trespassing'!

The various indents, bights and coves, between Sansum Point and Octopus Point are said by the B.C. 'Small Craft Guide' to contain oyster beds in aquaculture. We didn't see them, though.

Bold Bluff Point is barren enough, but doesn't seem all that 'bold'. Just south of it there is a cove with a big dock and a pier with many flower boxes and a flag pole—really quite attractive.

Burgoyne Bay: Who in the heck was 'Burgoyne'? Our faithful biographer, Capt. John T. Walbran, doesn't offer a clue in his book (see the bibliography). Could it have been named after the famous Revolutionary War general, John Burgoyne, who led the British Forces in Canada against the upstart Yanks? Want a 'trivia' item? Okay. General Burgoyne was also a successful playwright in England.

This bay would be a great place for visiting boaters, but logging operations have occupied most of the shoreline areas with log booms. There is a public wharf in the northern part of the head of the bay, but it's rather small: only 70 feet (21 M.) total moorage. Most of the water in this place is deep. You'll be in depths in the order of

The Lady Minto Hospital

The Gulf Islands have had a hospital in Ganges since 1914 when early residents felt the need for medical care without travelling to either Victoria or Vancouver.

The hospital originally opened its doors in a wooden building about one mile from Ganges Harbour. It is now a community center. The present hospital is about a half mile from downtown Ganges.

Lady Minto, the wife of the Governor General of Canada, the Earl of Minto, supported the Victorian Order of Nurses, a public home nursing service in the early 1900's. She campaigned throughout Canada for good medical care in rural and isolated parts of the country. She helped establish many 'cottage' hospitals.

The present modern facility was built in 1958 on land donated by a member of a well-known pioneer family, that of Gavin Mouat. The hospital has 50 beds: 31 extended care beds and 19 acute. There is an emergency room with a physician on call 24 hours; a cardiac observation room, a radiology department and lab; basic diagnostic services; consulting services with a laboratory and pathology link to Victoria; a physiotherapist and a full maternity facility.

There are eight active general practitioners and specialists, including one obstetrician, a surgeon and three anesthesiologists on the hospital staff. Patients from Galiano and Mayne are referred to Saltspring; those from Saturna and the Penders often are taken to either Victoria or Vancouver for health care.

100 feet (30 M) until you are quite near shore at the head. There is a narrow band of 30 foot bottom (9 M.) which could accommodate a few boats. When we were in there, much of the anchoring space was taken up by a big black Alaska-type freighter. Almost the entire north shore of this bay is covered with logs. Big brick-red mooring drums outline this area. One of them has a green light attached to it. Near the public dock, you will see the offices and shops of the operation. The name says 'Saltspring Log Sorting Co.'. There is a small fleet of yard-tugs tied up there. The interesting thing is that everything is painted a bright blue. The log booms on the south side of the bay take up some shallows that could be used for anchorage. There are only a few houses visible at the head of the bay. It might be a good place to over-night before entering the Narrows. It is protected from all but westerlies.

Octopus Point, across the Narrows from Burgoyne, has a pretty meadow on it. The light, flashing green, is mounted atop a mast. Near it you will see a locally well-known shipbuilding facility. There are two ways and a big shop building. In past decades, it turned out quite a few handsome work boats. Recently, it has not been in operation.

Grave Point on the Vancouver Island side, is about the northern limit of the Narrows. It is marked with a green light on top of a white pipe standard on a rock near the shore. The characteristic is 'flashing'.

Erskine Point is on the Saltspring Island shore directly across from Grave Point. It is adjacent to where Cranberry Creek comes down from Lake Maxwell. The delta created by this creek is called 'Cranberry Cove' if you want to pencil it in on your charts. This cove has a public boat ramp. The shores are quite steep around this nook, and there are no homes visible from the water. The center of this cove is deep: about 100 ft. (30 M.) but it shoals rapidly as you approach the head. It goes to about 10 feet (3 M.) in a few yards of distance. It's a good lunch-hook spot in nice weather, but we wouldn't want to live there.

The Point itself has a boat house and a big private boat ramp and pier.

Booth Bay: This is a spot that ought to be on your itinerary. Its chief attraction is **Booth Inlet** which intrudes into Saltspring Island for about 0.7 miles (1,200 M.).

A long drying reef makes the northern shore poor for anchorage. Like most of the coves on the Sansum Narrows side of Saltspring Island, it stays deep up to close to shore. Some anchorage is possible in about 50 feet (15.5 M.). The bottom is good.

The inlet is a delightful place to explore in a kayak or shore boat. Entering it, you pass through a cut. To the north you will see a beautiful old home on the shore, the Booth Bay Resort. They have an excellent licenced restaurant, 'The Bay Window'. There is no dock or floats, however. Once past the entrance, you will find the water in the inlet quite shallow. Clams and oysters are plentiful at low tide. When the current is flowing in the inlet, you will find water rushing through the narrow entrance like it is trying to fill San Francisco Bay. It swirls up over the shallow beds and the deepest courses are those on the southeast shore. When the water reaches its high, it pauses as if for breath and then it races back out.

There is a public beach on the north side of Booth Bay. From a road there is a stairway leading down to the beach.

Vesuvius Bay: A 750-foot (250 M.) reef strings out beyond the point on the south side of this port.

There are no volcanic mountains in the vicinity. The name came from an early survey ship, the 'H.M.S. Vesuvius' a 'paddle sloop' of 976 tons, 6 guns and a steam engine delivering 280 h.p.

The government dock has one float with 95 feet (29 M.) of space. There is a sign on it that says you can't tie up overnight; it is to be used for loading and unloading only. But boats do overnight there; some local boat-owners leave small boats there permanently. No one knows whether there is a dock-manager or 'wharf-monger' (as Zo calls them) to enforce the rules.

The inlet at Booth Bay.

The ferry slip there is rather small, because the ferries are small. Their chief purpose is to dart across Stuart Channel to Crofton, which they do very often. About 30 persons commute to Vancouver Island from Vesuvius daily, according to locals.

The dock from the public wharf is in good repair. It leads up to the parking lot for the Vesuvius Inn. This is a local pub that serves good Mexican food. Because of its popularity and the family atmosphere, you may have to wait for service on weekends. The Inn is rather famous among Gulf Island boaters.

There is another restaurant on the other side of the ferry approach. It is called the Seashore Kitchen and Restaurant. It has a hand-out counter for ferry passengers. It is also a licenced premise.

The head of Vesuvius Bay has a very popular public beach. Half of it is shell beach and half is lava rock. In warm weather, the water here can be quite pleasant. There is a stairway leading down to it from the road and the place is often well patronized.

A short walk from the dock is the Vesuvius Bay General Store. It is operated by Lynn and Zoe Woodside. They advertise their store as: "The tiniest grocery store on Salt Spring." They offer fresh produce, meat, cheese, bread, specialty items and shelf goods. They also have stamps, ice and fishing supplies. They are open from 10 a.m. to 7 p.m. each day.

Vesuvius Inn and the Government Wharf.

A Pastime for the Kiddies: Whale Walking

In Joe Garner's delightful book on early island living called 'Never Fly Over an Eagle's Nest', there is a photo of typical eroded sandstone and this cutline:

"In the early part of this century, gray whales still frequented the inland waters between Vancouver Island and the mainland. The whales would lie in the water and the waves would press them against this porous rock and help to loosen and remove barnacles from their bodies. The author remembers himself and two older Garner children, Ethel and Tom, tying a rope around a tree to lower themselves onto the whales' backs to help kick off the barnacles. While one of the children climbed down, the other two would stand up top to warn of any sudden movement from the whales. This pastime was considered great excitement by all three children."

Nowadays, we scold kids for playing on the dock without life jackets on!

Dock Point, like its neighbor to the south, has a drying ridge that extends about 1,000 feet (300 M.). It has fly-papered many a carelessly-operated small boat. If you intend to go 'around the corner' to the cove, go out into 30-fathom water before you turn in. We didn't see any kelp, incidentally.

Dock Cove is a little niche which offers good protection from prevailing winds. The only problem is that it is too good—practically the whole cove is filled with private mooring buoys. You could get so-so anchorage in about 60 feet (18 M.) at the entrance.

Parminter Point has a gunkhole of sorts behind it. One or two boats might stern-tie here, but they would have little screening from winds. The chart (#3442) identifies this point with a flagpole on shore. There is one, indeed, in the front yard of a nice house.

However, there is also another flagpole on a similar point near a similar cove about a half-mile northwest of Parminter. This one is partially hidden behind bushes and is not as evident as the charted one.

Idol Island would probably not lead you to idolatry. It is not an inspiring place. Now how did this one get this name? It is a several-acre wooded isle with rock shoulders at both ends. The shoal that surrounds the western end is about twice as large as the island. We didn't see any beaches to lure you ashore. There are some drying ledges on which to beach a shore-boat. There has been some talk about making it a provincial marine park, but for the life of us, we can't see why.

Stonecutters Bay has no visible signs of quarrying. It may have gotten its name from workers in one of the quarries elsewhere on the island. It has little to offer the visiting boater—a tight stern-tie might be possible. It does have an elaborate private float and boathouse, breakwater and an old marine railway. It has been a log dump in the past.

Grappler Rock: We won't make you wrestle with guessing the source of this name. (Foul! Foul!) It was taken from a British gunboat, the 'H.M. Grappler'. It was a 237-ton job with 3 guns, a 60-horse engine and was built in 1846. After 22 years of service, it was sold at public auction for $2,400. It was placed in coastal service and met an untimely end. It caught fire in 1883 off Seymour Narrows and was destroyed. 72 persons died. The story is that they were all Chinese workers who were on their way to the canneries.

The rock is marked with a white tower which is red-banded. The red light flashes once every 5 seconds.

Just off Grappler Rock, to the north, is **Grappler Reef** which dries at about 3 feet (0.9 M.). It has a good crop of kelp.

The shoreline here is a gentle arc and there are many attractive homes and cabins along it.

This whole expanse of beach along the west end of Saltspring south of Southey Point, could make you corroded with envy if you identify with the landed gentry. These posh homes should have spectacular sunsets. Across the channel, they can see the plumes of three tall smokestacks in the pulp-mill at Crofton. A less-than-paradisical note: when there is a temperature inversion or a strong west wind, the residents get more than a sniff of nauseating pulp-liquor.

Well, mates, we have brought you up the sundown side of Saltspring to Southey Point. Before we introduce you to the Central Gulf Isles, let's go back a bit and pick up the hardy souls who opted to run up the Saturna Island shore of Plumper Sound.

5. Saturna Island: A World Removed.

Boaters we have talked to from the States think of Saturna Island strictly in terms of the place 'where they have the lamb barbecue', often with only a vague idea of where it might be.

As you can see from the charts, it is the the most easterly of the Gulf Islands, lying north from Waldron and Stuart Islands in the San Juans, across Boundary Pass and the International line. As a matter of fact, it has a lot in common with those bucolic isles.

Saturna has about 280 fiercely-free souls living on its 12 square miles. They are friendly, open people who live there because they like its untrammeled ways. Most of them can do everything necessary to survive and live comfortably. They have in their midst musicians and artists, 'doctors, lawyers, merchants and chiefs' (as the doggerel goes) who came to the island to own their own lives; professionals turned handy-men.

And they do turn out a sensational lamb roast!

Before we get around to discussing this celebration, let's make an inventory of useful charts. We have an old U.S. chart, #18421, which we are told is not being issued any more. It covers the northern San Juans and the southern Gulf Islands, giving you a good look at the geography of the reefs and shoals off the east end of Saturna. (Remember, the Gulf Islands string out sort of west-northwest from the San Juans, not due north as you might think.) The next most useful chart is one of the Canadian Strip Charts #3310, Sheet #3. This one is pinched off just short of including some baddies that lie east of Tumbo Island. It does give you the whole of the island, however. The rest of Saturna takes two Canadian Charts, #3441—the lower two-thirds; and #3477 has the Lyall Harbour area.

Breezy Bay to **Saturna Point:** We might as well start out from the happy scene of our feast.

Breezy Bay is large and fairly shallow. It's a fairly good anchorage if you can get into about 20 feet (6 M.). The place deserves its name, it can get very breezy. There is a dock in the south side of the cove, which is called 'Saturna Beach', but it is used by the visitors to the Campbell place. If you drop the hook, try to get back into the area adjacent to the cable crossing.

Elliott Bluff, named after a captain of the British survey vessel 'Ganges', is high and has great rocky shoulders. Supposedly, there has been a colony of nesting guillemots there in recent years. You might scan the trees with binoculars, if you're of the birdwatching persuasion.

Payne Point has no impediments and you can round it towards Trevor Islet without concern.

Trevor Islet has one home on it. And there is a long dock and float off its southeast corner. You could pass between Trevor and Saturna shore in high water with a shallow-draft boat. We kayaked through and saw some gear and a boat which

The Lamb Roast

We began our exploration of the Gulf Islands on Dominion Day, which is July 1st—it's like our Fourth of July. That's the day of the big feast on Saturna. So we were there in Breezy Bay for the big feed. We were part of the crowd of about 2,000, most of them visitors, Canadian and Yankee. In order to get a chance to know the Saturna folks, we stayed on until the next day and helped the locals clean up the debris.

Jim and Lorraine Campbell and their daughter, Jackie, are the ones who put on this big feed every year. It began as a simple school picnic in 1950. On that day, they roasted three lambs and charged 50 cents to the Mayne and Galiano neighbors who came. It was remarkably successful, so they decided to make it an annual event. The next year, they barbecued 5 lambs. In 1985, they had to roast 26 lambs to feed the crowds who came. Refinements have been added. They have kids' sports events: bingo, horseshoes (how long has it been since you tossed horseshoes?), darts, balloons,

a 'coconut shy', a tug-of-war, a beer garden—and much more.

As many as 350 boats anchor offshore in Breezy Bay.

Proceeds go to the Saturna Community Club, which is used by all of the islanders for get-togethers from weddings to pre-school sessions.

As we helped stack knock-down sections of the booths and gather up beer cans, we got a chance to chat with the workers. We found they were proud of their island and their neighbors.

One very articulate woman, a school teacher in her 'previous life', told us why Saturna is different from the other Gulf Islands. She said they consider themselves a very cohesive community. This is due in part to the fact that there are few 'summer people' and 'visitors'.

"Everybody is involved in the community and has personal duties as volunteers," is how she put it. There is no 'elite' group on Saturna.

We can attest to the fact that they certainly know how to roast lamb, too!

apparently is used in the aquaculture installation in Boot Cove. Most boats should go out around Trevor Islet to Saturna Point.

Boot Cove: This lovely cove has a mud bottom and looks wonderful on the chart. There is enough room for quite a few boats. However, no matter how protected it looks, it isn't. Winds can funnel down a valley from Breezy Bay, and whistle through this nearly landlocked harbor.

There is an extensive aquaculture installation in the northwest corner of the cove. Oysters are produced there. The land off the beach around this cove is all private, but you can go ashore if you wish.

The entrance to the cove has an underwater power line, so don't drop the hook there, naturally.

Incidentally, Chart #3442 says there are 'ruins' at the head of the bay. We couldn't spot anything that looked like ruins.

There is a marker off Saturna Point, a red buoy marked 'U 58'. It's located on an 11 foot (3.4 M.) shoal. We suspect the buoy is there as a guide to the ferries which dock at Saturna Point.

Saturna Point: This is the communications center of Saturna Island. The ferry docks there, the government wharf is there, and you will find a little business center.

The public dock is small. There is 409 feet (124 M.) of space for moorage. The end of the float is reserved for seaplanes. The wash from the ferries isn't too disturbing; they are the smaller class of boats which service the island only twice a day.

In the early days, warships used these terraces for zeroing in their guns.

Islanders from all over the Gulf come to Saturna for the Lamb Roast.

If you don't find space at this dock, you could anchor in the harbour and dinghy up to the head of the bay where you will find roads leading to the place where Lyall Creek flows into the south shore. From there, you can walk up and see the grade school and continue on to the general store.

The community of Saturna is not your burgeoning metropolis. The Saturna Point store, which includes the post office, offers items for boaters such as charts, hardware, fishing gear, groceries and ice. Saturna Island Marina has gas and diesel fuel. Under the store is a neat little pub called The Lighthouse Pub, owned by Dick and Gloria Silverberg. On a nice day you can sit outside on the patio and enjoy the view up Plumper Sound as you drink or dine.

Just up the road from the wharf you will find the Saturna Community Center. You can see the fruits of the years of contribution by the lamb roast. A very modern kitchen is used and maintained by the Lions' and the women's club. Two halls, one of them quite large, are used for meetings and bridge club sessions. On Friday afternoons there is ladies' bridge, and every Wednesday evening there is mixed bridge. If you like to play, they assure us that visitors are welcome. The floors are bright and shiny, meticulously-kept hardwood. Needless to say, the people of the island are justifiably proud of the building.

If you like to hike, the road from Saturna Point is a pleasant stroll. The traffic is

Saturna Point shopping center.

The new St. Christopher's Church.

minimal. You will see a sign pointing to 'Boot Cove Lodge', the island's only resort, run by Mike and Debbie Graham.

Beyond the community center is St. Christopher's Church, a lovely little chapel set in amongst the trees.

Along the way we saw a sign for 'Carefree Court', and since it sounded like a motel or trailer court, we went down the driveway to check it out. Two delightful white-haired men greeted us eagerly. We had discovered a 4-unit, low-cost senior housing center. The two men, obviously happy to have visitors, showed us their neat, modern apartments. Then they bemoaned the fact that the other two units were empty and said that we should write in our book that they would be delighted to have a couple of senior ladies move into them.

About a mile from the ferry dock you'll find the Saturna General Store, sometimes called 'The Hat Store'. The walls are covered with hundreds of hats and caps of every size and color, all of them donated to Bill Lawson, who with his wife, Irene, own the store. Although 90% of the hats were handed to him by visitors, many were sent to him in the mail. They are *not* for sale, he says.

The store has space for things to sell as well. They carry general merchandise, groceries, canned and fresh meats and food, used paperback books to swap, fishing supplies—and it has the only liquor sale on the island.

The Lawsons have been on Saturna since 1974 and they love it. They keep the store open seven days a week in the summer and are closed Sundays in the winter.

Saturna Point to Winter Cove. Lyall Harbour: Entering this harbor, you will see the buoy marking Crispin Rock. You won't see the rock, because it's under 6 feet (1.8 M.) at lower water. It's a little east of the marker. The buoy is red and has a green band and a radar reflector and is marked 'UJ'. The red and green markings mean that you can pass on either side of it, of course. The light is red and flashes dit-dit-pause-dit. There is kelp off it toward the head of the bay and the kelp indicates where the rock is.

The entrance to Lyall Harbour has cables underneath. You wouldn't be likely to anchor there because the depths are too great.

The harbor provides good anchorage in all but a direct west wind. The bottom is mud and the depths near the shore vary from a drying flat at the head to about 16 feet (5 M.) near the shore and a big area that is about 23 feet (7 M.). There is a log dump at the south end of the beach.

The 'Hat Store.'

The harbour was named after David Lyall, a surgeon on the 'H.M.S. Plumper'.

King Islets are two small islands west of Lyall Harbour surrounded by rock ledges which dry at about 3 feet (1 M.). The larger of the two has about a dozen trees, the smaller has three scrubby ones. Not exactly regal, King Islets, but they look sort of pretty in the sun.

If you want to go between the islets and the shore, keep on the watch for a shoal that dries at about 3 feet (1 M.). Favor the islet side. We don't recommend it, but it's do-able.

Veruna Bay is a flat indentation between **Digby Point** and **Mikuni Point.** It has a big drying shoal which extends out at the head of this bay and the water is too shallow to anchor. There is no protection from the winds here. Forget it!

Mikuni Point must have been named after one of the industrious and well-accepted Japanese families that settled in this section of the Gulf Islands in the late 1800's. It is a peninsula that reaches out from the farthest west point of Saturna Island. One of the drying shoals that abound in this area is immersed much of the time and has only a small unnamed islet visible at all tides. The visible spots point like an index finger to the troublesome

Minx Reefs: (The dictionary says the word means 'a wanton woman'. We wonder who she was and how she got her name on those rocks!) They have no markers but they are dry until the tide gets to about 12 feet (3.7 M.) above datum, which makes the seals happy because they loll around on the rocks in the sunshine.

Winter Cove: This is one of the Provincial Land Holdings that is, as yet, an undeveloped marine park. It is still relatively unknown because it lies off the beaten path. Old timers, both Canadian and American, know about it and bemoan the fact that one of these days it is going to become as heavily visited as Pirates Cove. In other words, it is still a rare find.

The best way to wend your way into this cove is to go northwest along Minx Reef until you can look into Irish Bay on Samuel Island and see the beaches, then flip a U-turn and head straight into the entrance to Winter Cove. If you're a daring soul, you can tiptoe between the two sections of Minx Reef at low water, when you can see the drying rocks. Chart #3477 is a plans-chart and has a fine blow-up of the area.

There is lots of anchoring space in this cove. It was probably called 'Winter' because it is would be a good place to keep in mind to duck into during winter when there are storms and high winds.

As you enter, you will see a cove within the cove, off to the west. You will want to

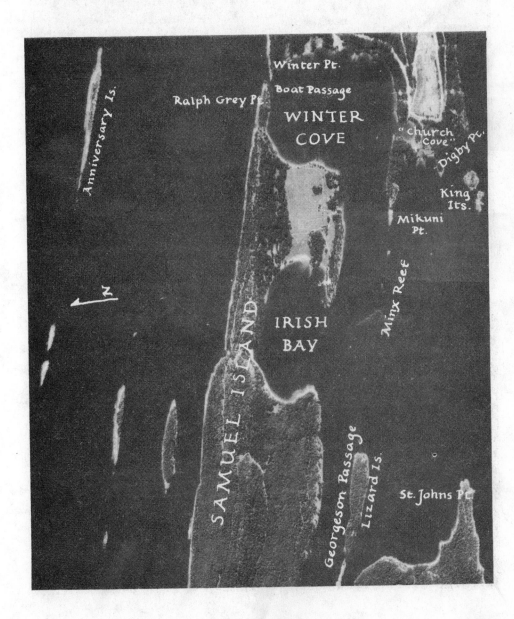

St. Christopher's Church

Pioneer Geraldine Hubert wrote of the church: "My uncle, Hubert Payne, was the parson, and he'd had this little church made from a boat-house in Winter Cove, and it was called St. Christopher's. But it was never consecrated, so in the end, when he went away, someone just went and lived in it. It would seat about 19 or 20 people. He would preach to us, and if we'd done something especially bad, I always felt the text was slanted at us.

"He used to go around the islands in boats, and he didn't know how the engines ran. His idea of fixing an engine was to give it a good swat with a hammer and then his head would poke up through the hatch and he would shake his fist at the sky and say "Oh, Jerusalem!" He couldn't swear, you see, he was a parson. But we really loved him very much.

(Expertise with engines must have been at a premium in those days.)

"My father didn't know much about engines, either, and his idea of fixing an engine was to take the spark plugs out if it wouldn't go, throw them on the wharf, pour gasoline on them and put a match on it. There used to be burn marks all up and down the float where Dad had been fixing spark plugs. Or he'd take a sledgehammer and hit the top of the engine a few mighty whacks. We used to sit in the stern of the 'Irene' and shiver and shake. But apart from that he was quite a mild man."

explore this spot, but we wouldn't anchor in there—the whole shooting-match goes dry at low tides. Drop the hook out in the main cove and dinghy in. At the head of this cove you will see a tiny church, called 'St. Christopher's', but there is no sign of the name. It was built originally as a boat-house for some Japanese residents.

There are several residences along the south shore of Winter Cove. There is a float for members of the Winter Cove Yacht Club, but no public moorage.

You would do well to study chart #3477 before deciding about the spot to drop the hook. Notice that near the park shore there is a boat launching ramp. Next to the ramp is the remains of an old wharf. That is on top of a shelf that extends from shore. To the right of the launch ramp you will see another shelf that is fairly extensive. Another rocky shoal clutters up the shallow water nearby. Across the cove, on the Samuel Island side, there are two more shoals to consider. So, the nearer the center of the cove you can get, the better. You will see markers on shore on both sides denoting an underwater cable. Only a turkey would anchor over that—your whole boat could light up like a Christmas tree!

Let's consider the park. It is a great place to go ashore. The 223 acre site was purchased by the province in 1979. In 1983, the Ministry put in picnic tables, trails, outhouses and a well. There is a billboard containing a map of the area. Unfortunately, overnight camping is not allowed. It's a short hike to a large gravel pit which was once operated by a company called B.C. Lightweight Aggregates. If you dig gravel pits (Heh Heh!) you might like to visit it.

There is a lovely three-quarter-mile trail through the woods and past swamps, out to the point which overlooks **Boat Passage.** This is a much more dramatic portal to Winter Cove than the one we mentioned above. We stood on a low bluff on the Saturna Island side and watched current boiling through this narrow gully at about 7 knots. We decided that, as novice kayakers, we wouldn't want to try that kind of excitement. We saw a fast outboard boat head through on the way to the fishing grounds outside. He had to rev up to full throttle to push his way through the chop and whirlpools. At slack water it is seldom still, but skippers with local knowledge and gutsy ones who are visiting have taken large boats through. This passage is a favorite for fishermen, but because there are two rocks in line with the opening on the inside and two directly in front of it on the outside, near **Ralph Grey Point,** it would be best to have a chat with some skipper familiar with bearings before attempting it. We went through there once, years back, in an outboard—at slack.

One of the Saturna boaters had this advice: "Look carefully before you try it. Once you enter it, you are committed. And if there happens to be a log in the middle, you don't have much room to dodge it." As a matter of statistics: it is 6 feet (2 M.) deep and 15 feet (5 M.) wide at extreme low tide.

Now that we have discussed the anatomy and physiology of Winter Cove, it is time to "turn the capstan 'round" or whatever, and let's go look at some spots on Samuel Island.

It's Boat Passage for occasional 'white knuckles.'

Samuel Island

Intriguing little Samuel Island, between Mayne and Saturna, was once recommended as the mid-point of a bridge which would connect all three islands. This was in the 1960's. It was the outgrowth of a petition to the government from the residents of Pender Island. They wanted a 50-60 car ferry, carrying 350 passengers to bring cars from the mainland or Vancouver Island to Mayne Island. They wanted a bridge to run from Mayne, through Samuel and end at Saturna. Then, they argued, the ferry wouldn't have to make the run to Saturna. The idea died a-borning, apparently. This scheme probably did not delight the more rural residents of the three affected islands.

Samuel Island has a remarkable tidal picture. There is a difference between the levels and times on the east and west shores. Tides for the west, facing Plumper Sound, are listed on Fulford Harbour soundings. The east shore, on Georgia Strait, has tides reckoned from Pt. Atkinson. The differences can be more than a half hour in time and over 2 feet in height. Check your tide books. It's fascinating.

The first settlers on Samuel Island were Ralph G. (Archie) Grey and his wife, Winifred. Winifred's sister, Mabel, lived nearby. The Greys ranched, clearing most of the south end and running sheep over the rest. A Japanese couple, Nakamura and Cormi, helped with the work on the farm.

The Payne brothers' families lived on Saturna. A daughter, Dora Payne, wrote:

"It was only a matter of maybe 200 yards of water between our place (at Winter Cove) and Samuel Island, and in the summertime, as soon as we got old enough, we used to swim across. The Greys used to swim over to see us, or we'd swim over to see them, and we would combine for picnics. I remember when there was something afoot, quite often they would collaborate with us, like the time we wished to get rid of a summer governess.

"The Greys had a horse which they kept on our place; it had been an Army horse, called 'Meatface'. We once got rid of a summer governess by getting her on Meatface bareback, then my brother giving Meatface a big whack behind. The horse bucked her off and that was too much for her. She couldn't stand that kind of treatment. She didn't, I think, appreciate our attitude, either."

Samuel Island is a privately-owned island, with a nice beach and a grassy meadow at **Irish Bay.** This is a tempting place to anchor because it has no perils in the entrance. It looks like a haven from winds. There are good depths in the southeast shores. If you happen to anchor in the 'wrong' side—meaning not properly predicting the wind for the night—it can be a dicey situation. We have talked to a number of skippers who had depended on the weather reports and had to hoist anchor in the middle of the night and ease over into Winter Cove.

Georgeson Passage is one of the lesser used entrances to the Gulf Islands from the Strait. It was named after Henry 'Scotty' Georgeson, a Gulf Islands pioneer. It is interesting to traverse either direction. It runs along the low bluffs of the almost straight southern shore of Samuel Island and the northern shore of Lizard Island. This is the preferred passage because it has a governing depth of 35 feet (10.4 M.).

Lizard Island has drying reefs at both ends. The east end has kelp to outline the reef. There is a dry rock at the west end which is the limit of the reef extending from the island. We had been told that we should never go between Lizard Island and the east end of Mayne Island. We thought that there must be some sort of rock or shoal in the passage that wasn't on a chart. We took our kayaks and lead-lined the water and didn't find anything noteworthy. It should be passable at all but minus tides. Incidentally, we found boaters who use it regularly—but they too said "Look out for the rock!"

Georgeson Passage, beyond the edge of Curlew Island, comes into a square-shaped bay with only one rock to worry you. It is out from the Samuel Island shoreline quite a distance and rather close to the deep channel of 50 feet (15.5 M.) to 122 feet (37 M.).

The shorelines in the passage are attractive. Where the channel narrows with Curlew Island, there is eroded sandstone and the beach which faces Grainger Point is white shell-covered.

The currents are half of those in Active Pass—3.5 knots at max, but they certainly seemed stronger than that when we went through in the 5-knot 'Sea Witch' against it. Slack and maximum flood times vary widely with Active Pass on which it is calculated.

At **Grainger Point** you will find two small islets connected by a ledge that dries. The B.C. Coast Pilot and other guide books recommend against sneaking through there, and we echo that advice.

Once out of Georgeson Passage, you face an alarming array of islands, islets, reefs and rocks.

As you head southeast in the corridor which will take you out to the Strait of Georgia or down along the seaward side of Saturna and Samuel, you will see a long, low island which, strangely, is unnamed. It is .1 mile (180 M.) off the Samuel Island shore. About one-sixth of a mile further north is a similar, but smaller island, also unnamed. This is the corridor between the two islands. Before you get to the island near Samuel, be on the lookout for a shoal with rocks; there is kelp to mark it. Incidentally, if you are new to using the plans charts, you will find it difficult at first to deal with distances. Since the detail is so large, about three times as large as the usual small-scale charts, you can find yourself on a reef which looked much farther away on the chart.

As you pass between these two sentinels, you may spot a several-mile-long process

Seal families on the Belle Chain Islets.

Samuel Island History

Before we leave this island, let's check on its history. It was owned originally by R. G. (hence: 'Archie') Grey. It had been named, decades before, for the surgeon aboard the 'H.M.S Plumper'. His name actually was Samuel Campbell. They must have been short on names to use first names!

Archie's daughter, Constance, remembers:

"My father did a tremendous amount of clearing. In one of these diaries I've been reading, he described it as really backbreaking and killing, but there was a satisfaction in it in all the different rhythm there is to it—and then blowing up the stumps and burning them and so on. He found wonderful, beautiful arrowheads and artifacts while he was ploughing. I think everyone did that in those days. They just ploughed up those priceless collectors' items.

"The only help Dad had, according to his diaries, was a Jap (sic) who lived on the island. But at the time of the year when you needed the most help, these Japs took off to the Fraser River for the fishing. Dad's diaries make you realize that if someone had been a slave in the West Indies, with someone standing over him with a whip, he couldn't have worked any harder. He worked from the minute it was light in the morning until dark at night."

Later, she remembers that he was "...able to run sheep and raise pigs and he learned to plough with oxen."

A later historic note: the island was owned during the 1930's and 40's by one E.P. Taylor who bred and trained some of his race horses there. Later, he sold it to Charles A. Lindberg's daughter and son-in-law who paid $48,000 for the 328 acres.

of reefs and rocks which are called the **Belle Chain Islets.** They end with an island that is named **Anniversary Island.** We saw families of seals and sea lions on its shores.

Along this route there are submerged rocks in clusters, but nature has kindly decorated them with kelp to keep you away.

When you are abeam Anniversary Island, which boasts of a few trees, you are off Boat Passage and you have made your 360 around Samuel Island.

Maybe you've noticed that we are now cruising down the outside of the barrier islands and we are, properly speaking, not in the Gulf Islands. But there are some features on the seaward side of these islands that might interest you, so we will continue down the shores of Saturna because we want to take you to a neat Provincial Marine Park.

The next geographical feature you should know about is a reef off the coast of Saturna—**Russell Reef.** It has the decency to clothe itself in kelp—so *keep off the grass!*

In the distance, to the east, you will see a rather big island about a half-mile off Saturna. You should see a cluster of boats of all sizes and designs, bobbing on the waves. The reef area ahead is a favorite fishing spot. As you get closer, you will be able to see that the south side of this island is a long, narrow peninsula and the north side is a line of rocks and reefs.

You are looking at Tumbo Island on the right and **Cabbage Island** on the left. The passage into the channel between them is rather narrow and fraught with dangers on both sides. If the fishing boats are out, you will have no trouble spotting the edges of the reefs because the boats haunt them. You should be steering a true-blue course of 90 degrees. The south chain of reefs has some dry rocks in it, and they can help you stay in the channel.

Another entrance to the park, taking you between the reefs, is suggested by the editors of 'Northwest Boat Travel, 8th Edition':

"The safest approach is to locate the end of the reef that extends northwestward on a line through Tumbo and Cabbage Islands and Pine Islet. This reef is approximately one mile long from Cabbage Island. A cut in the timber on the ridge of Saturna Island marks the end of the reef. By staying on the northwestern side of this cut, it is possible to head directly toward Saturna, and to turn to port on a line with Reef Harbour, proceeding east by southeast, approximately 105 degrees between the reef extending west-northwest from Cabbage and the reef extending west-northwest from the western finger of Tumbo." The above is a good tip if you are approaching from the Strait of Georgia.

Cabbage Island Marine Park: Okay. We give up. Why in the world is this island named 'Cabbage'? It's not shaped like a cabbage. It doesn't grow any that we can see. We didn't even see any sea-cabbage in the shallows. And there was no 'H.M.S Cabbage' in the history books.

It is owned by the Province of B.C. It's a park in an 11-acre wisp of Paradise. On the chart, the cove is called **Reef Harbour,** for good reason, as noted above. There are about eight mooring buoys. The bottom is good holding ground and the depths are conducive to anchoring. The head of the cove goes dry at low tides.

It is remarkable how the appearance of this park changes with the rise and fall of the tides! When the water is low, the reefs and rocks that flank the entrance appear. The rocky shelf that extends from Pine Islet to the main island becomes dry. When the sun is hot, the water in the tide pools becomes tepid, warm enough for swimming. Or you can sit on the beaches, close your eyes and imagine you are on a tropical island. Cabbage looks like its neighbor, **Tumbo Island.** There is no passage possible over the shoal that connects the two islands, except in shore boats. Tumbo is privately owned and posted. There is the remains of an old dock with a high concrete pier at the head of the bay. A sign reads: 'Tumbo Island Oyster Farm. Keep Off'.

Pine Islet has a driftwood-littered shore. We clambered over the logs at one point, looking for some place from which to photograph the boats in the harbor. In one spot, we found an old timber, piece of 12x12, possibly. It was studded with spikes. On an impulse, we put a quarter wrapped in a piece of plastic under it. If your kids want to have a treasure hunt, you might look for that timber and see if the quarter is still there. If it isn't, you might want to hide some goody under it so other kids can find it.

Burying treasure on Cabbage Island.

Tumbo Island History

In the 1880's, a man named Charles Gabriel went to live on Tumbo Island. He thought he could find coal, so he employed some Japanese laborers and sank a shaft. It is unclear whether he found any coal, as there is no record of any being shipped off the island. An old diary tells of a boiler at the digging exploding and killing an engineer and a contractor. The miners managed to get down 500 feet but water seeped in and made the excavation too dangerous.

Another character known as 'Jack', who laughingly called himself 'Jack the Ripper', lived alone on Tumbo in the 1890's. He was said to be a 'tough character'.

Winifred Grey tells this story of his fate: "It transpired that a wayfarer had put into Tumbo for the night, quite harmlessly; but that Jack had ordered him away with threats to shoot. The stranger, in self-defense, fired first, and without knowing the result of his action, had fled hurriedly to Miner's Bay to report the incident. The search party found poor Jack propped up on his bunk — dead — with an open Bible on his knees and a gutted candle beside him. A sad ending for a lonely man, who was probably a victim of nerves.

"Lack of evidence brought an acquittal for the stranger."

In the park itself, you will not find campsites, water, or garbage disposal bins—only pit toilets. During low tides, you can take a stroll around the island, a 20-minute walk, if you don't stop to beachcomb.

History records one early resident of Cabbage Island. He was Isaac Tatton. He bought the ll-acre spread for a dollar an acre in 1888. It was purchased by the government and several outdoors clubs in 1977 for $100,000.

Cabbage Island to East Point: You have a choice of routes. Leaving Cabbage Island, you can turn left (south) once you're past the reefs off Tumbo, or go right (north and east) around Pine Islet. If you go into **Tumbo Channel** you will find yourself looking at the Saturna Island forested bluffs and the wooded cliffs of Tumbo. Currents run fairly fast through this channel. There is a little nook just west of East Point on Saturna, where you might hide to wait for a southeast wind on Boundary Pass to die.

Boiling Reef: Now there's a name to give some thought. It is well named, too. It extends for nearly a half mile from East Point. There are tide rips, overfalls and eddies created by the shallow water. Only one little rock stays dry. The rest of the area has a respectable growth of kelp to alert you.

You pass Boiling Reef if you take the path down the north side of Tumbo Island. You pass **Savage Point** at the end of Tumbo and you will see **Tumbo Point.** In between these points is a very attractive cove. There is foul ground for three quarters of a mile from Savage Point and you would have to thread your way through the shallows that run from the point to **Tumbo Reef**—or go out around the reef and hook back in. We'd have to be very anxious to visit the spot and have calm weather and slack water before we would venture in there.

At this point, we have some problems regarding charts. The only one we could find that covered the area in question is the old U.S. chart, #18421. Using it, you will

Rosenfeld Rock

This rock got its name from a hapless ship that didn't avoid it. On "a dark and stormy night" (it didn't say that in the history book we read, we just threw it in for drama!) the sailing ship 'Rosenfeldt' ran up on the reef and there she stuck. She was loaded with coal. A year after the accident, she began to break up. Everything movable was taken from her by salvagers. A cabin was built on shore with lumber taken from her. In winter, hunters sat on her decks and shot ducks. Island fireplaces burned bright with the coal for many months.

The Belle Chain Islets

It was a bad winter—that of 1915-1916. The 'Kenkon Maru #3' ran aground on the Belle Chain Islets during the record-breaking snowstorm. The 3,700-ton ship, bound for Vladivostok from Seattle with a cargo of railroad ties and knocked-down box cars, stayed on the reef for nearly six months because of the rotten weather.

While the crew members boarded with the Thomas Bennett and William Deacon families, the ship's captain refused to leave the island, and the federal government had to hold an inquiry on Mayne Island—to finally convince the skipper to give up his island life and return to Japan.

East Point Lighthouse

It was built in 1887 and it was the second lighthouse built in the Gulf Islands.

James Georgeson, who came from Scotland, became the lighthouse-keeper one year later. He remained there until 1924, when his sons took over. James' wife was the first white woman to live on Saturna.

The Georgesons had nine children (an occupational concomitant to tending a remote lighthouse). Seven of them survived. They lived on $40 a month until their salary rose to $60—a munificent sum in those days. Every six months, Georgeson rowed or sailed a small boat across the Strait of Georgia to New Westminster for supplies. Rice was 2 cents a pound, flour was $1 for 49 lbs.

They supplemented their earnings with food from both land and sea.

He would scarcely recognize the electronically-operated lighthouses of this day if he should come back to earth. The B.C. Light List says the light now flashes:

"0.15 s; eclipse 14.85 s. High intensity flash superimposed every 5 s. White 149° through S, and W and N to 060°, red 156° through S. to 211° 30'. Emergency light. Hornblast 2 s, silence blast 2 s; silence 3 s; blast 2 s; silence 48 s."

Back then, the light had six wicks and burned coal oil. It operated on a pendulum system which had to be wound up once during the night, and flashed out once every half-minute.

see the outer limit of this Tumbo Reef system. The Small Craft Guide recommends chart #3462—but we couldn't find a copy of it.

You should go out around **Rosenfeld Rock,** a mile northeast of East Point, like the big boys do. This is marked by a green buoy with a radar reflector and it has a flashing green light. That buoy, marked 'U 59' is over the rock which has a depth of 9 feet (2.7 M.) and some friendly kelp. Currents in this area are often ugly.

East Point to Croker Point: Let us now focus our binoculars (senior citizens still call them 'field glasses') on East Point.

From a distance you can see unusual rock formations in the wave-eroded sandstone near the point. Keep your distance off—you could end up staying there permanently and people would build cabins from your planks. The lighthouse property is also a wildlife sanctuary.

There is a small cove, known as 'Fiddler's Cove' just outside the eastern end of Narvaez. It might provide anchorage in a northerly.

Narvaez Bay

It's off to Narvaez Bay — as they say in travelogues.

It's pronounced 'Nar-vay' the natives tell us. It was named in 1791 after Jose Maria Narvaez, who was 'sailing master' (pilot?) in command of the Spanish naval schooner 'Saturnina', which had 7 guns.

On the way there, you will see a little rocky hook, but it offers no security.

Matter of fact, Narvaez Bay, although it is free of impediments, is quite deep and offers little respite from waves and no protection from southeasterly winds. Anchorage is possible at the head of the bay.

It used to be called 'Deep Bay' at the turn of the century. It was the home of Andrew Robertson. He was an early live-aboard on his boat, 'Edith'.

Robertson was fond of children. When they visited, his idea of amusing them was to pick them up by their collars or belts and dip them into the sea and sometimes he left them under a trifle too long. Kids complained that getting past this merry pirate with his mutton-chop whiskers and his hard black hat and his macabre jesting was quite an ordeal.

Visitors remembered that his boat was 'leaded', the cabin top was sheathed with tin, giving her the appearance of a huge rickety old saucepan. When it rained, the noise below was deafening, but even more surprising was the sound of his chopping wood in the cockpit; often the axe hit the canopy, the sound echoing round the bay like an Anvil Chorus.

Meet a noble scrounger.

Monarch Head, a high barren bluff, is next. It was named after the 'H.M.S. Monarch', 84 guns, 2,286 tons, a third 'line of battle' ship stationed in these waters from 1854 to 1857. The water is plenty deep. The fishing should be good near these cliffs.

Java Islets consist of three bare and rocky projections. It is a glaucous-winged gull rookery. In 1985 an unmanned fishing boat was found on the rocks there, the engines still running and in gear. The fisherman was never found.

Bruce Bight was the site of a logging operation sometime in the past and old rusting machinery is still visible. There is a good beach. On a calm day, it might be an interesting place to explore. It is the namesake of Rear Admiral Henry William Bruce who was commander in chief of the 'Monarch' during its tour of duty in this area.

There is a rock off **Taylor Point** to be considered. It could 'unmake' your day.

Less than a mile away to the west is **Murder Point.** This was the scene of a grisly murder of a father and daughter in late winter of 1863.

Trueworthy Bight: was named after one of two men named Trueworthy: Billy, an Indian, or Charles, a white settler. History is not sure.

Keeping clear of the rocks and reefs west of Trueworthy Bight brings you to Croker Point: the last spot on our circumnavigation of Saturna Island. There is a light on this point, on shore, it is a white mast with a triangular daymark. It flashes red every 4 seconds.

And so, me hearties, we have made it around Saturna Island, which is indeed saturnine in appearance overall.

But don't let that stop you from enjoying the roast lamb on Dominion Day!

The Murder Point Massacre

Frederick Marks, of Waldron Island in the San Juans, set out in his small boat with his family of eight to move to Mayne Island. They were hit by a storm in Plumper Sound and Chris Meyers, of Mayne, went to help them. He took Mrs. Marks and five children into his boat. Marks and his daughter Caroline stayed with the family boat and all their belongings. When darkness fell, Marks and Caroline found shelter in a small cove on the Saturna Island south shore. As they sat by their campfire, a band of Lamalchi Indians attacked them. They shot Marks and chased the fleeing girl, whose nude body was later found by searchers, stuffed into a rock crevice. Marks' body was never found. The boat was reduced to splinters.

In the meantime, Meyers was alarmed and started back to search for them but couldn't find them. When the incident was reported, naval vessels were dispatched to investigate. The leader of the assailants, Umwhanuk, was found hiding in a cave on Galiano Island. He had in his possession a hair clasp known to belong to Caroline. Eleven Indians were charged with murder and four were convicted and hanged at Victoria in July, 1863.

The Two Trueworthys

In 1873, Charles Trueworthy homesteaded on 1,400 acres of land facing on Plumper Sound. He began to clear and develop his property and became the first permanent white settler on Saturna. In 1884, he sold the property to the famous explorer Warburton Pike, and Charles Payne, for $5,000.

Billy Trueworthy, the Indian, was a folk institution for the residents of the Gulf Islands for much of his life. He lived in a shack built for him by Pike on the shore. He was a legendary shepherd with almost unbelievable stamina during the annual sheep runs and roundups. Everyone liked him, especially the children of the islanders, who were captivated by his talents with sheep. He was also a bit of a scandal because of his connections with rumrunning and bootlegging.

Dorothy Richardson, a Saturna pioneer, said, "He was small and slight, and he had the most beautiful eyes, like brown velvet with a kind of sparkle in them. I can always remember Dad saying, 'Well, tomorrow we'll go over the mountain and see Billy.' That was the greatest joy to us. I can remember sitting in a ditch under some big walnut trees that grew there and he'd talk about the sheep. It was just something about the way he talked, and he had this soft Indian voice that just went up and down and on and on.

"I know how he earned his living...well, actually, he bootlegged. That's what he did, but he did it in the nicest kind of way."

Another pioneer woman remembered Billy. Geraldine Hulbert said she thought, "Billy Trueworthy was very quiet, except when he rounded up sheep. He ran, bending over a little bit, and you could almost see him with a spear in his hand going into battle, which of course he never did. Then he had a wild Indian yell that he used only when things got desperate. It was so terrible, this yell, that it must have been an old war cry from way back. The dogs would all crouch on the ground; they couldn't stand it. But he only used it if the sheep burst away and went trailing off in the wrong direction."

Constance Swartz, another pioneer, said, "He ran as fast or faster than any dog. He was just a legend the way he'd streak up and down Prairie Hill on Saturna Island. Why we're particularly interested in him was that when my father went to the Yukon gold rush in 1897, he left Billy looking after Samuel Island. So Billy had sheep to shear and to tie up and throw into the bottom of a boat and row them to the steamer, and so on; to see that the fences were mended and do all the chores, look after such crop as there was in those days. Billy was loved by everybody."

6. Mayne Island: Wellspring of Gulf History.

The rich history of the community of Miners Bay on this island makes it seem like the wellspring from which modern-day life in the Gulf Islands flowed. Its roots may not be as deep as some of the other, earlier settled islands, but it was a sort of Tigris-Euphrates center of activity, since it was a very habitable harbor on Active Pass, the well-travelled route from the mainland. For such an historic island, it has relatively few people even by Gulf Islands standards. The present population is only a little over 550.

Let's explore it together. You'll need charts #3442 and #3473.

St. John's Point to Miners Bay: We will start at St. John's Point on the far eastern end of Mayne. It is about a half-mile east of an interesting little nook that is a good gunkhole, it has good anchoring depth and a beach at its head. It certainly deserves a name. We decided to give it a name, 'St. John's Cove'. We won't be mad if you don't use it, though.

Further along to the west, there is a second hook with a drying flat at the point on Navy Channel where the submarine cable comes ashore a half mile east of Conconi Reef, known locally as **'Piggott Bay'**. It has a sandy beach piled with driftwood at the high-tide mark. You can ground a small boat there and enjoy near-warm water swimming in an incoming tide. It's a nice place to drop the hook and spend a pleasant afternoon. Take note of the cable on the bottom there. This nook is exposed to currents in Navy Channel which can run 2 to 3 knots. Winds up Plumper Sound might make it unacceptable as more than a lunch-hook anchorage. It's interesting to note that the tidal stream actually floods east through Navy Channel. It joins the Plumper Sound flow, mills about confusedly and then hustles out northward into the Strait of Georgia through the several passes around Samuel Island.

Active Pass, the crossroad of the Gulf Islands.

Active Pass Currents

If you are a fairly cautious boater, you will be careful of the currents in Active Pass and plan to make the trip at either slack water or fairly near to it.

The Small Craft Guide has good information on just how the currents work. One glance at the Current Atlas diagrams showing currents at the max and you can become an instant believer.

Active Pass is a deep but tortuous channel leading from Swanson and Trincomali Channels into the Strait of Georgia, between Galiano and Mayne Islands. The channel is about 0.3 miles wide in its narrowest parts, and there are no dangers at a greater distance than 0.1 miles from either shore, with one exception: a group of rocks, with less than 6 feet (1.8 M.) of water over them at 0.4 miles north-northeast of Collinson Point in Georgeson Bay.

Active Pass is not only used by pleasure craft and fishermen, it is the main artery for shipping, including freighters, tugs and barges, between the mainland and south Vancouver Island. In addition, it is used by the large, fast and maneuverable ferries of the B.C. Ferry System, linking Victoria, Vancouver and the Gulf Islands. There are often two ferries in the pass at the same time, and occasionally even three.

The Small Craft Guide recommends that the pass not be attempted under sail (without an auxiliary motor) because of the strong currents, absence of steady winds and the large ship traffic.

In the south entrance, off Matthews Point, the tidal stream is 5 to 7 knots on large tides, and 3 to 5 knots on smaller tides.

In the north entrance, opposite Burrill Point, the rate of the tidal streams is 4 to 5 knots on large flood tides and 3 to 4 knots on large ebbs.

On the flood tidal stream, there is a strong set into Miners Bay along its north shore, and on the ebb tidal stream there is a corresponding set into the bay along its south shore. Heavy freshets from the Fraser River increase the rate of the southgoing (ebb) tidal stream.

On strong flood tides, violent rips, dangerous to small craft, occur over an area extending from mid-channel south of Mary Anne Point, to Laura Point. Strong rips also occur near Fairway Bank and increase in violence during strong winds from the north quadrant. No violent rips occur on ebb tides.

On the Strait of Georgia side of Active Pass, heavy tide rips occur in the vicinity of Gossip Island, Lion Islets and Salamanca Point, particularly with the flood tidal stream and strong northwest winds. During summer months the effects of the freshet from the Fraser River and northwest winds which blow strongly almost every afternoon cause rough conditions along the west portion of the Strait of Georgia. Crossings to the mainland or travel along the east shores of the Gulf Islands should be carried out early in the day or last thing at night when the winds die down — usually.

Just to the northwest of Piggott Bay is a small rocky bight known as 'Gallagher Bay'. It's just below Conconi Reef and it's studded with some threatening rocks.

Conconi Reef: This rock is above water at 8 foot tides (2.4 M.) and it is at the western end of a full quarter-mile of foul area. Behind it are several beach homes. There are two dolphins and four pilings along the beach. It may have been a log dump at one time. The shallows west of the reef are covered by kelp. It might be possible for a skipper unfamiliar with the area to go behind the reef if he or she went very gingerly. Unless you want to visit someone who lives there, it hardly seems worthwhile, though. The light on the reef is a white tower with a red band at the top. It is an eclipsing quick white light. It got its name in 1860—Thomas Conconi was a paymaster on the 'Pylades'.

A cove with a nice beach and a beautiful white house is found between Conconi and Dinner Point where the marker indicates a submarine cable comes ashore. It is too open to be an anchorage.

Dinner Point is the southwest corner of Mayne Island. Two exposed rocks lie just off this point. No one seems to know how it got its name. A 'Dinner Island' in the San Juans got its name because a hungry one-time owner swapped it for a meal.

Dinner Bay is not named such on some charts, but it is the first possible anchorage on the Active Pass side of Mayne Island. There is a 15-foot (5 M.) contour which is deep enough to anchor except at very low tides. Here again, the ferry wash might be considerable, and northwest winds sweep into it.

Enterprise Reef extends from a red buoy, marked 'U 51', to the light on the most prominent part of the reef. It has 1-foot (0.3 M.) of water over it at lower tides.

The light tower on the reef is set on a rock that dries at 3-foot tides (0.9 M) It is a complex of red and white lights. The white light which is quick-flashing can be seen in all directions. The red and white alternating lights are on a lower plane and warn of dangers on the course to Active Pass from Ben Mohr light. The white flashing light can be seen on a sector from 107° to 110°—a safe course. The red light, indicating problems, can be seen from 110° to 121°. White light is seen in sector 121° to 123° 30'—safe course.

The reef was named for the Hudson's Bay Company's steamer, 'Enterprise', which was one of the earliest steam paddle vessels using the inland waters of the pro-

Village Bay ferry terminal.

Village Bay

An Indian village was originally located at Village Bay, possibly because there is a sulphur spring on the beach, which still flows from a sunken wooden pipe. The natives might have felt it was magical — some say today that the waters have medicinal powers. Others just comment that they 'smell bad'.

John and Louise Silva pre-empted the land and later sold it to John and Margaret Deacon who farmed the acreage. The Deacons also ran a summer resort and noted that a steamer would make a special stop at Village Bay. An advertisement in the New Westminister 'Columbian' said that Village Bay was "fortunate in possessing exceptionally fine beaches for bathing, while on the bay, boating is practically free from the danger of tide riffles (sic) and storms. In the vicinity also are fine mineral springs, containing valuable curative properties".

The present large B.C. Ferry terminal was built at Village Bay in the late 1950's.

vince. The 200-ton ship began trading in B.C. in 1862 and was lost in a collision with the steamer 'Rithet' in 1888 off Cadboro Bay.

If you monitor VHF channel 16 you will often hear the skippers of the B.C. Ferries announcing they are "just off Enterprise Reef heading north into Active Pass". Pleasure boats have no problem going between **Crane Point** and buoy 'U 51'—in fact, it will keep you away from the ferries as you enter Village Bay.

We discuss in detail the transiting of Active Pass in Chapter 7, Galiano Island.

There is good anchorage in **Village Bay** in a mud bottom. but the water is quite deep from centuries of sluicing by Active Pass currents. There is an extensive drying flat at the head of this bay. The only hazards are the ferries, winds and local mooring buoys. It is the site of the B.C. Ferry terminal, so the big ferries running from Tsawwassen to Swartz Bay stop there. There is a public boat launch ramp, also.

Time to concentrate on chart #3473 now.

Helen Point is the first narrow in Active Pass, eastbound. There is a wooded bluff above it. A quick flashing light on a white tower with a red band at the top is situated on the point.

It is interesting to note that lights in Active Pass do not follow strictly the convention of red to the right from the Trincomali Channel to the Strait. Probably this is to avoid confusion as to which way is 'from the sea'.

There is a ledge that is usually dry that bulks out from Helen Point. It has a red daybeacon on it. Beyond this ledge, near the Mayne Island shore, there are a couple of rocks that dry—they are close to shore and they have their banners of kelp.

Incidentally, Helen Point was named for the wife of Joseph McKay, the chief trader with the Hudson's Bay Company. She must have been quite a lady because the Admiralty surveyors named 'Nellie' Point in McKay Reach for her.

All of Helen Point is an Indian Reserve. Archaeologists from Simon Fraser University conducted a dig at the point in 1968 in which they found that the area had been occupied as early as 3,000 B.C. The local Mayne Island Museum and the Provincial Museum in Victoria have the artifacts on display.

Miners Bay — The Gold Rush Town

What a boisterous lusty village this must have been in the 1850's with the hard-bitten characters who were en route to the Cariboo gold fields! It was even known as 'Little Hell', at least among some of the straitlaced folk, because it boasted of two pubs. There were also two hotels, Springwater Lodge and the Mayne Island Inn. Yes, Miners Bay has a long history of tourism.

The Gold Rush era was not the beginning of transient visitors. In about 3,000 B.C. boaters came to these shores and beached their boats. They probably stretched their legs, fished, hunted, dug clams, pitched tents (do you 'pitch' tepees?) and enjoyed the scenery for a while and then went on.

In the late eighteenth century, strange-looking giant boats wended their way up the channels. Noisy men with white skins and sticks that held lightning came ashore and bargained with the original tourists. Sometimes friction arose and bloody little frays resulted. Records of those early European rubberneckers say that the people they met in the Gulf Islands were found to be more 'trusting and affable' than their northerly cousins.

A half century later, the English came in large ships and came ashore with shiny tubes they peeked through and made scratches on large sheets of marvelous birch-bark. They also parleyed and traded with the local folks who had settled down on the beaches.

These latter-day passers-by took great interest in the fact that the visiting groups, while looking very similar, spoke a number of different dialects. There were the Cowichans, the Haidas, the Songhees, the Saanich and a number of groups from further away.

Some of these white people stayed and built houses out of whole tree trunks and piled up stores of odd implements that only they had use for. They also traded glittering baubles to be used as ornamentation for the animal skins they collected each day.

Soon, more and more of the pallid people came and began to put up houses and plant crops and cut trees and herd strange looking animals. Many of the natives decided that the neighborhood was getting too crowded and went elsewhere. Others learned to live with and tolerate the newcomers.

In 1877, the white men who had displaced the original islanders from much of their land, graciously gave back 323 acres out near what is now called Helen Point. So people who speak Cowichan and are the descendants of the first visitors 5,000 years ago, have their own land, which the pale people call a 'reserve'.

Not all of the prospectors disappeared forever up in the Cariboos. Some remembered the beautiful little gem of an island and returned, most of them without pokes of gold. They settled down on Mayne. Many of them took Indian women as mates and began raising families.

Mayne folks are proud of the fact that almost all of those marriages (legalized to various degrees) were permanent. Indian women had the qualities inherited from centuries of living off the land. They had skills that made life more comfortable for their husbands. As the communities grew, they became respected members of the biracial society. To this day, Mayne Islanders, like most of the Gulf Islanders, speak proudly of their part-Indian blood.

There is a small bight just east of Helen Point. It has a rock in its center.

Naylor Bay is a large body between **Lord Point** and **Reserve Point.** The B.C. Coast Pilot says that anchorage is prohibited because there is a submarine cable there, but it doesn't appear on the chart and we didn't see any signs. We did see a number of Indian fish boats, however.

Miners Bay: This historic harbor has plenty of room for moorage. But, except for the area close to shore, it's very deep, and the shallow water is rocky. It is subject to the powerful currents which swirl in the Pass. As if all that's not enough, the B.C. super ferries, which ply the water regularly, usually manage to pass each other just off Miners Bay. The wakes they set up are uncomfortable to say the least. Even tied to the government wharf, allow plenty of extra line because your boat will roll as much as 25 degrees in either direction when the wakes from these behemoths reach you.

The government dock has only 72 feet (22 M.) of space, part of which is taken up with a seaplane float and a dinghy dock. Adjoining the public float is a gas dock offering gas and diesel, run by the same man who has the village service station. There was a marina here in recent years, adjacent to Springwater Lodge, but it has been abandoned. There is no water on the dock.

Miners Bay is a wonderful stop, nevertheless. It is the only business center on the island, although there is one other grocery store, the Centre Store, in the middle of the island.

If you get here and find the current against you in the Pass and have an hour or so to kill, you'll find this a rich stop.

And now for a look at Miners Bay in this day and age, as you see it when you leave the government wharf, where you have securely tied your vessel with lots of fenders and allowed for 'bouncing room'.

The first thing to your right is the still-standing Springwater Lodge—the very same one that housed the roistering miners on their way towards the gold fields back then. A deck has been added and you can sit at umbrella-covered tables as you quaff a cool one on a hot afternoon. Or you can eat on the old 'front porch' and watch

Miners Bay Government Wharf.

the boats in Active Pass as you dine. Overnight guests in this turn-of-the-century hotel will find they must share bathrooms, but the prices are reasonable and the place is heavy with history.

Just beyond the wharf there is a little triangular bench which was donated to the island by King George VI and Queen Elizabeth on May 12, 1937.

A block from the dock is the 'Trading Post', one of the most complete grocery stores to be found in the islands. It has cooler and freezer cases, with prefab meals, meats and other frozen foods, and is an 'agency' liquor outlet. The store is owned by

The beach at Miners Bay.

A watering-place since the late 1800's.

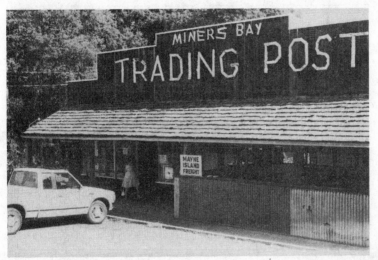

Here's the liquor store in Miners Bay.

Wayne and Connie Bryan, who have had it for 10 years. You can get fishing supplies, charts and stove alcohol there. There are two public phones outside the store. This is also an agency of Mayne Island Freight, in case you want something trucked in.

Across the street, at the intersection of Fernhill and Village Roads is 'The Root Seller', a bed and breakfast. The operator is Joan Drummond, who used to own the Springwater Lodge. She can accommodate as many as a dozen guests at one time and she fixes wonderful breakfasts. Not only that, she knows all kinds of trails and nature walks all over the island that she shows to her guests if they feel like a hike.

Just up Fernhill Road is a service station, a deli, the Plumper Pass Lockup-cum-museum and the Agricultural Building. In front of the museum, you will find a chart that traces the history of the island.

There is a delightful tea garden in the 'Robert's Chocolates' establishment, just off Fernhill Road. Robert Attwell, a dedicated chocolateer, produces candies that are scandalous. His wife, Silvija, operates the delightful tea garden and gallery, and also makes jewelry.

If you continue along Fernhill far enough, you will pass the present-day grade school. It's attended by more than 30 island kids, kindergarten through 7th grade. Another 20 or so, including youngsters from Saturna and Galiano, attend the 8th and 9th grades there. These off-island tads travel by water taxi.

Incidentally, almost all of the Gulf Islands high school kids are taxied to Saltspring to the only high school in the islands.

Farther along Fernhill Road is the fire hall, medical center, and tennis courts. The Centre Store, which is about a mile-and-a-half from the dock, is also about two miles from Horton Bay on the other side of the island. Dennis and Corrine Forster have operated this complete grocery store, which includes a laundromat, for about five years. They put out great ice cream cones, too—we tried 'em.

If you turn left on Georgina Point Road, from the Government Wharf at Miners Bay, you can walk all the way out to the lighthouse, if you're athletically inclined.

Plumper Pass Lockup

No visit to Miners Bay would be complete without a visit to the 'Plumper Gaol', a museum which once served as a lock-up for unruly islanders. It was used from 1896 to 1907 and history records only ten clients. You will find it fascinating.

The description of the lock-up, built in 1896 for $320 is:

"...a lock-up 15 feet by 23 feet, with one room and two cells cottage roof, walls of sized 2 by 4 scantlings, spiked every 18 inches, and enclosed with rustic floors of sized 2 by 4 scantlings set edge up, and spiked together and to sills."

The single front room in front of the cells was often used for a magistrate's court.

One cell now is kept as it was, so the general public can see what it was like in 'the old days'. The other houses a bottle collection. The court room has historical artifacts, including a portion of the remains of the wreck of the 'Zephyr'. In an outbuilding behind the gaol is an assortment of old farm and household implements. One of the most interesting is an old-fashioned stencil-cutting machine. You could stamp out your name or your boat's name. We did. It is considered proper to leave a contribution for the museum's maintenance.

Constables back in the 1890's and early 1900's did not have an easy time of it. We wonder how members of todays gendarmerie would look upon patrolling 600 square miles of territory — by rowboat! The Plumper Pass Museum booklet tells us that during the summers of 1893 and 1894, a police launch from Victoria assisted the constables in patrolling the Gulf Islands. But from 1895 onwards the only method of transportation for the constables was a 16-foot rowboat equipped with a sail.

And what a job they had to do! "Besides smuggling, cattle rustling and boat thefts, the constables had to investigate pit-lamping (Note: we cannot find out what the devil that means!), and the illegal sale of liquor to the Indians; deliver trading and liquor licenses approved by the Superintendent of Police, and report any outbreak of a communicable disease."

In 1903, a Constable Angus Ego on Galiano vaccinated 38 people for smallpox.

The museum is open to the public during July and August. It is operated by the Mayne Island Agricultural Society. There are friendly and helpful attendants on duty to answer your questions and explain the island's history.

Not many prisoners slept here.

An antique stencil press.

Mayne Island Time Line

In front of the Plumper Pass Lockup and Museum, you will find a board with a chart that traces the history of Mayne Island.

3,000 - 1,000 B.C. First Indian inhabitants.

400 B.C. - 1200 A.D. Second Indian period.

1200 A.D. - 1791 A.D. Third Indian—San Juan—phase. The Spanish arrive.

1794 Captain Vancouver checks Georgina Point.

1858 Prospectors use Miners Bay as waystop.

1861 Christian Meyers, first permanent white resident, arrives.

1872 The 'Zephyr' wrecked off David Cove. Captain and 1 seaman drown.

1874 Island officially surveyed.

1875 December 6, all Crown vacant land offered for sale.

1878 Wharf built at Miners Bay.

1880 First post office serving Pender, Galiano and Saturna also.

1883 First school.

1885 Large wharf built to accommodate sternwheelers. Lighthouse built at Georgina Point.

1890 Japs (sic) come to work in canneries. Springwater Hotel built. Larger school built.

1896 Lock-up built.

1897 St. Mary Magdalene Church built.

1899 Community Hall built.

1904 The 'Egeria' (British survey ship) arrives.

1912 Mayne Inn built to house brickyard workers.

1920 R. Hall and Japanese families raise tomatoes and chickens for export.

1923 Mayne Hotel burns. Lady Constance buys Point Comfort Hotel.

1925 Lady Constance starts Fall Fairs.

1927 B.C. Tel-building built.

1936 New cannery built.

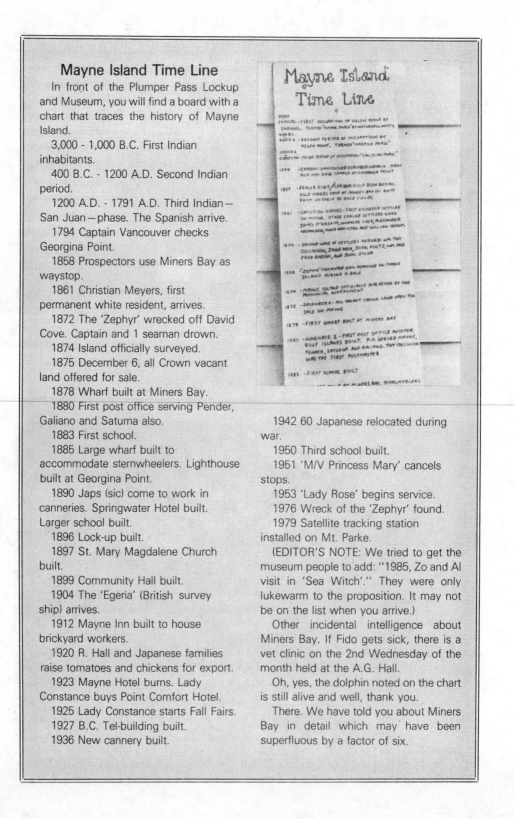

1942 60 Japanese relocated during war.

1950 Third school built.

1951 'M/V Princess Mary' cancels stops.

1953 'Lady Rose' begins service.

1976 Wreck of the 'Zephyr' found.

1979 Satellite tracking station installed on Mt. Parke.

(EDITOR'S NOTE: We tried to get the museum people to add: "1985, Zo and Al visit in 'Sea Witch'." They were only lukewarm to the proposition. It may not be on the list when you arrive.)

Other incidental intelligence about Miners Bay. If Fido gets sick, there is a vet clinic on the 2nd Wednesday of the month held at the A.G. Hall.

Oh, yes, the dolphin noted on the chart is still alive and well, thank you.

There. We have told you about Miners Bay in detail which may have been superfluous by a factor of six.

Her Majesty's Royal Navy versus Laura Point

Captain R. C. Mayne, Royal Navy (guess which island is named after him) wrote in his book 'Four Years in British Columbia and Vancouver's Island':

"On July 31st, 1860, we left for Burrard Inlet and Nanaimo in company with 'Termagant' and 'Alert'. As we steamed through Plumper Pass (Ed: now Active Pass) 'Termagant' met with an accident which well might have turned out seriously for her. In rounding the point in the middle of the passage, the current caught her bow and she wouldn't answer the helm. For a moment she appeared to be going stern on to the rocks, when she suddenly veered around a little, but not in time to clear them altogether. The rocky bank against which she had grazed (Laura Point) was fortunately sheer and steep; so that, although she heeled over so much that those watching her thought she must have capsized, she shot back into the middle of the stream, tearing up a tree with her foreyard and throwing it over the yard-arm as though it had been a broomstick."

Mayne Island Schools

The first schoolhouse on Mayne Island was built in 1883 and lasted only ten years. It was a simple, one-room structure, 18 by 24 feet, on an acre of land donated by Jacob Heck, in the center of the island. Classes began for the 20 youngsters in October, 1883, and their last names are a roll call of island pioneers: Robson, Bennett, Smith, Cook, Heck, Deacon and Collinson.

Mrs. Annie Monk was the first grade school teacher.

In 1894 a new larger building was constructed and it is still in use as the recreation hall of the Mayne Island Fire Department.

The newest school, built in 1950, has such modern conveniences as indoor plumbing, electric lights and a telephone. There are six classrooms, a gym, kitchen and an industrial education building, as well as offices and a medical room. Gone are the days of the one-room schoolhouse when a student lit a fire an hour before classes started each morning.

Georgina Point

William Tompkins 'Tom' Collinson, the first postmaster on Mayne, while strolling on Georgina Pt. found, under a stone, an English penny minted in 1784 and the remains of a seaman's knife. This gives credence to the vague references in Capt. Vancouver's diary that he and some of his crew went ashore in 1792 on a point on Mayne Island and spent the night of June 12th there.

On the way you'll see a house that was once a post office, later a store, even later, a doctor's office. You'll pass St. Mary Magdalene Church with an interesting 'Lych Gate' entrance (that's a famous gate in England, the sign says). On the church land is a wonderful old cemetery which contains the graves of such well-known personages as Lady Constance Fawkes, about whom more later. The graveyard overlooks Active Pass.

Miners Bay to St. Johns Point: Laura Point is truly a forgettable place. Its chief claim to fame is that it got a dramatic entry in the marine history books of the Gulf Islands.

The beautiful and historic Lych Gate.

The Point Comfort Hotel

A granddaughter of Captain Maude wrote that the hotel "was a wonderful place that he used as a private residence. Whenever you got tired of sleeping in one bedroom you simply move to another one. They had summer bedrooms at the front of the house, looking up the Gulf. I think it had about 60 rooms (actually, there were only 35). The dining room was a little larger than the Empress Hotel ballroom. It was a huge room. Then it had what we used to call the office, on the ground floor, where my grandfather used to sit. That was a kind of small hall with an open fireplace, and then above there was a parlour or sitting room on each floor above. There were three floors."

Commander Maude's son, Captain George Maude, also wrote about the mansion. "It was a beautiful hotel just about 600 feet from the lighthouse at Georgina Point...there was a wharf there in those days. They used to have a 24th of May celebration every year. They generally started at half-past 10 in the morning and had races. Then everybody would sit down to a big picnic lunch on the lawn and they'd have races most of the afternoon. Then in the evening a big dance would start..Mayne Island was the center of the Gulf Islands. All the people from Saltspring and the other islands all used to come over there and spend the weekends. There were two hotels and both had bars. Saltspring was just a drop in the bucket then, but it wouldn't do to tell them that now...the islands were alive in those days."

He goes on to describe parties and dances that would last several days. "It was a regular rule that they never stopped the dances before daylight because it wasn't safe to go home until daylight came." People would come from Orcas and Waldron for these parties, as well as from the other Gulf Islands.

Active Pass Lighthouse History

This lighthouse was the first built in the Gulf Islands. It was constructed by A. Fenney & Co. for about $3,000. An English chandlery, Chance Brother and Co., supplied the lantern and fittings for $1,600.

The first keeper was Henry 'Scotty' Georgeson. He fired it up on June 10, 1885.

Scotty was one of the six earliest settlers in the Plumper Pass district. He married an Indian woman, Sophie. The native women made good wives as they had been trained from birth to live in the wilderness, an ability that helped particularly during the early stages of homesteading. Indian women like Sophie preferred their own native doctors when they became ill, and Indian Tom from the Helen Point Reserve cared for Sophie until she became terminally ill.

A couple of months after taking over, Scotty wrote to his superior in Vancouver,

"As we have thick fog here lately all the time, I think it would be a great benefit to steamers for me to have a fog bell or horn, or something to guide steamers in the pass from the Gulf. If you do send anything of that kind up, please send instructions when to use it. I shall attend to it as punctual as I can. On Thursday night I heard a steamer blowing three distinct whistles steady all night in the direction of Gossip Island, but a long way off. I have not heard of any accident so far."

Scotty retired in 1920 and his son, George, took over the light. In 1910, the coal-oil (kerosene) lamp was replaced with a white vapor light (something like a Coleman Lantern, apparently). It was set to flare up every five seconds. In 1912, a 12-horsepower diaphone replaced the original steam foghorn.

In 1928 electricity came to Georgina Point and they installed a genuine 100-watt Edison Mazda bulb.

If this sort of stuff interests you, you might hike out to the lighthouse and get the brochure from which we gleaned some of this information.

The pristine white tower is 35 feet high (10.7 M.). There is a two-story keeper's house, a garage and several outbuildings. Just off the parking strip there is a visitor's display table where you can pick up a brochure, sign your name and even contribute to the welfare of this light. There was a big boat ramp there at one time and the winch is still there. However, the only boat we saw was a small Livingston with an outboard on it. There is not—we repeat not—a public toilet. There is also not one blessed place where a visitor can get a drink of water. After a several mile hike, those amenities would be greatly appreciated. Visiting hours are only from 1 to 3 p.m., so watch the time or your walk could be in vain.

The technical information about the light is as follows: it is visible for 12 miles. It can be seen in an arc from 055° to 253°. The steady white light is interrupted every 10 s by a high-intensity flash.

The horn is aimed to 025° and blasts every 30 s.

Just south of the lighthouse is rocky little **Maude Bay.** It was the site of the once-infamous Point Comfort Hotel which was built in the late 1800's as a mecca for the rich from Vancouver and Victoria. Somehow it never caught on and in 1890 it was bought by an Englishman who had served on Queen Victoria's personal yacht: Commander Eustace Downman Maude. Until the mid-1920's, the hotel was used as the private residence of the Maude Family. It was sold then to Lady Constance Fawkes and eventually burned in 1958.

The Grande Dame of Mayne

(From 'Lady of Culzean', by John Borradaile):

The rugged and fiercely independent islanders of the 20's came from all manner of backgrounds. Some were the descendants of pioneers, many with Salish blood; some were 'remittance men', black sheep of fine British families who were sent 'to the provinces' to live to spare the families any embarrassment; many were working class immigrants. But they all had one thing in common: just beneath the case-hardened surface of their personalities hummed an instinctual awe of royalty.

When Colonel and Lady Constance Hawkes came to Mayne Island in 1923, as guests of Commander Eustace Maude and his wife, Grace, the hardy folks of the island must have been fascinated.

They had watched the good Colonel and his lady for some years, with warm bemusement. It began when the Maude family moved into the huge wooden mansion that had served for many years as the 'Point Comfort Hotel'. It had already acquired some notoriety as the scene of noisy parties, legendary binges, questionable assignations and sundry derring-do.

The hotel had to close down in 1901 because of a drought that made the wells run dry. In that year, water or no, the Colonel bought the towering structure.

During the years of the Maude family's occupancy, one aspect of the Colonel's philosophy became clear—he did not believe in wasting time in maintenance. Within a few years after they moved in, the storms blew most of the shingles off the roof. Rain filtered into the rooms below, mostly the 35 or so bedrooms. The Maude family strategy to cope with this problem was simple. When a bedroom became too uninhabitable, they moved to another bedroom that had fewer leaks.

Mayne Island social elite remember a dinner party held in the sumptuous dining room, thirty by forty feet in area, which provided a spectacular view out over the 'Gulf of Georgia'. A storm came in, a volley of thunder pealed out overhead, the rain began to pelt the building. Sometime during the soup course, a huge piece of plaster fell from the ceiling, narrowly missing the head of Reverend Payne. The pile of plaster was quickly disposed of and the dinner resumed. However the rain now found a convenient drain and it proceeded to cover the floor with water.

The dinner continued without a moment's hesitation. The Commander's son, George, excused himself from the table, left the room and returned shortly with a brace and auger. He proceeded to drill a number of holes in the beautifully inlaid floor to scupper the water away.

Many of the neighbors remember Mrs. Maude doing her housecleaning wearing rubber boots.

Finally, the foundations of the building began to fail from rot. The doors to many rooms could not be opened. So the Commander did the natural (for him) thing. He moved the family out into a bungalow nearby.

It was the spring of 1924 when Lady Constance and her Colonel emigrated to British Columbia. They had sold their manor, the 'Elms', in Bedhampton, Hampshire in England. They wrote to Colonel Maude and asked if he would consider having them as paying guests. The crusty old gentleman went up to Culzean, found that a spate of dry weather had made the place somewhat habitable and that there were still rooms that were serviceable. He issued the invitation.

When the S.S. 'Otter,' which plied the waters in those days, docked at Miners Bay, practically the whole population was on hand to see the newcomers.

They were dazzled. The Colonel wore a black suit and a straw hat. Over his shoulder hung his leather water bottle, over the other shoulder was a canvas bag which contained sketching pads and paints. He carried his easel in his hand.

Lady Constance wore a black gown and over it a full length fur coat, the hem of which had been thoroughly chewed by her pet dog in England. On her feet, she wore high gumboots.

The crew of the 'Otter' proceeded to unload four huge packing cases and an array of suitcases and trunks. The onlookers helped load all of this freight into the truck of a local storekeeper. The furniture which had been shipped in the cases was put in storage in a dry shed. It contained priceless furniture, silver and Dresden China which Lady Constance had inherited from her mother, the Marchioness of Ailsa of Culzean Castle, in Maybole, Scotland.

The Colonel and his lady were installed in the habitable portion of the old mansion. Lady Constance could look out from her bed-sitting room and see tramp steamers from all over the world pass through Active Pass almost under her window.

The Colonel looked out over a fruit orchard and 18 acres of beautiful forest. This pleased his artist's eye. He had already become established in England as a portrait painter of some note. His canvases hung in many prestigious galleries and drawing rooms.

They set out to find a place to make their home in the new land. After searching around Vancouver Island for several months, they made up their mind. The old 'Point Comfort Hotel' had captivated them.

They bought it from the Maudes and contracted with a virtual army of workers, carpenters, plumbers, electricians and, of course, roofers. After six months of labor, the old building came back to life. There was running water and electricity and the doors all closed properly. Naturally, they disdained central heating. They retained all of the old fireplaces and box stoves.

They named it 'Culzean' after their barony in England.

Friends remember the daily life of the couple. Their morning started at the stroke of seven with a bath which, in winter, was icy cold. Breakfast was served at eight. It was eaten in the huge kitchen at a large oak kitchen table covered with oil cloth. After breakfast, the Colonel would read the Bible and lead prayers. After devotions, he would write letters or paint. Lady Constance would spend all morning in the kitchen, cooking.

The Fawkes family became deeply involved in island life. Lady Constance organized the first Fall Fair. The affair continues to this day.

Islanders remember that the aristocratic lady was very supportive of the Japanese farmers who came to the island.

The Lady of Culzean died in 1945.

The church on the hill on Mayne Island was filled with friends and neighbors from Galiano as well as the home island. They sang her favorite hymn, "For all Saints who from their labours rest."

If you stroll up to the church graveyard, you can see the large cross with the inscription:

In loving memory of LADY CONSTANCE FAWKES. Died Oct. 24, 1945. Aged 81. "And they shall be mine, saieth the Lord, in the day when they make up my jewels..."

The Don DeRousie family which tends the light gets its supplies and mail by helicopter and has a satellite dish for TV.

The brochure does not state what the salary is—or how to apply for the job when it comes vacant.

Georgina Point: This is truly another historic spot. It appears that Captain Vancouver came ashore here on one of his passages. It was named after Georgina Mary Seymour, the daughter of Sir George Cranfield Berkeley and the wife of 'Admiral, the honorable Sir George F. Seymour, G.C.B., G.C.H., Vice Admiral of the United Kingdom'. (How would you like to put that on *your* return address?)

As noted above, the lighthouse was established in 1885. It was equipped with a foghorn in 1889.

One look at a chart and you can see why it was an ideal place to put a lighthouse. The Small Craft Guide says it is: "..the north extremity of Mayne Island...is the northeast entrance point to Active Pass; it is fringed with rocky ledges and several rocks, with less than 6 feet (1.8 M.) of water over them, lie within 0.1 mile of the shore in the vicinity."

In other words, steer clear!

Off to the Cariboo Gold Fields!

It is said that "one had to be a real man to get to the Cariboo in those days over the pack trails, and a real man to stay there."

Travel was mostly on foot, with horses, mules, etc., to pack freight. Oxen were used also, but being able to travel only ten miles a day, were eventually sold to some local merchants for food. Probably influenced by a similar experiment in the U.S.A. (with much the same results) some enterprising business men even imported about twenty camels to carry goods. These continued for a while, causing horses and mules so much fright that they often shied and lost their loads. "This was overlooked when these packages were beans and bacon, but when the camels finally caused a pack train to lose a load of liquor, their operations were stopped by court order."

The miner's pack was supposed to include:

One sack (50 lbs.) flour, 10 lbs. beans and bacon; 10 lbs. (extra) flour; axe, frying pan, kettle.

Perhaps sheath knife, pannikin, sheet iron basin for gold pans—this was used at other times for baking bread.

Travel was, according to weight of pack, ten to thirty miles a day. Indians carried flour from Yale to Lytton by Hudsons Bay trail—any weight from 80 to 100 lbs. They travelled from eight to ten miles a day and were paid in gold dust. Women, too, carried packs, with perhaps a papoose as well.

There were stations on this long trail 120 miles apart, whether government-owned or connected with the Hudsons Bay Co. is not remembered. At some of these stations meals were evidently served—beans, bacon, apple pie, bread (no butter), cost $2.50. What happened if men returning from the gold mines 'broke' had not the necessary money to pay for such meals? They got them just the same. Evidently the miner's unwritten creed covered such.

Georgina Shoals has a rock which bares at 6 feet (1.8 M.). It's about 1200 feet (364 M.) offshore. No kelp around it that we could see. You can occasionally see the water breaking over the shoals.

Just off the shore on the Strait side of Georgina Point is a foul and nasty area containing reefs and several pinpoint dry rocks. It is excellent kelp-growing ground, though.

David Cove: The reefs that flank this small cove are formidable. One of them, at the east end, did in the poor old 'Zephyr'. This cove is sort of a three-fingered body which is filled with private mooring buoys and very little space to drop the hook. You wouldn't want to for very long though, because of the swell from the Strait. There is a rough boat ramp and a sort of public beach where the water was warm enough for Zo to go swimming. She was surprised to discover that she had two companions swimming with her—a couple of little garden snakes, which looked like miniature sea serpents.

David Cove is one of the few possible refuges on the outer shores of the Gulf Islands. One of the problems is that the area is filled with private mooring buoys.

The Squaw Man's Wife

"These native wives—so often without benefit of clergy," as Kipling puts it, adapted themselves in a surprising degree to the white man's ways—even learning to speak English more or less. One thing seemed curious in this direction. The mothers often spoke to the children in their own tongue, but the youngsters invariably answered in English. And while these wives might be docile, this did not mean subservient. Should conditions become too uncomfortable there was always the tribal reserve to fall back on, and hubby had to choose between seeking them there or having his domestic arrangements put out of gear. This used to amuse the white women who thought they were more independent in various ways than their white sisters. But such disagreements seemed to happen seldom and the union was, as a rule, kept loyally on both sides. As time went on, they might be moved, or persuaded to marry legally, and one of such events took place when the father and mother were married, and their grandchild christened on the same day."

David Cove

Two reefs which dry at 8 feet (2.4 M.) parallel the shore east of the cove.

Edith Point was named for the daughter of a Canadian Chief Justice. She and her husband-to-be, Henry Doughty, a midshipman, must have had it as a favorite place and named it after her. Okay. It didn't seem all that romantic to us. Entering Campbell Bay, swing wide around it because there is a nasty rock just off it; it dries at 4 feet (1.2 M.)

Campbell Bay is a big bay with good protection from Georgia Strait waves, but open to a long fetch in a southeast wind. There is a public beach at the head of the bay. It's popular with local residents who will hand-carry their small boats down a wooded path to the gravel beach for an afternoon row and swim. There is a resort community along the southern shore. Quite a few private mooring buoys take up much of the good anchorage depths on that side.

The Japanese 'Relocation'

In December, 1941, Bungoro Minamide, a respected farmer in Campbell Bay was getting ready to move into a fine new house he had just built.

John Nagata was starting his own tomato business, employing a new technique: circulating hot water around a greenhouse. They and two other Japanese farmers were roused from bed and taken to Miners Bay in the middle of the night. Their car keys were confiscated so that the families could not follow them.

Evacuation orders were issued in March, 1942 to remove all of the Japanese Canadians. They were given only hours to settle their affairs. A limit of 150 pounds of luggage was imposed on each family.

Kumazo Nugata, Secretary of the Active Pass Growers Association, wrote to the B.C. Security Commission, asking that caretakers be assigned to look after the extensive hothouse operations. He put in a plea that non-Japanese workers who had helped with the tomato industry be allowed to continue the work.

"On Tuesday, April 21, 1942, the CPR steamship 'Princess Mary' came for the fifty Japanese men, women and children who waited on Miners Bay Wharf. Most of the Mayne Island residents were in attendance to shake hands and wish them well. It was a sad time for all." (Vancouver Providence, April 20, 1942.)

After the war, the Japanese still believed they would be allowed to return to their farms. But legislation introduced in Ottawa in June, 1942, allowed returning servicemen to buy the confiscated lands. Mayne Island residents hid away precious belongings of their Japanese ex-neighbors. Some tried to buy the land and hold it in trust for them. In 1944, the government created legislation which made it a crime to buy and hold land for the Japanese. Their loss was permanent and irreparable.

This bay, named after the surgeon on the 'Plumper,' was the scene of an unhappy period for established Japanese residents in Canada, who were interned during World War II as were their brethren in the U.S.

Georgeson Island is less than one-half mile long. There is a drying reef which reaches out from the visible east end. It is the beginning of a series of reefs and rocks that extends for two miles in a southeast direction. You may pass carefully between the island and Campbell Point, if you stay close to Georgeson Island. It would be very unwise to trust to luck in going through the deep places between the reefs southeast of Georgeson Island. If you want to turn into Georgeson Passage, you should continue on a straight line about one-half mile beyond the last visible dry rock in this chain before flipping a "U-ie", as they say. Chart #3477 is a great blow up of this area.

Bennett Bay is a big area, but it is subject to waves and southeast winds from the Strait which funnel down the Samuel Island shoreline. The beach at the head has sandy spots among the rocky shores. It is a favorite sunbathing spot and is often warm enough for a swim.

'Mayne Inn', an historic hostelry, is located here. It was closed down in 1984, but there are plans to open it again. There is a long wharf for visiting boats on the southern shore.

Mayne Inn

Mayne Inn was built in 1911 because a brickworks was being established in the Bennett Bay area and it was felt there would be a need for a boarding house for the workers. It was called the 'Franco-Canadian Boarding House'. The enterprise never got off the ground. There were enough visitors to the island to keep it in operation because it had a bar. It was later named 'Arbutus Lodge'. Later, it became the 'Mayne Inn'.

In 1977, the company which then owned the Inn applied for permission to build a marina. They brought in pile-drivers and created one of the most extensive docks in the Gulf Islands—330 feet (100 M.) They may have been a trifle hasty, since the permit had not yet been issued, nor had neighbors been consulted about the project. A stop-work order was issued and the matter found its way into the courts. The Islands Trust, which administers the islands, prevailed, and the marina was never completed, although the wharf remains. There have been some bad times for the Mayne Inn, despite the fact that it has been a favorite watering-hole for locals and visitors alike. It may not be in operation when you get there.

Historic Pet Names for the Islands

Back in the pioneer days in the Gulf Islands, North Pender was known as 'Little Scotland', South Pender was 'Little England', and Mayne Island, because of its bars and hotels, was known as 'Little Hell'.

Mayne Island Taxes

Property on Mayne Island has always been a great investment, even back in the 1800's.

While taxes on property are somewhat high, 80 acres of waterfront property on Mayne Island carried a tax bill in 1879 of...75 cents!

Curlew Island History

Curlew Island, about 66 acres of rocks and trees, was a Crown Grant in February, 1893. James C. Campbell made his home there. In 1910, the brothers Bjornsfelt, Ossian and Gottfried, bought the island and Ossian had a home on the west side. There he kept goats and grew grapes. After his death in 1931, the island was used as a summer residence for the family.

Horton Bay: When we planned to visit this bay on the eastern end of Mayne Island, entering by way of Georgeson Passage, we did our homework and talked to local skippers. The things we learned were two: Be sure to go through the northern passage around Lizard Island, and look out for the submerged rock in the western end of the bay.

We also learned that it was named after one of the employees of the Hudson's Bay Company who sailed aboard the 'Otter', Robert John Horton. He provided local knowledge when Captain Richards brought the 'H.M.S. Hecate' to the region to do surveying in 1862. As a partial reward he had a bay named after him. It's a nice bay and a good moorage spot. Wherever he is, he should be pleased to know that visiting skippers take his name not in vain.

So we virtually tiptoed into the entrance, being sure that Lizard Island stayed to our port side. We agonized a bit over the fact there is a charted rock we couldn't

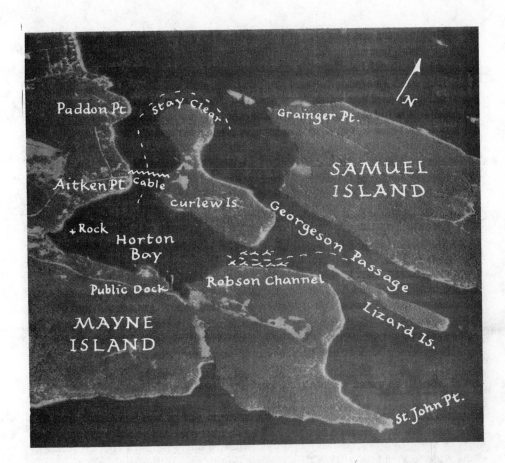

spot just off the shore of Robson Channel, but we saw some kelp which probably rooted in it. You will be able to spot it also. As a matter of fact, there are copious kelp beds in this channel, which you will see at low tides. You will probably want to steer through the path between the kelp, although it doesn't signal any badnesses, except at that rock.

If you go through at low tide, don't be surprised if your fathometer gets down to 10 feet (3 M.) when you go between Mayne and **Curlew Island.** It's shallow in there.

Once inside, you will see the typical government wharf, with more than the average amount of dock space, 410 feet (124M.). It provides garbage disposal only.

There is a sign on the pilings: 'Centre Store 2 Miles Groceries Shellfish Meat Ice Fish Tackle Licences Ice Cream Pop Laundromat'—that might conceivably tempt the ambitious to make the hike.

There is also a private dock which looks like a community facility. There are several liveaboard-type houseboats in this part of the bay.

We saw that the best anchoring space is at the head of the bay—the west end—where the famous rock is. We went down there anyway and dropped the hook in what we fondly hoped was a spot close enough to the southern shore to avoid swinging onto it.

In the morning, we got into our Easy Rider kayaks and explored the area. First we tried to find the rock. We dropped the lead line all around the spot but never found it. We did see a private mooring buoy which looked like it could be right over the menace. We debated it, hovering around in our kayaks. Would a local boater put a buoy right over a dangerous rock? The answer we came up with was: sure, if he tied off a small boat that only drew a foot or so of water. We gave up trying to help you avoid it. Later on, we were talking to a couple of Mayne residents who live on the bay. We asked one of them if he knew where it was. "Sure," he said. We asked him if he could pinpoint it for us. He waved his hand airily: "Oh, it's there all right!" Frankly I think it's a glitch on some surveyor's depth sounder. If you get a bead on it, please let us know so we can update information for our next edition.

Next, we decided to find out just what was hidden beneath the surface in the passage on the south side of Lizard Island. We must have drifted through that area a dozen times, dousing the lead line. We never found anything to justify the paranoia about that passage. Besides, the chart does not show any problems. We even met a local islander who uses that route regularly. So what's our advice? Simple. Go through Georgeson on the north side of Lizard Island. We believe in what our buddy Father Leche from Friday Harbor says—"Always err on the side of chicken!"

What else can we tell you about Horton Bay? Well, the water is warm enough for swimming—and Curlew Island has 'No Trespassing' signs.

We couldn't find any 'ruins' which are mentioned on the chart.

The 'piles' are a set of dolphins which must have held a big float at one time.

There is a public access at **Aitken Point** which is a cable crossing. It is a crude launching ramp.

Curlew Island has a very impressive float in the west passage between Aitken and **Paddon Point**.

When you round the northern end of Curlew to make the exit from Horton Bay, swing wide to avoid the rock. Off **Grainger Point** you will find a couple of exposed rocks, just like the chart says.

Aitken Point has a launching ramp.

The Monster 'Metric'

It is time for us to tell you that you have wandered innocently into the measurement mine-field. You are about to be dragged, cussing and snarling, into the world of metric—and we, who love you, are the villains who have lured you.

You see, we have it figured that by now you are well into our book and have spilled wine or catsup on it and can't take it back, and now we've got you!

We are about to make the grim announcement: you are going to be introduced to a new method of measurement. One that you were going to have to learn eventually, anyhow.

If it's any comfort, we hate metric too!

But Canadian charts are all going the scientific path and you will get your aft in a sling if you don't know how to pilot your boat according to the system.

Notice: Up until now, we have used the so-called 'English System' of fathoms, feet, inches and miles, and we have added the metric equivalents just to soften you up for the big punch.

In the next chapter, we are going to give you the metric figures first and the English in parentheses.

And Further Down The Line: we are going to make you go 'cold turkey!'—all metric!

Some day, you'll forgive us.

The passage between Curlew and Samuel Islands.

There is another propeller-inspecting rock, the chart says, almost in the middle of the channel between Curlew and Samuel. Nobody will spend much time hunting for it, though, because the current goes through Georgeson Passage like Billy Hell except for brief slack times. We would swing wide and keep in deep water, which is 43 feet (13 M.) at low water.

If you should go back down east through Georgeson Passage between Lizard and Samuel Islands, swing wide around the kelp-covered rocks at the east end of Lizard. Now you will find yourself back at St. John's Point. You have just done a dos-a-dos around historic Mayne Island!

How This Rhubarb All Started

The history of how come inches and meters is fascinating, we think. So, if you're interested—read on, Macduff!

Let's take the inch, and later on we'll take a mile, according to the old saw.

The inch was established by British tradition as "the length of three barleycorns". If you have any barleycorns in your larder, you might want to check this. You must admit that it is not a convenient method of measuring nowadays. You probably didn't know this, but you have been governed by barleycorn measure all of your life: the difference in length between any two successive shoe sizes (9 and 10, for instance) is one barleycorn.

Delving into tradition again: King Henry I of England, who held office from 1100 to 1135, decreed that the distance between his nose and the tip of his fingers was one yard. Unless someone wants to dig up old Henry and measure his bones, you can only guess how long that really was.

Well, subsequent generations fiddled around with the standard of a yard. In 1439, Parliament decreed that the yard could no longer be reckoned equal to 40 inches (barleycorn derived). Things went a bit bonkers then. The Scots used 37 inches as their yard. The British stretched theirs out to 45 inches. In 1527, cool heads prevailed and Parliament decided to go back to good old King Henry I's reach—about 36 inches. There it has stayed. As a matter of fact, in 1878, Parliament put a stop to guesswork. The Act of 1878 read:

"The straight line of distance between the centres of two gold plugs or pins in a bronze bar, measured when the bar is at the temperature of 62 degrees F. and when it is supported by bronze rollers placed under it in such a manner as best to avoid flexure of the bar..."

We wonder, what's going to happen to that rig when the English go totally metric? Will it end up in a garage sale?

Now at the risk of being called a fetishist: how about the 'foot'? Turns out that was the distance between heel and pinkie of a dude named Charlemagne.

So "whuffo metric?"

You can blame it all on poor old King Louis XVI of France. He wanted to establish a strictly Gallic unit of measure which would be called the 'meter'. He got this idea when he was in something of a fix. He was in prison awaiting a date with the guillotine. But, nevertheless, he sent out a final royal proclamation, directing two engineers, Jean Delambre and Pierre Mechain, to come up with something. They did, in 1791. The 'meter' was set at 'one ten/millionth of the length of a quadrant of the earth's meridian' that is, an arc between the Equator and the North Pole.

Another interesting note: a meter is the exact length of a pendulum that will swing in one second at the 45th parallel which is in Paris—or thereabouts.

Why? Damm'fweno! Ask Daniel Boorstin, who quotes it in a book called 'The Discoverers'.

You are probably reeling with all this smart-alecky stuff, but we have one more last item to lay on you. Since you probably don't want to go out with a humongous steel tape and measure the meridians, science has established the final word on the meter.

"Equal to 1,650,763.73 wavelengths of the red-orange, light given off by Krypton 86 isotope under certain conditions."

Satisfied? You do have a supply of Krypton 86 on board, don't you?

(NOTE: This will teach you to be more careful and not spill wine on your books and make them unreturnable.)

7. Galiano Island: A Shoulder Against the Sea.

It has been described as a huge rock thrust up from the sea. Like the other barrier Gulf Islands, it seems to have broken free of the earth's crust deep in the Strait and been driven upwards with the sharp fractured side forced high in the air and the seaward side low and rocky and lacking in breaks in its bleak profile. Over the centuries, the force of the waves, driven by the funneling winds, have carved marvelous bas-reliefs and grottoes. As you pass along the inner shore of Galiano and Valdes, the northwesterly barrier islands, you keep feeling that once a race of titans created a rock tapestry with strange frescoes.

Galiano is about 18 miles long and two miles wide at its broadest spot. Fissures in this forbidding rock at both ends create passages for boats from the mainland to the Gulf Islands, Active Pass at the eastern end and Porlier Pass at the western extremity.

The island was discovered by the Spanish explorers in the summer of 1772. The same territory was being investigated by the English under George Vancouver in the 'H.M.S. Discovery'. The captain of the 'Sutil' was Dionisio Alcala Galiano, of the Spanish Navy. It would appear that the Spanish exploration was not for the purpose of annexing land to the Spanish crown, but just to explore. The British, however, made no bones about laying claim. As a matter of fact, when the captain took possession of an area, part of the ceremony was turning a piece of turf. That may be where the term 'turf' meaning 'ownership' got its start.

At one point, the two captains met and apparently had an amicable discussion.

Galiano might have been better at gunkholing than he was at fighting. Later, he was in command of the 74-cannon battleship 'Bahama', which was captured at the Battle of Trafalgar.

Let's consider the Galiano Island side of Active Pass first.

Active Pass—Collinson Point to Whaler Bay: Unless you are at the helm of a fast boat, you will want to do some checking of the currents before you set out to take this entrance to the Gulf Islands. It's relatively simple. The flood current goes from the Gulf area into the Strait of Georgia. The ebb current pulls back into the inland waters. It's a little over two miles long, so you should be able to negotiate it in less than half an hour at slack. If you're the antsy type, you may want to provide a time cushion by approaching the pass while there is still a little ebb against you. Then the actual slack will find you part way through. Theoretically, you could go through at any time on a flood current, but it might get hairy. Boats do not steer well in a following current of 4 knots. The B.C. Small Craft Guide suggests you do not attempt going through this pass under sail unless you have an auxiliary engine.

The pass is a beautiful and heavily-travelled area. The B.C. Ferries go through from Tsawwassen to Swartz Bay and return. They always announce on Channel 16 VHF that they are entering the pass and invite response on that channel or on Channel 11, the traffic control frequency. This communication is meant primarily for deep draft traffic like tugs with barges and log-tows and freighters. We suppose that small craft skippers could use the service if they wished. If you are the skipper of a 26-foot Bayliner, it might make you feel like you are commanding a deep sea vessel.

The sea carves friezes on the sandstone walls.

Active Pass, Always Active.

Early Galiano residents took their culture when and where they could get it, as did other Gulf Islanders. One anecdote tells of a "fine concert organized by a summer visitor of charm and distinction. Artists wore evening dress though some had to come along woodland trails to the hall. All went smoothly, the organizer introducing each item of the programme with apt and pleasing comment, until suddenly, glancing down, she exclaimed, 'Goodness! I've forgotten to change my shoes!' For there, below her elegant green evening gown, protruded running shoes, large and weather-stained".

That same evening a group of Pender Islanders prepared to leave the concert from Georgeson Bay on Galiano. "Returning from the concert, they groped their way down to the wharf in the dark and waited while Mr. Spencer Percival rowed out to his launch which was anchored a little way out. They heard the engine start, then stop, and then followed a long, long silence. It was a summer evening, but the breeze through the pass grew chilly as midnight approached and the party waited shivering and in growing anxiety for no reply came to their repeated calls. At length, from far up the pass came the welcome 'chug-chug-chug' of the engine and soon they were all safely aboard the 'Sunbeam' and hearing her skipper's cool reply that it had been merely a matter of the current catching her before the engine had properly warmed up."

Big B.C. ferries ply Active Pass.

The pass makes a dogleg, as you can see from Chart #3473.

Now that we have made it all sound so simple, it might be well to look at some 'howsoever's'.

On a large ebb tide, there is a counter-clockwise eddy (the Canadians say 'anti-clockwise') which will run westward for a time at **Collinson Point,** which is a steep, rocky bluff at the foot of Mt. Galiano.

The light just beyond this point, which marks shoals and rocks, is Galiano Light. It is a white circular tower with a green band at the top. The light is also green and flashes every 10 seconds. You can pass between these shoals and Galiano Island in about 12 M. (39.5 feet).

Georgeson Bay has a shoal with depths of 1.8 M. (6 feet) at lower water. Because of the currents and the wakes, it would not make a satisfactory anchorage except in emergencies.

Matthews Point was named for an English family which used to live near it. There are high bluffs along this stretch. It has a drying ledge and just off the ledge you will find **Salalikum Rock.** It is visible at 1.5 M. (5 feet) tide. Another rock nearby is lower, it shows at 0.6 M. (2 feet). The midchannel point just off Matthews is the spot at which all current references are applied.

The point at which the cable comes to the surface on the Galiano side has a very attractive beach. There is a triangular daymarker on the shoreline just before you come to **Spire Rock.**

Mary Anne Point is steep and rocky. It was named for the daughter of an old Scot who worked for the Hudson's Bay Co. in the early 1800's. The light tower there has a green top and a quick-flashing white light, 7.5 M (25 feet) above high water. Nearby, a home has a long dock and a flagpole.

There is a small shell beach just south of **Scoones Point,** which has an abandoned cable crossing terminal. Paul Scoones was a charming old gentleman who lived near there and entertained friends with his collection of over a thousand gramophone records in the mid-1850's. A drying reef extends from this point about 220 M. (660 feet) into the channel. It is visible at 1.5 M. (5 feet).

Bellhouse Bay lies between Scoones and Burrill Pts. A rock which is awash at 1.5 M. (5 feet) is in the middle of the entrance. Even without this menace, it would not be a good anchorage because it dries at low tides.

Burrill Point is the site of Bellhouse Park. There is a reef lying in wait just south of the point. It comes up for air at 1.6 M. (5 feet). There is a triangular daybeacon on the extremity of the point.

Bellhouse Park is not a marine park. There are sloping meadows and a beautiful view of the Georgina Point Lighthouse Station. Benches have been provided for sightseers and picnickers. It's only a little more than a half-mile hike from Sturdies Bay, which is the best place around to leave your boat, tied securely to a government wharf.

Sturdies Bay: This is the only real community center on Galiano Island. It is also a B.C. ferries terminal, the last stop between the Gulf and the mainland. There is a small public dock with 48 M. (158 feet) of space and a crane. This is the spot from which skippers can drop off weekend visitors to take the ferry back to the mainland, and they can breathe, "Ah-h-h, alone at last!"

The public dock is tucked back behind the wing walls of the ferry dock. The ferry wakes and the constant wave action of the Strait can make for a restless stay. There are restrooms in the ferry waiting room at the head of the dock, but the finks lock the area after the last ferry leaves. You can get drinking water from a hose on a spigot behind the terminal.

Just beyond the public dock is a long wharf belonging to the Galiano Lodge. There is some transient moorage available at this dock. The dining room in the lodge opens at 7:30 a.m., so you can go up and get breakfast early in the morning. It is also a 'licenced premise' and you can get drinks with your meals, even on Sundays. They also have tennis courts and a swimming pool.

When you pass the ferry ticket booth, you will come to a fast-food trailer which serves fish dinners and also sells fresh fish and scallops.

The road from the ferry heads inland and at the first corner you will find an information kiosk—which, strangely, is closed on holidays. About a block from the ferry is Madrona St. Turn left and you will find the post office for Galiano. It opens at 7:30 a.m. to accommodate ferry patrons, but it closes at 8:00 a.m. It reopens at 10 until noon, then closes until 12:30. From 12:30 until 2:15 it is open again. There is a public phone booth there.

There is no gas float at Sturdies Bay.

Next to the post office is the Sturdies Bay Garage which sells some grocery items, ice and fish as well as fishing gear. It also sells propane, a hard-to-find item in the islands—but only offers it once a month!

Across from the garage and next to a real estate office is a neat little shop called the 'Dandelion Gallery', which was founded in December of 1984 and features the

Beautiful woven goods at 'Dandelion Gallery.'

work of 19 Galiano artists and artisans. Among the many attractive items, we found some extraordinary woven articles there. There are several other galleries on Galiano.

Continuing down the road, you will come to a deli which offers food items and it is also the island's liquor store.

Beyond that is a delightful and historic old store building called 'Burrill Bros. Store'. The stained glass transom over the door says 'founded 1903'. Bob and Carole George have had the place for the past 7 years. They offer most staples, some fruits and vegetables, frozen and fresh meats, delicious bakery items from the Trincomali Bakery on the island, ice cream, natural foods, and a few sundry items. Check the charming little tea-room section of the store, it is a glassed-in sitting room with comfortable chairs and tables for tea, cocoa, coffee and conversation.

Continuing up the pass from Sturdies Bay, you come to Enke and Rip Points. A daybeacon is located on **Rip Point.** Both of these points are of importance only in locating **Fairway Bank** far out in Active Pass. It lies about 80° and 750 M. (2,475 feet) off **Enke Point**—in a line between it and Georgina Point. It is in 9.1 M. (30 feet) of water, so it probably wouldn't be much of a hazard to the average small craft. It has no kelp to indicate it, but the B.C. Small Craft Guide says that you can see tide rips over it.

Rounding Rip Point, you can pass, with care, between Cain Peninsula and Gossip Island to enter Whaler Bay.

Whaler Bay: It got its name from the fact that whaling boats that plied the Strait of Georgia would lay over there, according to old timers. Chart #3473 gives you a good picture of the problems involved in entering it. There are rocks off both sides

Burrill Bros. Store

Joseph and Fred Burrill left Yorkshire in England and came to Galiano in 1896. They bought 80 acres of the rare farmland in that year. They began to till the land and they did quite well as farmers. Because they had been raised to be very provident, they kept a good supply of necessities on hand at all times. Neighbors kept coming to the brothers to borrow or buy things. So, in 1903, they built a small store on their property. Later, business became so good that they built another, larger store building. The old place became a feed-shed. By 1947, the business had become so prosperous that they could afford to move the present building to the Sturdies Bay area. For many years they had the only telephone on the island. That same old instrument is still on display in the store.

One of the most charming yarns about the store is this one. An Indian brought in a beautiful salmon to exchange for groceries. The Burrill Brothers welcomed the fresh fish and asked what he wanted in exchange. "Two of those," was the reply. The Indian pointed to the shelves where there were tins of canned salmon.

Some Notes on Galiano Island Cruising

Since most pleasure boaters end up at Montague Harbour at least once a year, either at the park or the marina, we offer some random information about the island.

First of all, and this is a biggie to many boaters—there are no public showers on the island. If you want a bath, you have to go to one of the resorts.

And there is no laundromat. You may have to learn to wash your clothes like the old pioneers did, by trailing them on a rope behind your boat.

If you are a golfer, you will find a course where visitors are welcome and there is a small greens fee. It is quite a hike from Montague, but not so far from Whaler Bay.

The population of the island is about 700. About 60 of them are kids who attend school on the island, from Kindergarten to grade 7. The older kids go to high school on Saltspring Island and travel by water taxi every morning. (This may be of interest to kids in your crew.)

If you arrive at Montague from the end of July on, the blackberries on the road between the park and the ferry landing are delicious.

Galiano has a resident doctor, and a fine water ambulance service in case you should get hurt or ill.

Way off the beaten track for boaters, about two-thirds the distance from the eastern end of the island and inland, is the 'Trincomali Bakery'. It's in a private home. It produces marvelous bread, pastries, cakes, pies and all manner of seductive fatteners. However, it isn't necessary to hike to the place, the goods are sold in all of the island stores.

We met the brother of the chief baker, and he points out proudly that this is a Cottage Industry success story, and we can understand it.

At the latest count, we noted about seven resorts or lodges, and three bed and breakfasts. If you intend to meet visitors at Montague and don't have room for them aboard, you might consider one of these places. Most of them will send a car for visitors.

There are, of course, four real estate offices. The island has six arts and crafts galleries. You can take day tours, and there are also horseback trail rides available.

of the entrance. **Gossip Island** has one rock at the edge of the passage and there is one in line with the straight edge of Cain Peninsula's northwest shore. Fortunately, both rocks have their garlands of kelp.

There is another rock and reef on the north side of the passage at **York Rocks.** They too have kelp.

Local skippers have some information to pass along that will prevent embarrassment and hull repair work.

At the north end of Active Pass, go out toward the **Gossip Shoals** light until you can look west straight down the passage. The Gossip Shoals light is a green buoy

This is the "red roof house" you're looking for.

with a flashing green light and a bell and radar reflector. It is marked 'U 47'. The B.C. Small Craft Guide says that because of the strong currents and wave action, the buoy may wander a bit. The shoal has rocks with less than 1.8 M. (6 feet) over them at lower water, but going into Whaler Bay you shouldn't get too close to the buoy.

Once you can see clearly down the passage, get out your binoculars and find a house with a red roof on the shore south of **Twiss Point.** This place is partially hidden by trees from some viewpoints. (There is a house nearer Twiss Point that has a brown roof and is in plain sight. If the owner ever decides to paint his roof red, too, there'll be hell-to-pay in Whaler Bay).

Head for that red roof. We ran a course of 280° but we won't guarantee that. Watch for the wisps of kelp over the entrance rocks—there won't be much, maybe one or two wisps. These rocks can pop up at 1½ M. (5 feet) at lower water and they are in 10 M. (33 feet) depths around them.

The whole shoreline of the **Cain Peninsula** is dotted with summer homes which have a front seat to watch for turkeys who run aground.

Keep on this red-roof heading until you can look to your left and see the red railings of the public wharf, then turn left.

York Rocks off the west end of Gossip Island are pretty much above water all the time. **Lion Islets,** beyond them, are quite picturesque. There is a single, solitary wind-swept tree in the middle of the largest one.

The reefs west of **Cain Point** are also pretty much in evidence most of the time. There is one rock that stays dry at all tides.

As you come down the entrance to the bay, skirt along the private docks on the west side. The water will get shallow in here. You may be reading 1 ½ to 2 M. (5 -6.5 feet) at low water and still be in the fairway.

The government wharf has 185 M. (610 feet) of space but transient boats often raft up here because there are usually quite a few commercial fishing boats tied up. A crane has been provided for their use. There is not much swinging room in this section of the bay. If you can't tie up and you want to stay near the float, you should stern tie. This is good protected anchorage, though.

Off **Murchison Cove** you will find better depths for anchoring, although not as much protection as down near the wharf.

When leaving Whaler Bay, you reverse the process, of course, keeping the red-roof fixed on your backstay or flag mast. You can take a bearing on a prominent rock just off the headland at Georgina Point and keep a few degrees north of it.

Whaler Bay.

Wharfingers, Alas!

In Canada, the folks who tend the government wharves, help berth private boats and collect fees are called 'wharfingers.' In some ports, especially the small and remote ones, you may never see one.

Americans find the word quaint. One U.S. lady we know had a hard time coming to grips with the new word. She called them 'wharfmongers,' as in 'fishmonger' or 'ironmonger'. We pointed out to her that the term 'wharfmonger' was perilously close to another 'monger' which was considered an insulting term.

Turns out that the Government agency which administers the wharves and the Ministry of Fisheries and Oceans (how's that for an impressive title?) has decided that the usage, as applied to dock managers in small-boat harbors, was not proper. So the signs that direct you to contact the 'wharfinger' will be changed to read 'Harbour Master'.

Alas! Will the next word to go be 'wicket'?

The south finger of **Gossip Island** has a tall flagpole which is a good marker. Shoreward from the pole is a pretty gazebo and a bench. The 'public wharf' on Gossip, noted on chart #3473, is no longer public.

Since the northeast shore of Galiano Island has little to offer in the way of anchorages, we will not take you around that way. As a matter of fact, we didn't make that trip this time because it seemed to have little to offer.

So, instead, we will retrace our steps (our 'wake'?) and take you to one of the most popular gathering spots in the whole Gulf Island Archipelago—Montague Harbor.

Collinson Point to Montague Harbour: The shoreline of Galiano Island between Collinson Point and Phillimore Point is high, rocky and forested. It is good fishing territory, being adjacent to Active Pass.

Phillimore Point: It was named after Henry Bouchier Phillimore, who was a Lieutenant aboard the 'H.M.S. Ganges'. What did he do to get his name appended to such a prominent spot? Nobody knows. The light is on a tower with a red top. It quick-flashes red. It can be seen for 5 miles.

The 'dinghy dock' at Montague Marine Park.

Julia Island is privately-owned and is quite a nice spot. Some local skippers go between Julia and Parker Islands. The water is plenty deep enough. But you have to be in a heck of a hurry to do it, because the normal entrance to Payne Bay is wide and deep and fair.

Payne Bay has a private wharf at the southeast shore. There are a number of mooring buoys in the shallow water at the head of the bay, but not much room for transient boats because the controlling depth is 14 M. (46 feet) up close to shore.

The channel going from Payne Bay to Montague Harbour has a power line which crosses it at a height of 38 M. (125 feet). There are two abandoned submerged power lines with faded markers on shore.

Winstanley Point has a cove behind it which is often used for day-stop moorage. The point has a triangular daybeacon.

Montague Marine Park is a provincial park of 87 hectares, or about 35 acres.

It was once called 'Stockade Harbour' by the settlers. The natives had attacked the Hudson's Bay trading vessel, 'Otter' here. Some of the renegades lived in a cave in the bay.

Although not a part of the park, there are other anchorages in the west end of Montague Harbour that are worth considering on Parker Island.

There is a cove on the east side of the T-shaped peninsula of Parker Island. The chart shows a dolphin, and it's there. We have seen boats tied to it and there's enough water. On shore, you will find a fascinating array of ruins. There is an old barge on the shore that looks permanent. It's noted on the chart. Next to it is a series of floats that are in fair condition. They are not marked 'Private', although they are undoubtedly owned by some private party. There is also the remains of what once

Montague Provincial Marine Park

35 acres is plenty of room for 31 camp-sites and beachcombing and the Gray Peninsula which has great hiking trails. In the park's east bay you will find about 15 mooring buoys and space to accommo-date another couple dozen boats riding on the hook. During the height of the tourist season, your best chance of find-ing a free buoy seems to be in the morn-ing about 10 a.m. or in the evening about 5 p.m. we've found. If you have to anchor, you will find it difficult to get rode space in among the buoys unless your boat doesn't draw much water and you can get in close to shore. The ad-vantage to this position is that you can quickly pull up the hook and take over a buoy when someone leaves.

There is a dinghy dock, but it is limited to boats of 7 meters or less. You will pay an overnight fee for space at this dock, about $7.50, which is pretty steep.

Campsites on shore also cost $7.50 per night.

Incidentally, if you have guests who want to camp out on shore and they find that the spaces are all filled, they can pitch their tents in the area which is sign-ed: 'No Camping'. That space, to the north of the main camping area is used as an overflow area, the signs notwithstan-ding. Even though there is no picnic table or fire pit at these spots, you still get to pay $7.50 per night.

Still, there is plenty of good drinking water and enough toilet facilities and a few old apple trees for the kids to ravage.

Montague has long been a favorite destination for families because it is a great spot for kids. They can swim or fish off the dock, prowl the beaches for drift logs to paddle on without the worry of strong currents or steep bluffs. There used to be good oyster picking in the

shallow bay that goes dry at low tide, between the campground and the Gray Peninsula. But now most of the oysters are gone and there are signs warning of pollution. The price of success, we guess.

You will notice that there is also good moorage, although not so protected from west winds, on the west side of the spit. If you look at the 1:18,000 blowup of the area on Chart #3473 you will note that the beach on this side is divided by a short reef. The northern shoreline has a launch ramp and the beach is pebbled. It is better for anchorage because it has better depths. The longer beach on the south side, opposite the tide flat, has a pleasant sandy surface and is ideal for swimming. Also, it is not a heavy anchorage area, as it is on the other side of the spit with a couple dozen boats contributing to the pollution.

There is a reef and three little rocks in a line off the west point on the Gray Peninsula. Those are stinkers. Our friend, Horst, the lifeboater, has yarded a few boats off these rocks. Swing wide around them.

The only other hazard in the Marine Park that we can think of is purely mental: the half-dozen power lines that stretch over the anchorage in the buoy-section of the harbor. They are 38 M. (125 feet) overhead. They look plenty substantial. We, however, always feel a little paranoid about them—wondering what would happen if they broke. Of course they would fall sputtering and hissing on our deck!

The water's never too cool for kids to swim at Montague.

was a big wharf. The beach is muddy and not very inviting. We didn't notice signs on the beach, but we were told that the land is for sale.

Opposite this Parker Island cove, you will find a longer cove on the west side of the spit. The portion near the bay's head is somewhat shallow. A nor'wester could sweep in there and make life troublesome.

There is a relatively flat cove on the west end of Parker Island, just north of **Wilmot Head**. We have seen boats anchored there, but it didn't look very safe to us, too many rocks on either side.

Parker Island like most of the islands on Trincomali and Stuart Channels is high and cliffed on the southern edge. Parker has cable crossings at each end. At the south, there is a big power terminal with towers and transformers that feed the lines strung over Payne Bay, which carry power from Galiano to Saltspring Island.

The northern end has another cable—also going to Saltspring. It comes up out of the water in a concrete causeway and rises up to towers on top of Parker Island that lead to the lines that fly across Montague Harbour.

There is a big orange sign, reading "Danger. High Voltage. Submarine Cable." Right nearby is another sign reading, 'For Sale'. It would be interesting to live there. You'd worry about your kids flying kites or climbing over fences, but you certainly wouldn't have to worry about getting electricity for your house.

The Marina at Montague

One of the few places in the Gulf Islands where there is a marina and a provincial park within walking distance of the ferry terminal is Montague Harbour. It is convenient to meet friends who want to come aboard by catching a ferry to visit aboard your boat at Galiano.

The marina, which we used as a base in that area of the Gulf, is called 'The Marina at Montague'. It offers transient moorage with electric hook-ups—you have your choice of 15, 20 or 30 amps. There is a gas float with Chevron regular and diesel, the only gas dock on the island. There is even water on the dock.

At the top of the dock there is a store which is attractively arranged and offers a remarkable supply of food items. It features both fresh and frozen meats. On the shaded sundeck you will find a snack bar, ice cream counter and a display of fresh fruits and vegetables arrayed in a shoreside dinghy. Shirley Coulter, with her husband Rick and their son T.J. who run the store, explains that when she cruises, she always develops a hunger for fresh vegetables and fruit. They had often found none available, or else in scant sup-

ply, when they visited dockside stores. The difficulties involved in transporting and storing perishables like these do not make their handling very profitable, but she is proud of the fact that her green grocery has become well-known among Gulf Island boaters.

Shirley, an excellent cook, has recently added a lunch counter where she serves home-made breakfasts and lunches.

The people who work in the store and on the docks are dressed in shirts that say 'Staff' and they are well-trained and courteous.

The marina is the site of the annual Thundermug Races. A sea-going 'Thundermug' is a basic outhouse installed in a fast boat. These bizarre little craft go zipping around the buoys just outside the marina on race day. It's Galiano's version of the infamous Nanaimo 'Bathtub Races'.

Of course, there's a barbecue on the beach on race day.

The marina also hosts a salmon derby and other island events.

It's a clean and delightful place to visit.

The Coulters at the Montague Marina

The passage between Wilmot Head and Sphinx Island is over 7 M. (23 feet) deep and quite fair.

Sphinx Island has a nice house in the waist of the island and the area is posted.

Now, let's consider the southeast end of Montague Harbour which has a lot of space for anchorage. There is a big area in the 9 M. (30 feet) depth range. The only drawback to this part of the harbor is the good fetch of west winds which whistle in over the low spit in the Park.

There is a government dock in Montague. It is almost hidden between the ferry dock and the Marina. It has 103 M. (340 feet) of dock space, but it seldom has any openings.

There is a public phone just above the government dock, which joins the ferry ramp. This ferry goes to the other Gulf Islands and to Swartz Bay on Vancouver Island.

Trincomali Channel, Montague Harbour to Porlier Pass: Continuing west out of the harbor, you pass Sphinx Island and then you have to make a few minor decisions: should you go between Sphinx and Wise Islands? Or between Charles and Wise Islands? Or how about between Charles Island and Galiano? Rest easy. Passage is okay in any of those places; just watch out for the rocks off the east and west ends of Wise. We also spotted a triangular daybeacon on the west end of Wise which wasn't on our brand new chart. Wise Island is completely subdivided and there are summer homes all along the shores.

Ballingall Islets, which look like a tug and barge when you approach them from the west, are in reality a bird refuge. You can go fairly close to these two islets, and you will find them fascinating. One is a roosting place for gulls, the one farther west is a cormorant refuge. They are completely white from the accumulation, over the centuries, of birdlime dropping from the nesting birds. There are a couple of old dead trees that have been coated with white guano, and the sight of the coal black cormorants roosting in their branches is spectacular. So is the noise—and the smell. The rocks off Ballingall are covered with kelp.

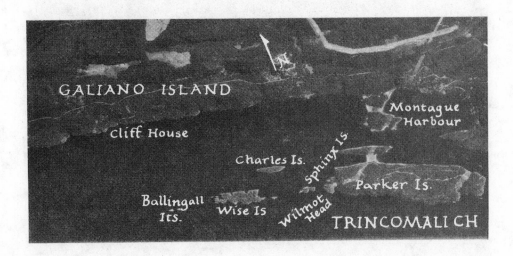

Meanwhile, on the Galiano side of the channel, about a mile and a half west of the marine park, a road comes down to the shore line. Near there is a small beach and above it is a fascinating house perched precariously in among the rocks. It is bleached and weatherbeaten. There is a path from the house up over a knoll to the beach.

Retreat Cove is actually divided into two coves by a drying flat that connects Retreat Island with Galiano. In the east head of the cove is a small government wharf with 49 M. (162 feet) of moorage. The float is tucked back behind the dock. There is a bed of kelp that extends from Retreat Island into the entrance to this cove. As usual, when in doubt, it is well to avoid it.

Right behind the public wharf is a private one with white railings which is connected to the shore by a dock and a very long staircase. There are a couple of private mooring buoys in the cove, which limit anchorage. It is customary in small public docks like this one to allow boats to raft up. If you arrive late, it might be well to ask courteously to tie up, but you ought not be refused. Even with a space at the dock, the spot is not a guaranteed retreat. Winds in the Channel could really stir up the boats.

Retreat Island is connected at low tides to the main island by a spit. It is posted and a house is being built on it, overlooking the channel.

The cove to the west of the government dock has a rock and a reef in the middle of it. Some anchorage may be possible near the spit. The west cove has a house with a pleasant meadow, a boat house and a flag pole. There are some dolphins which may

Ballingall, an island really for the birds.

Retreat Cove.

have been part of a projected Japanese fish-packing plant that was scrapped after the Japanese-Canadian internment during World War II. There is a very choice beach near the house.

Although a road leads along the ridge above the shore west of Retreat Cove to a spot near Spotlight Cove, we did not see any houses. A niche just east of the cove has a cluster of homes and cabins. One has a flagpole on a rocky point. There is a remarkable-looking house perched high on stilts in this area.

Spotlight Cove offers no anchorage. The water is shallow and the area is described in guides as having log rafts in it. We didn't see any. There are rocks in the entrance. Spotlight Cove is another small Galiano community. It boasts a video store and a flower shop.

There is an unnamed cove about 1½ miles northwest of Spotlight Cove.

You might call this shallow indentation 'Spanish Hills Cove'. It could be a refuge in a southeast gale, but it is not much of a summer gunkhole. Kelp covers much of the entrance. The flagpole noted by the chart is there. Behind it is a triangular marker indicating it is a 'fishing boundary', probably the eastern limit of the Porlier Pass fishing area.

North Galiano Public Dock: It looks new and in good condition. It probably was built to serve the growing community at the western end of Galiano. The dock has a stiffleg crane which is in good condition. It is the best public crane we saw in the Gulf area.

At the top of the ramp is the 'Spanish Hills Store'. It is open every day but Tuesday, except during July and August, when it's open every day. Of course, we visited the spot on a Tuesday in September, so we didn't get a chance to talk to the proprietor. Its hours, the other days, are 10-5, according to a sign. There is a public phone booth across the road from the store. Across the cove from the dock is a boat launch ramp. Like Retreat Cove, this one has a line of kelp intruding into part of the entrance from the west shore. There is a flagpole on a rock on the west side.

Porlier Pass: This is only ¾ of a mile from one end to the other. Although the area is cluttered a bit, it should pose no problems if you figure the slack currents.

Chart #3473 is a big-scale blow-up which makes it look easier than one of the small scale charts.

Who was 'Porlier'? Well, our historic guardian angel, Capt. John T. Walbran, is not much help. He says that in 1791 the name 'Boca de Porlier' was assigned by Capt. Jose M. Narvaez of the Spanish exploration boat 'Saturnina'. Capt. Walbran says that 'Boca' means 'mouth'. But about 'Porlier' he offers nothing. However, the Small Craft Guide comes to our rescue: Antonio Porlier was an official in Madrid in those years.

Let's take it feature by feature.

Alcala Point got its name from Dionisio Alcala Galiano, a Spanish naval officer involved in the exploration. His last name got put on the island. His first name is on a point which we shall consider in a bit, and his middle name got hung on this point. If he had had a nickname, it probably would have been tossed in the pot, too.

The daymarker listed on the chart eluded our scanning. The point is a boundary of the Indian Reserve. There are some houses on the top of the point.

The two coves between **Alcala** and **Virago Points** might offer some refuge if the currents were not too strong at the time. The north, unnamed, cove would protect you from a southeaster. There are rocks and reefs along the southwest shore of this peninsula; they are marked with kelp.

Romulus Rock was discovered first by the German steamer 'Romulus'. All 1,722 tons of her hit the rock in 1893 on a trip from Nanaimo to sea, loaded with coal. The ship was not sunk, however. Capt. Walbran, our historian, who died in 1913, found the rock in Porlier Pass in 1893 and gave it the name.

The rock was a nuisance and was later removed by blasting. The shoal remains, but the water is about 7 M. (23 feet) deep even at the shallowest. We wouldn't fret over it, if we were you.

North Galiano Public Dock from the Spanish Hills Store.

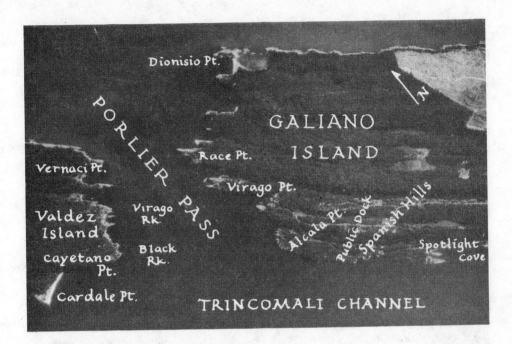

Virago Point is the first of two lighthouse stations in the pass. It got its name from the rock in the channel which nudged the keel of the 'H.M.S. Virago' in 1853. The 'Virago' was a 'paddle sloop of war'. She tipped the scales at 1,060 tons. She had 6 guns and a 300 h.p. engine. She got off the rock when the tide came in. The captain of the 'Virago' and a pilot named Capt. Stuart of the Hudson's Bay Co. were not held accountable for the accident because the rock was 'unreported'.

So much for nomenclature. Now let's look at the Virago Point lighthouse. It is short, squat and four-sided. It has a red cupola with a yellow light. There is a large sign on the structure warning small boats of less than 30 M. (100 feet) not to impede the passage of large and deep draft boats.

It flashes yellow and can be seen for 10 miles. It forms a range with the front light at Race Point. There is an emergency light on both houses. They are white lights that operate automatically whenever the main light fails for some reason.

Lighthouse Bay is in the Indian Reserve. There was a marina there at one time, but the docks are in bad condition. The Indians now use it for their boats. Power lines are buried in the entrance and in the head of this cove. The shores are rocky and there are kelp beds at the entrance, but no hazards.

A lighthouse-keeper's residence and outbuildings are on the rocky shores of the bay at the entrance. There is a wharf and a tall radio tower.

Race Point was named for the swirling currents, of course. The lighthouse is a twin of the Virago Point Light. It has a horn which points 240°, that is nearly west down the passage towards Trincomali Channel. It has a flashing yellow light that matches the one on the rear station. The two yellow lights are in a vertical line only on 196° 30'. It also has a quick-flashing white light which intersects the Virago Rock range white light.

The Porlier Pass Lighthouses.

The pattern of the **Virago Rock Light** throws a quick-flashing white beam from the middle of the channel to the east and a quick-flashing red light from the center of the passage westerly, where there are rocks and shoals all through the passage. The tower is cylindrical and has a green top. It has a solar panel. It is mounted on a reef that dries at 0.6 M. (2 feet). Another rock which has 1.6 M. (5 feet) over it at low tides is just southeast of it. Kelp surrounds these rocks. There is a wreck between the two rocks; it is not the 'Virago', of course, but we don't know its identity.

Boscowitz Rock dries at 0.9 M. (3 feet). Who was 'Boscowitz'? Please, no Polish jokes!

There are some glorious coves and beaches between Race Point and Dionisio Point. Anchorage would be delightful as long as the weather remained calm. Shoals reach out from the sides of these coves for about 300 M. (990 feet) and at points the depths are only 0.6 M. (2 feet.) They grow a good crop of kelp, fortunately.

At the northerly entrance to Porlier, on the Valdes side, you will find a green bell buoy with a flashing green light. It is labelled 'U 41'. It is in 29 M. (96 feet) of water, but it stands just east of Canoe Islet and its associated reefs. This is good fishing territory.

There is an unnamed rock which dries at a shocking 0.3 M. (1 foot) between Race Point and **Vernaci Point,** which was named for a lieutenant on the Spanish schooner 'Mexicana' in 1792. The cove south of it has a driftwood-strewn beach and a clearing.

A second cove to the south has a house with a dolphin and a piling.

The next finger south is part of an Indian Reserve. Reefs extend quite a distance from the area south of this Indian Reserve point.

Black Rock could give you a 'bad day', but a daybeacon is mounted atop a pipe which is set in a pyramidal concrete base. The marker appears to be a piece of plywood which was not painted red. There are drying rocks on both sides of the marker and cormorants roost on them.

That closes the file on Galiano Island.

The Porlier Pass Light

The post of 'Keeper of the Light' in most of the Gulf Islands area lighthouses has been a family franchise since the early days. The first keeper at Porlier Pass was Frank 'Sticks' Allison, who held the job from 1904 to 1941. His wife was the daughter of another lighthousekeeper, Henry Georgeson from Active Pass. They had two daughters, Devina and Frances. Both of these women married subsequent Porlier lighthouse-keepers.

The recollections of these two women are fascinating.

DEVINA BAINES: There was no fog alarm or anything at Porlier Pass in those early years. Being an old sailor, my father was interested in boats and ships and everything. In the foggy weather, when he would hear the boats blowing out in the Gulf or out in the channel, he'd get himself up on top of the hill where the sound would travel, and get an old coal-oil tin and a stick and he used to beat away on this tin can to show the boats as they came closer where the pass was. The captains soon got to know the sound of his tin can in the fog.

Eventually they gave us a hand foghorn and we used that until recently when they installed our new electric foghorn. The hand foghorn worked on a bellows deal. It was just a small box, about the size of a packing case like they used to put coal-oil tins in years ago. It had a handle on it and a horn out the front. The harder you moved the handle back and forth, the louder sound you got coming out of it. It had quite a different sound.

In those days we listened for boats to blow. As they got closer and they were wondering just where the pass was, then we would go out and blow the foghorn to them and listen. They would blow first, then we would listen and listen to their echo die out. When it died out across the pass and we couldn't hear it anymore, then we would answer with one.

A long blast on our foghorn; just a nice long blast so that it would carry and re-echo and sound from across on Valdes so they could pick up where the sound was coming from. In that way we used to direct them either out or in through the pass. Then if they were coming from Vancouver, coming through, when they got beyond Virago Point we used to give them three little short blasts which said goodbye to them, and they would answer. It was the same going the other way: when they went from Race Point we would signal goodbye to them. You soon got so that you picked out the whistles on the dfferent boats and you could tell if it was the old 'Qualicum', the 'Nitinat', 'Nanoose' or 'Swell', any of those old-time boats. They all sounded different.

FRANCES BROWN: When Daddy first came in 1902, the lighthouses were the same buildings that are still standing today. The lamps were brass lamps, and they burnt coil-oil. These lamps were filled in the morning and the chimneys polished and the wicks trimmed. Then in the afternoon as the sun went down, the lights were lit and you stayed in each light tower for 15 minutes or half an hour until it warmed up—it took quite a while—and waited until your wick burnt up and came to the height where it wasn't going to flare and yet was going to be high enough to show through the magnifying or prismatic glasses that surrounded the lamp. Then you left it overnight and it burned all night if things went well. If a draught came in, you ran into trouble and had to go down and relight your light. Those wicks were in operation in these lighthouses right up until my father retired in 1941.

We lost the 'Peggy McNeill' out here. That has always been one of the mysteries of Porlier Pass. We don't know just what happened to her. She was towing two coal-barges when she came out. It was quite a calm night, although it was a strong, strong tide, and Daddy and I watched her come down the inside shore there—this was around midnight—and then we went to bed. We didn't hear her go through the pass. Two days later her two scows were picked up off Gabriola Pass. There is no record of what happened to the 'Peggy McNeill'. One of the bodies was picked up towards the north end of Valdes. The only presumption is that she got caught in the strong tide-rip off Race Point here and was completely capsized and sank before the men had a chance to get off. The 'Peggy McNeill' is just one of our mysteries.

There are quite huge whirlpools in Porlier Pass and there seems to be a drop-off. Fishermen could probably tell you more about that. I don't know too much about that, but there seems to be quite a deep hole off Race Point there in one spot. (Our note: There is a drop from 30 to 42 meters there, a drop of about 40 feet.)

If you don't know how to handle your boat, you can get caught in the whirlpools. But you never see any of the Indian folks getting into trouble out there in their canoes. They can go across at most any stage of the tide. They know exactly where to go and which way to catch the eddies. I wouldn't say the same for other people. We don't seem to be quite as good at knowing the tides as they are. It's not so important in these days but in the old days they travelled more in rowboats. They had to watch the tides. ('Gulf Islands Patchwork.')

The Hummingbird Pub

Now we just have to tell you about 'The Hummingbird Pub', because we think that no visit to Montague Harbour would be complete without a visit to this happy place.

We were sitting in the cockpit of the 'Sea Witch' which was moored on a buoy down in the park, when along came an aluminum boat with a smiling young man at the tiller of the outboard motor. He handed us a brochure and told us we should come and visit his pub. When we said we might do that, he asked "Are you really Jo and Al?" and then he said, "You can catch the Pub bus at 5 o'clock up in the parking lot," and he waved toward the road at the entrance to the park.

When he left us, he went to all of the other boats in the harbor. We wondered if he had guessed their names as well.

That kind of welcome was hard to pass up. Besides the menu looked good and the prices seemed reasonable.

So, at 5 p.m. we stood at the gate to the park along with other curious boaters. We had all sort of dressed up for the occasion — at least, clean shirts and jeans.

It came right on time, an ancient, bright red Ford 30-passenger bus. Emblazoned on its side in large white letters was 'The Hummingbird Pub'.

We climbed aboard and found that the bus driver was George, still the big smile. He collected 50 cents for the round trip to the center of the island. After the bus lurched into motion, the stereo music system started. All the way out to the pub, we kept time to the music and sang along with old Fats Domino songs.

Some of the hills on Galiano are fairly steep and the bus would be shifted into compound low and the engine would howl as if in pain and the wheels would turn at a turtle's pace. We passengers had all become friends within 10 minutes and we all volunteered to get out and help push. But George assured us it would not be necessary...he thought.

Sure enough it crawled to the top of the hills and we began again to sing, lustily, "I found my thrill...on Blueberry Hill..." When we arrived at the big old turn-of-the-century house tucked back in among some trees, we got out and moved as a group up to the entrance.

We shared a table with some young people who had sat across from us in the bus. We chatted with the people at the other tables nearby. We had a delightful dinner, one captain's plate and one tortelloni. Since it has a licence, we could have cocktails before, after and during dinner.

The place is ideal for families. While children are not allowed to enter the restaurant because of the liquor licence restrictions, whole families can eat at picnic tables out in a pleasant yard. There is also a volleyball court and when the place is crowded, as it often is in summer and there is a wait to be served, impromptu volley ball games spring up.

George and Vera, a happy and warm-hearted couple in their late 20's, started this little jewel of a place in 1984 and they say it has been phenomenally successful despite the fact that it is way out in the boonies. They told us that before coming to Galiano, they had operated a charter service in the Grenadine Islands.

We thought the food was tasty and the bill was modest.

And we think you will be missing a bet if you don't visit 'The Hummingbird Pub'.

Not 76 Trombones—A Gross Of Them

American visitors are charmed by the fact that almost all Canadian products have information on their packages in French as well as English. Over time, you pick up quite a vocabulary in French. Sometimes the Francophone equivalent is surprising. Take, for example, paper clips. The French word is very descriptive: 'trombones'.

Winstanley, the Fisherman

Edward George Winstanley was one of the gold rush prospectors who came through Miners Bay in the 90's, went to the Yukon, made their bundles and returned to the tranquility of Galiano Island. He had a home on Arbutus Point. On one trip in 1905 he came home with a buckskin bag of gold nuggets. He was an ardent hunter and fisherman. His slogan was, "When the tide goes out the table is laid for breakfast."

The Gulf Islands area has quite a few liveaboards.

8. Wallace and the Secretaries.

That title sounds like a TV sitcom, doesn't it? Well, actually it's a catchall to include Wallace Island, the Secretary Islands, Norway Island, Reid Island, Hall Island, and little old Mowgli Island. Quite a mixed bag, eh? Yes, there are lots of hunks of real estate but not many good gunkholes in this area. That's why we're lumping them together. Actually, our favorite anchorage is in there.

Let's start our round trip at Panther Point.

Panther Point is the far southeast tip of Wallace Island. It has a reef that is the nail of a finger pointing east. There is a dry rock at its tip. The daybeacon is a triangle with red areas, mounted on a mast set in concrete.

From this point on, if you intend to explore the two coves on the Houstoun Passage side of Wallace Island, keep close to the shore of the island.

Wallace Island became famous because a man with a dream and a flair for writing bought and developed it and wrote a delightful book about the endeavor.

A reef system parallels the southwestern shoreline. A flashing red marker is the eastern extremity of this system, and it continues with varying depths for about 1.7 miles west to a rock which is exposed at 3 M. (10 feet.)

The passage between this reef and Wallace Island is fair.

We spent a whole afternoon hand-line fishing for salmon (or cod...or anything!) in this passage. Hand-held lines are the most practical in kayaks. You may be pleased to know that we left the fish population totally undiminished.

Conover Cove: The first entrance is this cove. It is 1,000 M. (0.6 miles) from the Panther Point daybeacon. It's a tiny hole in the wall.

Once you are inside, you will get the feeling you are in somebody's front yard. You will see an extensive development facing you. There is a long dock, a boathouse and some cabins along the shore. This is part of a condominium arrangement of about 50 people, according to one member we talked to. It began as a fishing resort

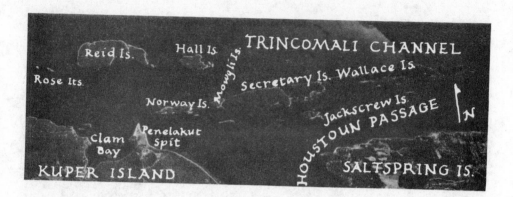

under Conover's ownership. He had big plans for the area. Unfortunately, the planned development of the island ran afoul of regulations of the Islands Trust which administers the islands' land use.

This delightful cove gets plenty of use during the summers, nowadays. Members, most of them from the Seattle area, fly in by private plane or come in by fast boats to spend a weekend or a few days.

At the west end of this cove, you will find the remains of an old boathouse and some discarded floats.

At both ends of the cove water is quite shallow, and boats often anchor there without checking the depths and end up hard aground at low tides.

Anchorage is possible with short rodes near the center of the cove. There are no inviting beaches.

'Princess Harbour' is not named on the charts, but is well-known to Gulf Island gunkholers. It is the long, narrow and well-protected cove west of Conover Cove. It is one of the most delightful spots in the whole Gulf Island area, so is quite popular. There is space for about six boats to anchor at one time if they all observe conventions. The beach at the head of the cove is very inviting and you can get a few oysters and some small clams there. Crab traps do fairly well here, also.

As you can see from the chart (#3442 is best), getting into this cove is not a piece of cake. The area west of the anchorage is foul and only the initiated try to enter that way. Our advice to skippers who want to go into Princess Harbour is to proceed west along the shoreline from Conover Cove until you are beyond the point, then allow for some shallow rocks off the point and swing wide, making a right turn, heading east, when you can see clearly down the inlet.

There is a beautiful fieldstone house on a small point just opposite the entrance. It has a small breakwater. A reef extends from the point on which the house sets but the end of it is marked with a stick. The house was Conover's until he moved off the island to try his hand at developing another island area. There is one other house and dock in the harbor. All land above the high tide line is private. A sign on the shore of the finger reads:

"Warning: Dogs Chasing Our Sheep Will Be Shot"

In calm weather, boats anchor at the end of the string of rocks extending westward. One rock in this area is dry at 0.3 M. (10 feet) and should be located before dropping the hook here.

Wallace Island

This is one of those beautiful little islands that dreams are made of. David and Jeanne Conover bought it in the early 1950's. They discovered, sadly, that sometimes it might be best to leave dreams as dreams. The book, 'Once Upon an Island', chronicles the problems the couple ran into both in developing the island, in fighting poverty, hunger—and sometimes each other—trying to turn the place into a resort. They were divorced 20 years later after the struggle was over.

Conover, who died in December, 1983, also bought Secret Island off Prevost. He, it is said, intended to give this island to an old flame, Marilyn Monroe. He always claimed to have been the man who 'discovered' Marilyn. He wrote a book about that phase of his life, entitled 'Finding Marilyn'. When the star married Joe DiMaggio, he decided against making the island a gift to her.

Wallace Island burned over in 1930, but is now full of lovely second growth timber: fir, cedar and arbutus. Deer are plentiful in the woods. Berries are lush in late summer. Fishing is good in nearby waters. The coves are rich in shellfish and crab.

As you now know, it was once called 'Narrow Island', but it was renamed 'Wallace' in 1905 by a Captain John Parry.

The "Conover House".

Swing wide around these rocks.

Princess Harbour was not named for any royalty, but because Jeanne Conover, on first seeing the cove, said she thought it was large enough for one of the Princess ships (like the 'Marguerite') to enter and anchor. We suspect that notion was born of a moment of girlish enthusiasm.

Only shore boats at high tide should attempt to go between Wallace Island and South Secretary Island.

From a private dock in Princess Harbour.

Jackscrew Island: Want to guess about this name? A 'jackscrew', as you probably know, is a lifting device like a house-jack. Maybe some beachcomber found one on shore there and assigned the name to it. It is a several-acre island with an impressive house on the beach on the west side. Near the house are several small outbuildings. There is a dock, but no float. The light at the southeast corner is a red-banded tower and flashes white.

Passage behind Jackscrew Island is possible in 5 M. (16 feet) depth but is tricky with rocks and reefs and clutter. If you insist, stay center in the passage.

We'll tell you more about South Secretary Island when we make the trip down the Trincomali Channel side. The south shore has some very alluring beaches, though.

There is a big home near the spit connecting the two Secretary Islands.

Travelling west along North Secretary Island, you will see a remarkable reef which is not named, but is clearly marked on the chart.

Passage is possible between North Secretary Island and Mowgli Island in 5 M. (16 feet) of water. Be on guard against a small shoal which dries at 4 M. (13 feet) off the southeast end of Mowgli.

Mowgli Island: Wasn't he a character in Kipling? Please don't say you don't know because you've never 'kippled'! It is a nice looking island, but appears to be uninhabited and doesn't offer any incentive to passing boaters to visit. Locally it's known as 'Spike Island'.

The reef which lies off Mowgli and North Secretary probably should be called 'Mowgli Reef'. It is marked with a red triangular daybeacon on the west end. It is a

Poor Old Panther!

The Griffith family on Saltspring Island used to tell people they would never forget the stormy Sunday in 1874 when they stood in their front window and watched the Clipper ship 'Panther' drift helplessly up Trincomali Channel to her destruction on an outlying reef on the southern end of what was then called 'Narrow Island'.

Panther left the coal dock in Nanaimo with her decks nearly awash with 1,750 tons of coal for San Francisco. She was towed by the Tug 'S.S. Goliath'. Crossing Boundary Channel, they ran into a gale near San Juan Island. For several hours, the tug tried valiantly to find shelter, but finally the sea began to win the struggle.

In the boiler room of the 'Goliath', the engulfing waves began to fill the space until the poor fireman trying to keep the steam up had to stand in his waist in cold salt-water. At almost the last minute, the towboat captain reluctantly gave the order to cut the hawser and turn the clipper ship free to fend for itself.

Captain Balch of the 'Panther' approved of the measure. He set his crew to raise canvas immediately and began to run before the gale. Somewhere during the flight, on the morning of the 18th, the ship hit a rock (history does not indicate which one). The pumps were started, but they discovered nine feet of water in the hold so the captain decided to run for Trincomali Channel and try to beach it.

After two hours of desperate pumping and sailing, the 'Panther' struck the reef which now bears its name. The distance to the shore was only a hundred yards, so the crew got a line ashore and after saving themselves, attempted to save some of the movable contents.

They put up a crude building to shelter themselves and the gear they had salvaged. Later, they and their belongings were rescued.

The 'Panther' was a total loss. It lay for years on the rock until the sea gradually pounded it into invisibility.

The 'S.S. Goliath' reached Seattle safely.

There are butter clams in Princess Harbour.

very photogenic reef, as reefs go. Rock faces slant up from the water's edge on both sides, making it somewhat prism-shaped. The top of the ridge is fringed with moss-covered trees, brush and grasses. It is a fascinating sight. Some day we plan to anchor nearby and go prowl it. There is a spectacularly-twisted and split arbutus tree at the southeast end. A reef which dries at 1.5 M. (5 feet) continues out for about 100 M. (330 feet).

Norway Island is a beautiful place. We were told it was owned by the Canadian Ambassador to China. Signs say it is for sale, though. We wanted to buy it on the spot, but we would first have to take back the deposit beer bottles to make the down payment, and we didn't have time. So, will you please buy it and invite us to visit? We fell in love with it.

There is a mean reef, marked with a black daybeacon at its east end, off Norway Island's southeast corner.

At the northeast tip is a small cove made by a natural breakwater. The rock has a triangular red daybeacon. There is a flashing yellow light on the west tip, which is privately maintained and is probably used to direct the owner home from the sea. As you approach this point, you see the house. There is a sign saying 'Welcome - Norway Island'. Nice touch, isn't it?

The granddaddy of all driftwood fences.

Reid Island: There are reefs and rocks at the east end of this island. One dry rock even has trees on it. The reefs are visible at low tides. This island is also for sale, according to signs posted all around it. There is a little house almost completely hidden in a rocky indent. A pebbled beach has pilings which may have supported a boat house at some time. The narrow bight is protected from northwest winds. On the west end of this area, there is a nice house and a cabin with a dock. A shoal is detached from the east point of the island. The southeast end, behind the rocks and reefs, is apparently a camp ground of some sort. We saw a lot of tents and beachcombers.

Another shoal lies off the west end of Reid Island. Passage between this shoal and the Rose Islets is possible with care. You should go in a northeasterly-southwesterly direction between the shoal and the islets in water about 20 M. (66 feet) deep.

The **Rose Islets** are a rookery for cormorants. The surface is dead and drab and is decorated only by a bit of brush on top. Along the shores of the Rose Islets, if you look carefully, you will see grey, loaf-shaped figures—sunning seals. The rocks off the east end of Rose Islets are covered with kelp.

We are now, as you may have noticed, heading east along Trincomali Channel, having just circumnavigated Rose Islets (where we got skunked in fishing, but then we get skunked everywhere!)

On the northern face of Reid Island there is a picturesque driftwood fence and a rustic cabin. From this point along the north shore, you will see a number of homes along the beach. At the indentation in the island, there is a sign which reads: 'Trincomalee Reid Island, B.C.'

The cove at the southeast end of Reid could be a pleasant lunch hook stop if you want to ease in between the shoals.

Hall Island: There is a cove at the east end of this island; kelp rings the entrance, but it looks fair. There is a fine home on this cove, and it has a dock and float.

The east point on Hall Island has a triangular daybeacon.

Returning along the Trincomali Channel side of the Secretary Islands, the shore of North Secretary Island offers no attractions for passing boaters.

The separation point between North and South Secretary Islands is a favorite anchorage spot. If you are accustomed to stern-tying, which is customary in this area, you will find it quite pleasant. You have your choice of the eastern shore where you will see the late sunset, or the western shore where you will get the sunrise. There are some impediments to this area, though.

At the western end off South Secretary, there is a reef extending well into the entrance. About 12 M. (40 feet) from the end of the visible rocks there is a shoal that is submerged at high tides and pokes up somewhat alarmingly at low tides. It is surrounded by kelp. So when entering this cove from the north, be sure to steer around the several areas of kelp. There is a kelp bed over the reefs on the north shore off South Secretary Island, just outside the entrance. We lead-lined the depths at 6 to 9 M. (20-30 feet). We have a suspicion that the charts do not show all of the reefs in this area.

The spit between North and South Secretary Islands is dry at all but the highest

Stern tying saves anchoring space.

tides. There is a handsome wooden sign reading 'South Secretary, Private'. (It really is East Secretary, by the compass, but we decided not to quibble.) Both Secretary Islands are posted.

Chivers Point on the west end of Wallace Island is a pretty parklike finger of land. There are kelp beds to keep you off the reefs. The point was named for Jeremiah Chivers, who in 1889 received a crown grant for the 145-acre Wallace Island. The old pioneer died in 1927 at the age of 92. He is buried on Saltspring Island.

There is a cabin at the small cove halfway down the north side of Wallace Island. Some ugly rocks, awash at 0.5 M. (1 ½ feet) dot the landscape at the east end of Wallace Island making it not advisable to stay close to the shoreline there.

A drying tide flat fills the cove at the east end of Wallace Island behind Panther Point.

Okay, that's our rubberneck trip around the Secretaries. Not too many places to anchor, but some interesting scenery.

Well, don't just stand there, throw me a fish!

9. Thetis and Kuper: Six Meters and a World Apart.

One historian describes these two islands as "...the two most inhabited (of the Gulf Islands),...which at times become one, since the short narrow channel dividing them goes dry at low ebb tide."

Even though a narrow canal has been dug to improve the passage between the islands, it still goes dry at low tide and shore boats have to be portaged for a hundred meters (330 feet) or so.

Thetis was named after the 'H.M.S. Thetis', a frigate of 36 guns which was stationed there to maintain order in the area in 1850.

Kuper was the name of the Captain of the 'Thetis', Augustus Leopold Kuper.

Thetis is a retirement community with many beautiful homes, but the only commercial establishment is the Telegraph Harbor Marina, which has a grocery store. There are several Bible camps on the island. There is no liquor store on either island.

Kuper is an Indian Reserve. The Penelakut Tribe lives there. They have something of a history of being fractious. There is a Catholic Church, but no commercial establishment on Kuper Island.

The B.C. Ferry stops at both islands, at Preedy Harbour on Thetis and in Telegraph Harbour on Kuper.

Let's approach these islands from the southeast, where Stuart Channel and Houstoun Passage join.

North Reef is a sandstone razorback about 1 M. (3 feet) high. It has a white circular tower with a white light flashing a 3-group: three quick flashes followed by 6½ seconds of eclipse. This reef is the southeast end of a foul ground system that ends with Escape Reef to the northwest. The depths between these two reefs shouldn't trouble you unless your keel is more than 2.9 M. (10 feet).

Escape Reef has a daybeacon which is mounted on a mast set in a concrete base on the rock. It is a red square, indicating port hand passage.

Sandstone Rocks is connected by a shoal to Tent Island.

Tent Island is an Indian Reserve. For years, it was a favorite stopover for boaters. The Province leased the land from the Indians as a provincial park. In recent years, the lease has been dropped and the Indians have placed the uplands off limits to tourists. Boats still anchor in the cove and folks still go ashore to swim in the warm waters off the beach.

It would not make a good overnight anchorage in a westerly, however. The spit between Tent Island and **Josling Point** dries at 1.6 M. (5½ feet) so it could be crossed in a shallow draft boat at high water. If you try it, be on the lookout for a rock which is in the center of the Stuart Channel side and is visible at 0.9 M. (3 feet).

Lamalchi Bay: At the head of this bay there is a non-Indian enclave, with several attractive houses. Temporary anchorage on a calm day is popular and the water is usually warm enough for swimming on sunny days in summer. The bay dries almost completely at extreme low tides.

This bay was named after a tribe called 'The Lamalchi', a branch of the Cowichan tribe. They had a village in this bay in 1863 when the English authorities aboard the gunboat 'Forward' came into it to hunt for the murderers of Frederick Marks and his daughter (see that story in Chapter 5). The Lamalchi fired on the boat killing a young seaman, Charles Glyddon. The ship returned fire and several Lamalchi were killed. A week or so later, a party of marines went ashore and completely destroyed the village by burning it.

One of the men of the village, A-chee-wun, was implicated in the murder on Saturna Island. He was also accused of leading the attack on the 'Forward'. The historian, Captain Wallbran, writes that when he was finally hanged, the Indians were relieved because he had been something of a tyrant to them as well as a danger to the settlers. He boasted to his tribe that he had killed eleven white men.

A school for ghosts?

The Lamalchis dwindled in number and by 1905, there were only 15 of them left on Kuper. In that year they joined the Penelakuts who numbered 149.

Author Bill Wolferstan says that the bay was taken over by a religious group in the 1880's. They had 100 acres of land on which they established 'The Company for the Propagation of the Gospel in New England and the Ports adjacent in America'. In recent years it has been used as a base for a Gestalt Institute and an Ecological Centre.

Augustus Point has a rock just offshore which dries at 0.6 M. (2 feet).

There is another rock off **Active Point** which is in 1.8 M. (6 feet). Stay offshore if you are heading for Telegraph Harbour.

The beach between Active and **Donckele Point** is very inviting. We have seen many boats anchored there. Watch for the two rocks off Donckele Point. This point must have been named after Father Dunkell, a Catholic missionary who devoted his life to the Penelakut Indians.

The unnamed bight just beyond Donckele Point is a mudflat at low water. There is a log skid at one side, an old wrecked fishboat up on the beach and a dolphin on the north side. Log booms may be found in this area at times.

The government wharf on Kuper is tiny and in poor condition. There is an old ruined tin shack on it. Local small boats take up the space at the float.

The M.O.H., Ministry of Highways, ferry dock is of no interest to visiting boaters.

There is an imposing brick edifice on shore behind the ferry dock. At one time, it was an industrial school operated by the Roman Catholic Church for the Indians. Now it stands vacant, the windows mostly broken out. A resident told us that the government refused to fund the continuation of the school so it was abandoned.

Telegraph Harbour: These may be the most protected waters in the Gulf Area. It is a long, narrow inlet. Along the east shore, there are a few houses of Indian families. The Thetis Island shore, however, is well populated.

Chart #3477 will give you plans in this area.

Halfway down the inlet, there is a series of pilings which bisect the passage. The passing boaters are shunted off to the east. The other corridor leads to a gas dock and a marina. In recent years, the Thetis Island Marina has had troubled times. When we were there, in 1985, it was not pumping gas. It continued to offer moorage, however. At one time, the marina had a restaurant that was known for its cuisine, as well as a store, laundromat and showers, and a playground for kids. A nice spot.

The inlet widens somewhat at the head. There is anchorage space for more than a score of boats in 3 M. (11 feet) of water.

Telegraph Harbour Marina seems to be flourishing. It offers moorage at very tidy floats. There is a restaurant, post office and grocery store connected with the marina. The gas dock has complete fuel service. There are showers and a laundromat, garbage facilities, launching ramp, bait, tackle and charts. Propane is not available.

Telegraph Harbour Marina.

The cut really runs dry at minus tides!

Boat Passage, between Thetis and Kuper, is famous for its challenge to skippers. Remarkably large cruisers and even deep draft saiboats have negotiated the tricky slough at high water. The entry on the Telegraph Harbour side has a beacon and tide-indicator scale, but it is badly worn and virtually unreadable unless you are familiar with it. The beacon is red, so the scheme is "returning to Telegraph Harbour", which is an arbitrary denotation. The cut is about ½-mile long.

The narrow cut has a B.C. Tel cable under it. At low tides, as we said, portions of it are completely dry. The rest of the passage has a little water in it at zero tides. It looks like an irrigation ditch at low water. The banks are all soft mud. At high tides, the whole area is covered with water and it looks like a big bay. About halfway through the passage, a creek intersects it.

Aside from feeling your way along between the two red daybeacons which mark the channel, the biggest hazard is eel-grass. Be sure to check your sea-water strainer after running this passage. There is scuttlebutt that says that in previous years the Indians would put sticks in the shoals so that boaters would go aground and they would be charged high prices to be floated free by Indian boats. We think this practice, if it ever really existed, is no longer a danger.

The Clam Bay entrance to the passage has two beacons, one is black and square, indicating starboard passing. The tidal current in the passage floods to the east and ebbs to the west.

Leaving Telegraph Harbour, returning to Stuart Channel, swing wide around **Foster Point.** It has a shoal reaching out 100 M. (330 feet). If you are heading for

Preedy Harbour, take a bearing on the red topped tower off Hudson Island which is called 'Hudson Island North Light'. It flashes red. A dry rock west of this light has a red triangular daybeacon on a mast. In line with these two markers is a third, the Preedy Harbour Daybeacon, also red. It is fitted with a radar reflector.

Alarm Rock is an extensive reef just southeast of Hudson Island. It has a white tower and it flashes 2 short in succession. Stay outside this light when returning to Stuart Channel.

Preedy Harbour: The government wharf at Preedy was in poor repair when we visited (1985). The float is three-sided. It has about 15 M. (50 feet) of moorage, most of which was taken up by small boats belonging to residents. The walkway to the top of the dock had a loose plank which tilted up when stepped on and it could drop someone onto the float below. We hope it is repaired by the time you visit.

The ferry dock does not have any tourist facilities near it. You will find a bulletin board with a map of the island and a list of the residents and their locations. The only commercial establishment on the island, outside of the marina, is a coffee-roasting plant. Much of the island has been subdivided. There is one resort, Overbury Farm Resort, up near **Crescent Point** but it has no dock.

The beautiful building and grounds that you see near the ferry docks is the 'Capenwray Harbour Bible Centre'. It is an inter-denominational school offering intensive Bible study, according to the staff.

Preedy Harbour ferry dock.

Preedy Harbour would offer some protected moorage. There are some favorable depths in the northwest head and down near the peninsula at the southeast head. The ferry wakes would be disturbing, though.

Hudson Island is private and posted. There is a cove at its east end which has a large private float. The remains of a once-elaborate dock can be seen across from this float. The light on the drying reef northwest of Hudson Island is not located on the edge of the channel between Hudson and **Dayman Island.** It is called the Preedy Harbour Light, a tower with a red band at the top and a quick-flashing red light. It is in the center of the reef which may be submerged at higher water.

Stay close to the green buoys off Dayman Island, 'U 33' and 'U 35'. This is the route of the Chemainus-Thetis ferry. There are extensive shoals and reefs west of Dayman Island. If you exit Preedy Harbour passing Crescent Point, stay in the 11 M. (36 feet) contour which is in the center of the passage.

False Reef in Stuart Channel, is not false at all. It's very real and several boats have been hauled off it. It has a rock that dries at 0.9 M. (3 feet). A daymark on a mast indicates the preferred passage is to the right.

No difficulties should be encountered in cruising along the southwest shore of Thetis. Be aware of the oyster culture farm about half-way between Crescent and **Fraser Point.** Stay well off Fraser Point because of the two rocks just before you reach the point. Then you can slip along the western shore of Thetis and enter North Cove. Do watch out for foul ground about 0.3 miles east of the point at the outer edges of the cove. There are two rocks with less than 1.8 M. (6 feet) of water over them.

North Cove offers anchorage in 10 M. (33 feet) in a square-shaped bight between two fingers. This cove is a refuge from the often unpredicted southeast winds that

---

Cufra Inlet

This slough is lovely and serene, with green waters reflecting overhead trees. The only sounds you hear are those of your canoe or kayak as you slip through the water, or the birds who are annoyed at your intrusion and will scold you roundly.

The inlet narrows and shallows the farther you progress, and then widens once again into a small lake-like bay.

You almost feel like you should be in an English punt, the man wearing a suit and a 'boater' hat, the woman relaxing in a white lace dress, holding a parasol — with Handel's 'Water Music' filling the air.

can whistle up Trincomali and Stuart Channels. It is exposed to northwesterlies, however. There are aquaculture facilities in North Cove.

There is a Christian camp in the small cove in the southwest corner of the area, which has a private dock. The camp is run by a group called 'Pioneer Pacific'. A resident told us that the group owns 'quite a bit' of land in this area.

'Cufra Inlet', almost a mile long, cuts into Thetis in a southeasterly direction. It's a perfect spot to paddle a kayak or shore boat. There is a breakwater near the mouth of the Inlet which extends from the east shore and provides shelter inside for a private moorage. The whole area is an oyster aquaculture farm and taking of shellfish is illegal.

A submarine cable crosses the Inlet.

Pilkey Point at the northwest tip of Thetis has a shoal extending from it, but passage may be made between it and the Ragged Islets by staying in the middle of the opening.

Ragged Islets is a nice poetic name for this cluster. There are three dry rocks, one of them being enough above water, 11 M. (36 feet), to support some vegetation on its top. The red triangular day-beacon is on the northwest end of the reef. It is on a mast from a concrete base.

The northern shores of Thetis offer no interesting features except some attractive homes. There is a boat launch ramp just west of Leech Island.

Leech Island is fairly high and wooded. It is shaped like an old-fashioned flat iron. There are submerged rocks and drying reefs northwest of it. They are flagged by kelp. There is a private dock on the west side.

Clam Bay: This is a very popular anchorage and there is quite a bit of room for transients. Powerboats frequently moor here waiting for water to rise in Boat Passage.

Incidentally, the plans in Chart #3477 are in such large detail that it can become confusing. Clam Bay is nearly a mile across. **Rocket Shoal** in the center of the bay has five rocks with 1.8 M. (6 feet) of water in lower tides. They are marked well with kelp.

Centre Reef farther out in the bay, has one rock that dries at 0.6 M. (2 feet). It is marked by a conical red buoy, numbered 'U 42'.

You can easily pass between Leech Island and Centre Reef, just stay in closer to the Leech Island side.

Most boats prefer to anchor on the Kuper Island side of the bay, although we like the Thetis side, even though a chartered sailboat did drag anchor there and snuggle up to us unexpectedly one night!

If you decide to anchor near Leech Island you would do well to stay clear of the dry ridge off the western shore. There is a dock on the Thetis Island shore here. A marker, a red flag, near the dock, probably was installed by the resident and indicates a rock to be avoided.

The winds can help you make a decision, however, in finding the best protection.

The beach on the Kuper Island side is an oyster-cultivating area and is marked by a log boom in the 10 M. (33 feet) contour. This boom takes up much of the space. Signs warn that taking shellfish in this area is illegal. The tribal police watch the area in fast boats. There is some moorage at the southeast end of the bay beyond the log booms.

Penelakut Spit is a long, low white beach of clamshells with several areas that dry at low tide. One island is connected by a road to the main island. Another fishhook shaped dry area extends out into Houstoun Passage.

Off the spit to the east is a shoal that dries at 1.8 M. (6 feet) so stay wide around the foul ground and favor the Norway Island shore.

On a hill above the Spit area, you will see the Catholic Mission, a beautiful sight, towering over an Indian village.

Continuing east down Houstoun Passage, watch for kelp which hangs onto about a half dozen rocks about 400 M. (0.2 miles) off the eastern Kuper shore.

An interesting note about this area: the B.C. Small Craft Guide says that passage between Norway Island and Penelakut Spit should only be attempted with 'local knowledge'. There are some shoal areas, as you can see from the chart, but favoring the Norway Island shore, as we advised, should take you safely through. Go on slow bell and watch your fathometer. You can do it. We did it.

The Kuper Island shore on Houstoun Passage has no refuges or anchorages.

As you approach Tent Island, stay well offshore. Watch for the marker off Sandstone Rocks. This is the **Tent Island Reef** Daybeacon; a triangular red board on a mast.

To recapitulate our introduction to Thetis and Kuper: there are some beautiful and interesting areas to see and a number of good anchorages. Telegraph Harbour can be terribly overcrowded on weekends. It might be well to consider some of the other anchorages, even though they are not so well protected.

Capenwray Bible School in Preedy Harbour.

10. De Courcy Islands: No Ties to Land.

These five northernmost islands form the top of the Gulf Islands Area. Beginning with Pylades Island on the southeast and ending with Mudge Island and Dodd Narrows, they represent the most untouched and uncommercialized lands in the archipelago. There is no ferry service to connect them to the mainland or Vancouver Island. There are no stores or marinas, no electric power or telephones. Good anchorages are few. With the Nanaimo metropolitan area growing exponentially, there has been talk of bridging between Gabriola and Vancouver Island through Mudge Island over Dodd Narrows, which would tie rapidly-developing Gabriola Island to Vancouver Island. Other short spans would connect Link Island and De Courcy. The scheme sounds like a nightmare to the fiercely independent and self-sufficient islanders. Only Ruxton Island and Pylades Island would be immune to encroachment.

Let's begin the exploration a bit to the south.

Danger Reefs represent the junction of Trincomali and Stuart Channels. One of the rocks dries 1.2 M. The light is a tower on the north end of the large arrow-shaped middle rock. It is a quick-flashing white light visible for 5 miles. Canadian Coast Guard recommends giving this light a one-half mile berth when crossing south of it.

Tree Island is 300 M. off the south end of Pylades. It is diamond-shaped and has a number of trees. There are the remains of an old shack on it.

Pylades Island was named after the screw-corvette 'H.M.S. Pylades' which was on scene around 1859. One of the officers on board was the son of author Charles Dickens. Pylades, in case you care to trace the name further, was the close friend of Orestes, the son of Agamemnon. The island is very hilly and has a beach and drying shoals off the northeast corner. There is a small islet with trees and brush, just off Pylades' north shore, Whaleboat Passage. It used to be called 'Indian Island'.

We got into our kayaks and paddled out of Whaleboat Island Park into the

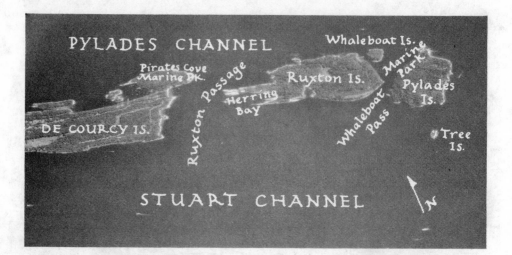

passage between Indian Island and Pylades. It's all shallows and reefs in that area, but very beautiful and quiet. Even in mid-summer we were the only boat anchored at the park and there were no homes or other people around. We paddled down and partially around Pylades. We went ashore on a small shell beach in a tiny cove on the eastern shore and decided that it was a beautiful place to visit but we wouldn't want to ride long at anchor there.

Whaleboat Passage between Pylades and Ruxton Island is passable and fair at most tides. There is a rock in this passage near the Pylades shore which dries at 0.9 M. There are two rocks off 'Indian Island' with 1.8 M. over them at lower tides.

Whaleboat Island Marine Park: It is a 7-acre undeveloped park with room for several boats to anchor. The best spot is in the narrow channel that separates Whaleboat from Ruxton Island. There is a rock in the cove which dries at 1.5 M., and it would be advisable to find this rock before setting out scope.

There is no beach on Whaleboat Island, it is steep and rugged and rocky. Shore boats can be taken out on ledges in the anchorage so you can clamber up into the island, which has no facilities. The Parks Service says there are no good camping sites on the island and we believe them. Some rugged kayakers we met said they found a spot to pitch their tent, but we didn't find out where. The highest point on this tiny island is 49 M. which is about 160 feet.

The island was added to the marine park system in November, 1981. Up until then it was Crown land known as 'Eagle Island' locally. If you're a sun lover, be prepared to have the sun set early at Whaleboat Island Park as it hides behind the high hills on the Ruxton Island side of Whaleboat Passage.

Ruxton Island: The whole southeastern end of Ruxton is steep and forested with a hill of 18 M. dominating the entire end of the island.

There is a dock on the Ruxton shore opposite the park with a sign saying 'R.C.Y.C.', which is the Royal City Yacht Club of New Wesminister, B.C.

There is a very small cove, **West Bay,** on Ruxton's southwest shore and a house has been there for several decades. There is no anchorage. The cove is filled with private floats and mooring buoys. West Bay is nearly unusable at low water.

It's tiny, but the almost-white, fine sand makes the beach at Herring Bay one of the most inviting in the Gulf Islands area.

Herring Bay on the northwest corner of Ruxton Island is one of the most attractive moorages in the Northern Gulf Islands. It has become quite popular in the last few years and acts as an overflow for boats that can't find space at Pirates Cove. This is one of those lovely places we thought we had exclusively since we discovered it years ago, but now we realize everyone else knows it, too.

It is made up of a cove and a passage between a reef that extends 0.2 miles off the island, and the northwest long finger of Ruxton Island. The reef has a red triangular daybeacon at its northwest end. There are several summer cabins in this cove. Anchorage is in 4.6 M. to 9 M. Entrance can be made on either side of the reef with the marker. The easiest and safest course is to come in along the side of the reef, and head straight southeast into the bay. There are beautiful white sandy beaches on the reef which are uncovered at 3 M. They are great for swimming, sunning, beachcombing and just lazing about.

Ruxton Passage, which separates Ruxton and DeCourcy Islands, is deep water connecting Stuart and Pylades Channels. There is no problem navigating the passage. There are two coves with summer cabins on the south end of De Courcy Island. Boats anchored in those coves are protected from most prevailing winds. The squarish cove southeast of the peninsula of Pirates Cove Park offers a nice beach and plenty of room for anchorage in 2 M. to 6 M.

Avoid

"U36"

Dinghy Dock

White Range
(Priv)

PIRATES COVE
MARINE PARK

Dinghy Dock

Private Dock

DeCourcy Island. Pirates Cove Marine Park: This is a favorite of most cruising boaters in the Gulf. The problem is that during much of the summer, it becomes 'wall-to-wall' with boats. We have been here in the off-season and had the whole cove to ourselves. It was a 'dream come true' spot.

The entrance to this park is made difficult by a poorly-placed black beacon. Some charts, like #3443 corrected to 1985, do not even show the markers for this entrance. The port-hand marker is placed shoreward of the reef it warns of. This drying reef continues northwest for 100 M. At most tides, the reef is covered. What this means is that, going northwest up Pylades Channel along the north shore of the park, you must continue far beyond the black beacon before turning southwest to enter the cove. However, the owner of a home on the beach has apparently provided a range marker on the rocks in front of his house. It is a white-painted arrow which points at an 'X' on a post near the house. So, proceed along the channel until you see the arrow pointing at the X, then follow the indicated course. When you can see the dinghy float on the northern side of the cove, turn toward it and keeping the red buoy marked 'U 36' to the right, head for the center of the cove.

Unofficial range marker.

Pirates Cove

The 38-hectare (76-acre) park was born in 1966, thanks to the Council of B.C. Yacht Clubs. There are nine camping and picnic areas on shore, lots and lots of trails, two octagonal dinghy floats and a traditional hand pump for drinking water.

It's a lovely park. Trails wind through uncluttered forests of arbutus and evergreens, often just above the shoreline. There are all kinds of seabirds and landbirds in the trees and in the air, and if you're there in the off-season, you can easily hear them.

The water in the cove is warm for swimming, but do it early in the morning before another 75 boats arrive.

The park does not include quite all of the cove. There is a private dock at the west end. The park does include a cove on Ruxton Passage, and it has a sunny beach, pleasant for an afternoon's sunbathing.

The two islands that flank the northwest entrance to the park are also private.

Now that we've told you how to actually get into Pirates Cove without tearing holes in the bottom of your boat, we simply have to give you the wonderful quote by Peter Chettleburgh, who wrote the definitive book on B.C. Marine Parks, 'An Explorer's Guide to Marine Parks of British Columbia:'

"Entering Pirates Cove requires a certain amount of caution. Indeed, don't under any circumstances come into Pirates Cove too close to the porthand day mark at its entrance. It is one of the few local aids to navigation which works notoriously well in reverse, luring boatsmen onto the rocks much like those eighteenth-century, beacon-lighting plunderers on England's south coast."

Anchorage is in 1.2 M. to 3 M. in the cove. But be advised that the holding quality of the rocky bottom is poor. That makes it important to back down on the hook until the line gets tight and the boat begins to slew around it. There is a second dinghy float on the south shore of the park. There is no moorage at these octagonal floats for cruising sized boats. Notice there is a shoal that extends into the anchorage from the shore just beyond the outer dinghy float. On the shore near the inner dinghy float you may find ringbolts set in the rock which you can use for stern-tying.

By the time you get to this inner harbour buoy, you have made it safely through the tricky entrance to Pirates Cove.

Although it is not as secure from winds, the bight northwest of Pirates Cove is potential anchorage. Most of the good depths are occupied by private mooring buoys, though. There is a reef, which is 0.6 M. to 0.9 M., in the center of the bight, but it is indicated by kelp.

Northwest of this bight there is a long island which is connected by drying shoals on DeCourcy's north shore. Temporary anchorage might be had in the shallows northwest of this island. There are drying reefs and rocks which intrude into Pylades Channel quite a distance at the northwest end of DeCourcy Island.

The separation between De Courcy Island and Link Island is a good spot for anchorage. Once past the shoals off the northwest end of De Courcy, the entrance is fair. This is called 'Orgy Cove' by some Nanaimo sailors for reasons which might stimulate the imagination. The depths are fair: 0.9 M. to 2 M., but again much of the bight is taken up by local boats. Only shore boats can go between the islands here at high tide.

And if you look at the waters between Link and Mudge Islands at high tide they don't look too bad. But that passage goes totally dry and is a mess of rocks and mud.

The reach that is formed at the entrance to False Narrows is wide and fair for anchorage but is not protected from winds up Pylades Channel, or currents running through False Narrows.

We wondered why we made such poor time in Pylades Channel one day, and then checked our handy-dandy B.C. Small Craft Guide. Lo and behold, the currents in the channel sometimes reach 2 knots—which is a lot if you're in a five-knot boat. The flood sets northwest and the ebb southeast in Pylades Channel. Of course, the current is on its way to or from False Narrows, where it can run as much as about 6 knots.

If the combination of the bad reputation (pretty much undeserved) False Narrows has and you want to test your navigation skills, the Narrows is a real challenge. If you decide to try it, check the tips on page 209.

What's a "tide book?"

Brother Twelve

Greedy gurus and Machiavellian messiahs are not strictly modern-day phenomena. The Gulf Islands had their share of 'Rajhneeshes' and 'Moonies'. One colony of early 1920's dropouts had its centers near Nanaimo and on DeCourcy Island. It was the settlement created by the almost mystic powers of a man called in British Columbia history, 'Brother Twelve'.

The first record of Brother Twelve is about 1899. We find him working in the Dominion Express Office in Victoria. People who knew him then described his "piercing, electrifying eyes". He must have been very much like Charles Manson. His eyes were "like pools of fire with an unnerving ability to cast a long and hypnotic look at those he met". He was known as Edward Arthur Wilson at that time. Later, he took the name of Julian Churton Skottowe Amiel de Valdez. He was also called less charitable names.

One morning Edward Arthur Wilson walked into the office of his boss at the Dominion Express Office and demanded a 100% increase in pay. It was naturally refused. People who knew him at that time thought that it was a tactic to salve what vestiges of conscience he might have had and justify his embarking on a life of chicanery and enslavement.

He set out to see the world. He went to England and India.

He told shipmates that he had been born in India to an apostolic Catholic Church Missionary who had married a lady from Kashmir. She was of royal birth, he said. Certainly, there had been some exotic lineage: he had dark, swarthy skin. He claimed to have become familiar with the mysteries of the Eastern World.

He was a small, wiry man, about five-foot six. He affected a well-trimmed, pointed beard.

He said his visits to the Orient taught him to be a mystic. He claimed to have become a swami and a seer. He collected books on theosophy and studied them.

His studies included marine skills and he obtained mate's papers in a short time. Then he became a Master Mariner.

His next exploration took him to Genoa, Italy. There he came into the mysterious cult of the 'Eleven Masters of Wisdom'. He studied their teachings and passed a series of extremely difficult tests and became accepted as one of the Masters. He became 'Brother Twelve'. He was proclaimed as an ambassador of the Messiah and, as such, was gifted with messianic powers.

He wrote a small book entitled 'The Three Truths' which outlined his dogma.

In 1927 , he moved to Southampton in England. There he announced he would hold a meeting for the local people to hear his plan for a new society. The people of the town flocked to see and hear him. After his first meeting, his supporters begged to learn more of his plans.

He told the assemblage that he was the only man living who could complete the 'Sacred White Circle'. He then went into a trance, so he could "reveal a golden opportunity to a chosen people." He was wrapped in white. He put on an unforgettable display, wailing and groaning and apparently undergoing dreadful pain. While Brother Twelve communicated with the spirits, the crowd waited breathlessly. Finally he came back to consciousness and shouted that 'a great guiding message' had been given to him.

"Doom!" he shouted. "Civilization will crumble. I am the Chela. Follow me to British Columbia and we will found the earthly branch of the White Lodge. I have never been to that place, yet the Masters of Wisdom have disclosed to me the exact spot in North America where we must lay our foundations."

He called for a pencil and paper. He proceeded to draw some kind of diagram. The audience was completely rapt. None of the people present could interpret the diagram, but they all knew it was sacred and significant. They could see some sort of intricate map.

He told them he was fated to go to a Nirvana and found a colony which would be called the 'Home of the Aquarian Foundation'. All that was needed now, he said, was to acquire enough money to bring the dream to reality. His admirers wasted no time in amassing a considerable sum of money.

Mr. and Mrs. Alfred H. Barley, a chemical engineer and his wife, handed over $100,000.

With a few workers, he went to the town of Cedar in British Columbia — a half dozen miles south of Nanaimo. When the settlement was completed in 1927, the Southampton converts came to the new world. In that year, there were over 8,000 members of his cult who were contributing.

During the early days of the institution, conditions were not bad, and it was easy for the leader to bind his disciples to him. His first step was to warn one man against the other. By methodical brainwashing, he brought them under his complete control. The faithful believed that he would destroy their very souls if they were disobedient.

Many of the new colonists came from very well-to-do backgrounds. For example, Sir Kenneth McKenzie of Tunbridge Wells, England was one of them. Mr. A. Laker, a wealthy newspaper editor of a British Publication called 'The Referee', emigrated. Maurice Von Platen, a millionaire builder of organs from Chicago, moved to Canada. Joseph Venner, a publisher of a newspaper in Akron, Ohio, also joined. Bob Kieshner, an ex-secret service agent, also succumbed. A man who made millions in the poultry and egg business showed up.

Neighbors of the commune expressed wonder that so many intelligent and successful people could be so victimized. They pointed out that newspaper pictures of him were very unimpressive. His eyes stood out in startling contrast to his bony, scant-whiskered face.

One resident said, "He was only a little guy, but he acted like he owned the whole world, including me!"

"He was a brilliant man," said another. "He could have been successful at any line he chose."

A woman added, "How he appealed to those women, I simply can't understand. He just looked like a repulsive old man to me. He had a large wart on his cheek. The whiskers couldn't hide that!"

A Mrs. Mary Connelly came from North Carolina. She was 62 years old, and a grandmother. She left behind her good name as the leader of a posh circle of society in her town. She was immediately accepted, along with a check for $23,500. We will hear more of this woman, later.

Brother Twelve went east on a recruiting trip. He met up with a Mrs. Mynite Baumgartner in Clifton Springs, New York. At a meeting, he told her she was the reincarnation of the Egyptian goddess Isis. He explained that he recognized her because he was the reincarnation of Osiris. She was apparently easily convinced. He told her that fate had decided that she was to rule the group at his side. They returned to Cedar to take over their thrones.

There was an impediment to this happy coronation, however. Brother Twelve already had a wife in the colony. Her name was Alma. When she expressed displeasure at accepting the new consort, she was accused of 'lacking trust'. She suffered a dreadful beating and was ejected from the colony.

Mary Connelly entered the sacred confines of Cedar to meet appeal after appeal for more donations. She gave $1,500 for an engine for his boat, $10,000 to purchase the DeCourcy Islands, and many other sums for a number of purposes.

A new building was needed, he told her. While his earthly body had rested in the 'House of Mystery' his spirit had received new revelations, he claimed. The Masters of Wisdom, in their ghostly supervision of the colony, had noted the lack of privacy which was needed for a true refuge of brotherly love. He had therefore been instructed to secure, in the DeCourcy Islands, a school and a great castle, to be known as 'Greystones'. In this magnificent estate Mary was to have a nice little home.

Mary agreed. She later got the home, but at Cedar. Brother XII sold her a small house, built with her own money, and charged her three times the actual value.

Shortly thereafter, he decided a part of the flock should move to Valdes Island.

Since Mary was running short of money, the Chela decided she was a nuisance. He had her moved to Valdes and assigned her to a miserable shack.

Legally, all was tied up neatly. His foundation was registered under the 'Friendly Societies Act'. Under the charter, Brother Twelve held all powers.

On Valdes they built the mansion called 'The House of Mystery'. This was his personal domain.

The settlement worked assiduously at becoming self-sustaining. There was a community water system and a large community hall (which was bugged with microphones). There was an efficient Delco lighting system.

His consort, Mynite (aka Isis) became pregnant. She was destined to give birth to 'the Second Christ', the flock was told. When the fateful day arrived, the cult all gathered in breathless anxiety. After the birth, it was discovered that the child was a girl. Brother Twelve raged and ranted. The colony was in turmoil. Brother Twelve told them that the misfortunate child was the product of 'their doubts'. Poor Mrs. Baumgartner was labeled as 'demented'. Isis was rejected because she had proved faulty. Her mental condition became so serious that she went into a deep depression. She was removed from the colony without ceremony and put in a nursing home in Victoria, where she was adjudged insane. She was transferred to an asylum and all trace of her was lost to history. No one knows what happened to the unfortunate girl baby.

As more people flocked to the two settlements, a new ruling was decreed. Men and women, even husbands and wives, were to be segregated. When one family came from the U.S. and the wife was forcibly separated from the children and their father, the woman went to the Nanaimo police. The gendarmes came to the island paradise and were met at the dock by Brother Twelve who told them she was "a poor, deluded woman". But she was immediately reunited with her family. The police were satisfied and left. The man and his wife realized that their days with the cult were numbered. They found a boat and escaped one dark night.

Brother XII now found another consort. She was Mabel Skottowe. History does not record where she came from, but the Chela installed her as his companion and secretary. She was renamed "Madame Zee."

"She is my eyes, my mouth, and my ears," he told his followers. "What she says, you are to take as coming from me." She was also his bed-partner.

Ex-cultists later remembered her as a dazzling young woman with shining hair. She became a devil in woman's form, they said. She would dress in skin-tight pants and high boots, naked above the waist, and would wield a bull whip over the workers without mercy. Rumor had it that orgies took place in the 'House of Mystery'.

Poor old penniless Mary Connelly was removed from Valdes and sent to DeCourcy to one of the outposts. She was dropped off on the beach with her belongings and forced to carry her furniture and bags to a shack. When she finally got her things installed, she was ordered to paint the building completely.

When she complained that she couldn't reach the area of the rafters, she was beaten for her laziness.

Madame Zee took instant dislike to a new couple who arrived. Mr. and Mrs. George Crawford were young, and Mrs. Crawford was beautiful. They handed over their life savings when they arrived and were put to work under the whip-wielding overseer. Zee singled out the woman for special cruelty. She was forced to work in fields which had to be cleared and was not even allowed to use tools. Shortly, her health broke and she was taken from the fields and became a goat-herder. She became sick from exposure to the weather and she and her husband were expelled from the community.

Word of the conditions in the two island enclaves reached Victoria, and Brother XII became leery of investigation by the authorities. He ordered that fortifications be built on DeCourcy. These took the form of earthworks which were invisible to approaching boats. When they were completed, they were manned around the clock. A case of rifles and ammunition was shipped from Edmonton. Women guards were stationed in lookouts. When a suspicious craft appeared, the dauntless leader would take refuge in the woods in the center of the island. Guards would fire over the heads of possible intruders. Many people still living in the Islands claim to have been shot at by Brother XII's riflemen.

Another young couple came to the island. They had accepted an invitation from the guru to visit. He was attracted to the beautiful young wife. He and Zee persuaded her to return with her husband to Seattle from where they had come, then leave him and return to the colony.

She showed up a few days later, and disappeared into the House of Mystery with the Chela and his concubine.

The young husband didn't take his abandonment with resignation. He went to Chemainus where he borrowed a boat and rowed back to the island to get his wife. He was caught by the guards and held at gunpoint overnight. The next morning, the colony's boat took the man over to Yellow Point, near Cedar, and dropped him.

The husband finally went to the R.C.M.P. The police launch brought him back to the island. Brother XII denied any knowledge of the woman. After the man and the policeman had left, he ordered the wife to be taken to a lonely beach on Vancouver Island and dropped off.

For some unknown reason, the couple never filed charges against the mystic.

Cracks in the edifice built by the charlatan began to appear. One of the faithful, Bob Englund, told other members that he had gotten access to the record books and had discovered that vast sums of money that had been contributed had disappeared. Another member, who had been an attorney before coming to the group, also encouraged the members to take action.

Robert Englund found the courage to go to Nanaimo and talk to the police. The prosecutors had heard continuous rumors about the group's finances but had no hard evidence to act on. Now they felt that they had a case.

Another splinter group went to an attorney, Victor B. Harrison, who had an office in Nanaimo. He agreed to help them bring civil actions.

Brother XII discovered the revolt and sneaked aboard the ferry 'Princess Elaine' and fled to Vancouver. The police were waiting for him on the dock. He was returned to Nanaimo.

But the foxy leader was prepared to take the initiative. He went into court and accused Robert Englund of stealing $28,000. He pointed out that the terms of his charter put him in complete control of the funds. Englund was arrested.

People still remember the trial. It was called "the most bizarre legal proceeding in the town's history."

There was a strange array of witnesses on both sides. A kind of magic descended on the courtroom. Some of the witnesses fainted on the stand. Some faithful held 'magic trinkets' in their hand to ward off the evils of the law. Some wilted into incoherence under Brother XII's gaze. Many forgot the facts of the case.

In a strange twist of fate, Mary Connelly, the poor woman who had been defrauded and misused by the group, appeared as a witness for Brother XII! She testified that her money had been indeed an unconditional gift.

The eerie drama came to a climax when the prosecutor, Tom Morton, began his summation to the jury. In the midst of his oration, he suddenly and inexplicably became mute! He floundered pathetically, swayed, and then dropped heavily into his chair.

The verdict: Robert Englund was found guilty and sentenced to serve a term in Ocalla Prison Farm. He went to jail and was lost from history.

But Brother XII did not escape unscathed. His charter was revoked. He returned to his remaining flock and held a number of meetings to assure them that he was still in control and that the discipline must become even more stringent. The members knelt in a circle and accepted his orders. They promised to return to "duty, sacrifice, patience and faith".

In order to build up his population and funds, he made regular visits to Vancouver where he courted the susceptible —especially the women. Without questioning his power and prophecies, they turned over their money to him.

He had a yacht built in England. It was a 'Grimsby Fish Trawler' in type. He named it 'Lady Royal'. In it, he and Madame Zee set sail from England to Panama. In that country he hired two natives to work for him for minimal wages. When the boat arrived in Nanaimo, it was met by a man with a truck who took on board a number of wooden crates. The driver told people that he thought each crate held about $3,000 to $4,000 in gold, judging from its weight.

His paranoia increasing, Brother XII began to fear that invaders would go around his battlements on DeCourcy by going through the small cut between that island and Link Island. He gave orders to take 25 sticks of dynamite and blow up a tree so it would fall across the narrow passage to block it. The huge tree merely shuddered at the blast and remained standing. The guru's fury exploded. He was said to have become nearly insane. When obscene words and curses failed, he stood speechlessly thrashing his arms in rage.

Long-suffering Mary Connelly came back into the picture again. She had a change of heart and went back to the authorities. She told them that she had misled them at the trial. She had not made her gift unconditionally and wanted her money back.

The Nanaimo police had begun to assemble a dossier that had some substance this time.

Item: a 76-year-old ex-school teacher, Sara Tuckett, who had donated thousands of dollars was ordered to commit suicide by jumping off a cliff. She refused and went to the police.

Item: one of the elders had been directed in a letter to 'kill by etheric assassination' the Honorable R. H. Poley, Attorney General for British Columbia; Hon. Joshua Hinchliffe, Minister of

Education; E. A. Lucas, a Vancouver barrister; and Maurice and Alice Von Platen, a wealthy California couple who had left the cult.

The elder, who had been trained by the Chela, was at a loss as to how to kill by 'etheric assassination', so he waited for the master to teach him.

In a training session, the leader uttered dark incantations and summoned the soul of the chosen victim to stand before him. Then the mystic attempted to sever the spirit with vicious slashes of his hands, like those of a kung-fu artist. The subject did not die, however.

Item: one disenchanted member escaped, but feared for the safety of his family which he had left behind. From Galiano, he phoned to Vancouver Island and hired three launches to meet him on a beach on DeCourcy at midnight. He then returned to his family and they all labored to carry their belongings, plus what they thought was a fair share of the supplies they had contributed, down to the rendezvous.

Under the cover of darkness, the family loaded the bundles and boxes onto the launches. In the early morning, they landed on Vancouver Island. They were the only ones to completely recoup their investment as far as history records.

They went to the authorities and filed a complaint.

The leader became aware of these defections and became frantic. He began a wholesale house-cleaning and evicted a number of members who no longer had anything to contribute. Strangely, none of these rejectees went to the authorities. They simply faded from the area and returned to pick up their previous lives.

Clyde Coates recalls that his father, a neighbor of the colony, told the story many times of being summoned to the compound and hired to transport, on his boat, many heavy boxes. As they were taken on board, Brother XII kept track. The Coates' boat was then driven to the 'Lady Royal' which was at anchor and the boxes transferred to its hold.

As his payment, Coates was allowed to return to the island and remove and keep a vast quantity of supplies. Coates owned a store and he sold the surplus items off during the next few years.

The final act in this drama took place in court in Nanaimo. This time, it was the unsinkable Mary Connelly appearing as a witness against Brother XII. By this time, the goings-on in the islands were known all across Canada and the trial opened with reporters from most major newspapers in attendance.

Even with all the evidence, the outcome was not a clear vindication of Mary Connelly or a defeat for the guru. She was granted a token settlement only.

When the authorities came to serve the writ on the swami, he had flown the coop. He and Madame Zee were not to be seen. The police found everything in shambles. The buildings had been dynamited and wrecked. The water tanks were riddled with bullet holes. The doors to the 'House of Mystery' were smashed; even the fruit trees had been uprooted. The beautiful 'Lady Royal' was found on the beach. It had been dynamited.

It was ten years after the breakup of the colony that the fate of the spoils was discovered. News came from Switzerland that a man had just died there during World War II, leaving 50,000 pounds in a Swiss bank. Routine investigation detemined that it was the long-sought Brother XII.

Legal proceedings began to restore the loot to its rightful owners. As far as can be determined, the process has not yet been completed.

One more fascinating item remains. Some $240,000 has not been accounted for. There are people who still believe that it is buried somewhere on DeCourcy Island.

If you decide to ask for permission to dig (it is all private property now), you might take your shovel in hand and go ashore on DeCourcy Island near the passage to Link Island where some of the old outbuildings can still be seen.

11. Valdes and Gabriola Islands: The Northern Seawall.

Valdes Island shields the De Courcy Islands from the sea. It is like a ridge on the moon—almost totally uninhabited. A third of it is an Indian Reserve. Loggers are among the few who have explored it. A number of old logging roads lead up into the hills. The only homes are found near the bays and point on Porlier Pass, at Shingle Point, on Gabriola Passage and a tiny community at a cove on the north shore near **Detwiller Point,** called **'Starvation Bay'**. It has no ferry service.

Gabriola Island, to the west of Valdes, is a rapidly growing retirement and summer home territory. Roads follow much of the south shore of the island down to Gabriola Passage. The relatively low land at both ends of the island has made it attractive to farmers and retired homeowners. Strictly speaking, it is not one of the Gulf Islands, but we have included it because of the worthwhile spots on Gabriola Passage and the anchorages on the west end in **Fairway Channel.** It has frequent ferry service.

Valdes Island: By now, you have become familiar with that name. He was a famous Spanish explorer of this region in the 1790's. The names he designated for many of the features have stuck through nearly two centuries.

We have discussed the bays and points of Valdes in the Porlier Pass section of a previous chapter, in order to provide continuity in information about traversing the Pass.

Let's pick up the Valdes shore west of **Cardale Point.**

There frankly isn't much to offer a boater on this coast.

The cliffs are steep and wooded from Cardale to Shingle Point. In the rocks just before you reach Shingle Point we found a formation that looked like a modern sculpture of a human face. An outcropping looks like a brow, beneath it are two small triangles resembling eyes and a large triangular nose. Once we saw that

Find the man's face.

tableau, we began looking for more figures and thought we saw a lot of them, but our imaginations were in high gear by then.

Nearing Shingle Point we saw a rock onshore with a big white letter 'W' and on an adjacent rock there was a big white splotch. We couldn't imagine what it meant. It apparently doesn't indicate 'Water' because there is no sign of fresh water or a spring there.

Shingle Point: This is a small Indian Reserve on a beautiful sloping beach. A logging road ends at the shore on the east end of the Reserve. There is a nice home here. Signs on shore warn that "Trespassers will be prosecuted under Federal Reserve Law."

On the point itself, there is an attractive gazebo on the beach. Behind it, there are two houses. One of them is blue and the other resembles a mountain chalet with a TV antenna. Since there is no power tie with Vancouver Island, it must be powered by a generator. A triangular day beacon near the house indicates a fishing boundary.

Leaving the Reserve, the shoreline gets a little steeper but flattens out again at Blackberry Point.

Blackberry Point: There is no habitation here. The logging road that leads to the Reserve ends here. Bill Wolferstan, an author who writes for Pacific Yachting Magazine, mentioned in his beautiful pictorial and cruising guide of the Gulf Islands, that there was a point on Valdes that was called 'Strawberry Point' locally. It was the site of some ancient Indian burial grounds which have been badly

Shingle Point Indian Reserve

desecrated over the years by marauding yachtsmen. We wondered if it were the same point.

As we neared shore, we saw some signs of campsites. We could see a log suspended from the fork of one tree to the trunk of another. Beneath it were old boxes. We stopped and kayaked ashore.

On the west end of the flat point there is an old hulk that must have been there for decades. The shore above it is a very pleasant meadow. We hiked down the logging road toward the other end of the point. At one point we saw a box with open ends, chicken wire and a hasp. It looked like some kind of animal trap. There were fire-pits. It is possible that small boat crews had gone ashore and camped there.

Near the hulk is a rock that is one of the most fascinating natural formations we have seen. It is probably 15 M. long by 3 M. high. Standing on top of it, you can see that it has been split by the elements into several curved sections that look like heavy flower petals carved out of stone. In the fissures between the sections the crystal clear sea-water flows in and out. It has a look of magic about it.

The water is shallow enough to anchor off a drying reef, but it would only be a lunch-hook stop.

The cliffs west of Blackberry Point and across from Pylades Island have the most dramatic sea-carving we have seen in the Gulf Islands. For a mile or so, the sandstone has been blasted by the waves which have created shell-shaped holes of various sizes. Interspersed are sharp geometric figures. From a distance, it looks almost like some kind of Egyptian frieze. You can make out almost any picture you can imagine. There are serpents and human faces and rampant animals. Be sure to have some color film when you pass this area.

Chart #3443 will show you that there is nothing but flat steep coastline on the south shore of Valdes up to Gabriola Passage.

As you near Gabriola Passage, you can turn to Chart #3475 for plans in this area.

There is a bight about ¼-mile east of Dibuxante Point. The dolphins that are mentioned there are staging areas for log booms. There are also some private mooring buoys in the area.

Dibuxante Point: That word means 'draftsman' in Spanish. The spot was named by the Spanish explorers for their mapmaker whose name was de Cordero. A reef extends 150 M. into the entrance to Gabriola Pass. On the tip of this drying ridge there is a white tower with a red band on top. It has a quick flashing red light, visible for 6.4 miles.

The cove northeast of Dibuxante Point has a couple of pilings in a small niche between two reefs. We did not see the private beacon listed on the chart.

Wakes Cove has a private breakwater and dock and offers little space for anchorage because of private mooring buoys. It is open to northwest winds.

Cordero Point is also named for the Spanish mapmaker. The passage narrows to 91 M. here, between Valdes and Josef Point on Gabriola.

Kendrick Island: The point facing the Passage has a sign welcoming members of the West Vancouver Yacht Club. The main island, which lies in a northwest to southeast direction, is part of a chain of islets and drying reefs. The dock and buoys of the yacht club are in the bay which is called 'Dogfish Bay'. A resident of Valdes told us that there was a bottomfish processing plant there at one time. This is a good sheltered moorage.

The northeast shore of Valdes has only a couple of bights with local names. The first one southeast of the reefs off the north boundary of the Indian Reserve is called 'Cable Bay'. The cove at Detwiller Point, about 2½ miles northwest of Porlier Pass, is called 'Starvation Bay'. There is nothing of much note from Detwiller to Porlier Pass except some reefs which are as much as 0.4 miles offshore.

The Strawberry Point rock and beach.

Gabriola Passage: This is a popular shortcut between ports in the Vancouver City area and the Gulf Islands. The maximum current on both ebb and flow can be as high as 8 knots. It would be well to wait for slack in this passage in Silva Bay or Dogfish Bay when coming in from the Strait. Pirates Cove and the anchorages in Ruxton Passage are good holding areas when waiting in Pylades Channel for slack water. The critical area of Gabriola Passage is about 2 nautical miles.

Although the Passage is narrow at one spot, there are no hazards in the fairway. You can get in deep you-know-what among the numerous islands and reefs east of the pass, however. So be on the lookout for **Thrasher Rock, Gabriola Reef,** etc.

There are two favorite anchorages on the Gabriola side of this passage, Degnen Bay and Silva Bay.

A tug labors through Gabriola Pass.

Degnen Bay petroglyph.

Valdes History

The south end of Valdes with the northern tip of Galiano form the boundaries of Porlier Pass (Cowichan Gap) through which salmon travel in season on their way to the Fraser River. A small community of Indians owns a limited amount of land on both sides of the pass for a fishing station. A pioneer wrote: "It used to be a pleasant sight on a summer morning — after daybreak — the best time; to see the little canoes being paddled, shuttling backward, forward and across the swift current towing the salmon lines; surrounded by such beautiful scenery. Not always a very safe occupation though! They say one reason for letting even their boys' hair grow fairly long, was that if by accident they fell overboard from one of the canoes — and most of their travelling was carried out in this way — it made their rescue easier.

"A mile or more northward from the pass a native named Ce-Who-Latza, Valdes Chief, had his home on a harbour partly protected by a little peninsula.

"This intelligent Indian had acted in early days as a sort of pilot among the very difficult and unknown channels our gunboats had to navigate at times, and thereafter wore a naval cap. Also, in greeting, he gave the naval salute — with gravity and dignity as if to the manner born. His sons were skilled boatbuilders, and each — there were several of them — played some musical instruments to form a band of sorts. The priest used to pay periodical visits to this little community — they had even a private cemetery on their land, which was doubtless a government grant. Also in the very early days when ships from Mexico perhaps found their way here. Someone had most likely given Ce-Who-Latza a cow or calves of their special breed, for as they multiplied one saw cattle, mild enough in appearance, but with great and rather fearsome wide spreading horns — not to be seen elsewhere — I think these must have all disappeared by this time. The family, in imitation of their new neighbours, built themselves quite a big house, which outwardly was fairly true to type; but once indoors it was seen, not to be divided into rooms, but followed more the pattern of an Indian community lodge.

"Apart from these two native districts, Valdes as well as the DeCourcy group nearby, belonged to an ex-captain of the

At times, current boils through Porlier Pass.

Royal Navy, who after retiring from Her Majesty's Service commuted his pension, a practice fortunately since forbidden, to take up interest in Virginia, U.S.A. The venture resulting unsatisfactorily, this family whose name is among those counted by Heraldry to be the oldest traceable in British history, came out to British Columbia and was given a grant of land on the island already mentioned. For their home, they chose the northern shoreline of Valdes, which forms with its neighboring island lying across from it, as it were, the narrow Gabriola Pass. This was about ten miles or so from Nanaimo, their nearest town in point of contact.

Here they lived for some years, and as travelling was always by water, it was noticed that though the two sons were experienced enough in managing their boats, the Captain himself did not seem to acquire skill in adapting himself to small craft of the kind, and had to be assisted in getting out of difficulties from time to time—someone making the remark that he might get into them once too often.

"This happened under circumstances which might have overtaken the most experienced. There is in winter and spring at times a dreaded northerly wind in these parts; the kind which as you may be rowing on a quiet water and happen to lift your eyes, can see in the far distance a black line across the channel; making one grip the oars firmer and consider themselves fortunate if they are near enough shore to reach shelter before the fierce wind reaches them.

"It was such a storm which overtook the captain on his way back from Nanaimo where he had gone in his sloop to receive packages and heirlooms from England. It was known he had started homewards; but except that his sloop was found wrecked on the shore of a distant island, no trace of its owner was ever found—or its contents.

"In time to come a young granddaughter's name—the same as his own—came into sad prominence; when, during the Great War, the Germans bombed one of the hospitals at Etaples in France, where she was among the nurses, and was one of the casualties. A tablet to her memory has been placed in St. Paul's Anglican church, Esquimalt.*

Captain Valdes

Commander ('capitan de fragata') Cayetano Valdes, of the Spanish Navy, commanded, in 1792, the exploring vessel 'Mexicana', and in 1791 had been first lieutenant with Captain Alessandro Malaspina in the corvette 'Descubierta' (Discovery). In the summer of 1792 Valdes, in the 'Mexicana', under the orders of Galiano in the 'Sutil', assisted in the examination of the channels between what is now Vancouver Island and the mainland. After returning to Nootka, the vessels sailed for Acapulco and San Blas.

Promoted to captain, circa 1795, his name appeared in that rank with Galiano. He was present at the battle of Trafalgar, where he commanded the Spanish line-of-battle ship 'Neptuno', 84 guns. This ship, like Galiano's, was captured by the British, but when a gale came on at the close of the action, she was wrecked between Rota and Catolina, when many of the survivors of the battle lost their lives. The island was named by Captain Richards, 'H.M.S. Plumper', 1859.

The homey Degnen Bay government dock.

Degnen Bay has the familiar red-painted government dock. The approach is made by continuing in the passage until you clear the islet in the entrance and can see down into the bay. The point across from Dibuxante is not named. It is a small Indian Reserve. Passage should not be attempted even at high water between this point and the tiny islet in the entrance; it is shoal. Note there is a reef which dries at 1.7 M. in Gabriola Pass at the entrance to Degnen Bay. Stay near the cliffs on the northeast side as you enter the bay.

A mud flat fills the west head of this bay. The foreground of this flat has anchorage in 1.2 M.

The public wharf in Degnen Bay is well-known as the most hospitable one in the Islands. It is overseen by a very warm and gregarious lady, Jane Wardiel, who decorates the float with hanging flower baskets. She occasionally comes around with delicious homemade goodies. There is 124 M. of moorage. This is also the site of a famous petroglyph on the shore near the north end of the bay.

There is room for anchorage in 7 M. adjacent to the dock.

It's a very popular spot.

Josef Point is quite high and rocky. There is a reef-filled bight just northeast of this point but local knowledge says it is very poor anchorage and the currents are very tricky.

Drumbeg Provincial Park is a 20 hectare (50-acre) park about a mile south and east of Degnen Bay. It is not a marine park.

Silva Bay Approach: The preferred route from the Gulf Islands to the Strait is to go east around **Rogers Reef**. The reefs you see on the chart that extend out from shore and north from the lights have less than 1.8 M. of clearance at lower water. The passage between Breakwater Island and Rogers Reef is deep and free of hazards. Kelp beds are found on the north and east side of the reef. The light is a white tower with a quick-flashing white light and can be seen for 5 miles.

Breakwater Island is windswept and low and you can see the Strait beyond it in spots. It has a flashing red light which can be seen down the passage. At night, head toward the light and keep the Rogers Reef light to port.

As you pass along Breakwater Island you will be able to see the white tower of the **Tugboat Island Reef**—head toward it.

On the shore of Breakwater Island you will see a big log crib. We couldn't find out what it was used for. You will be looking out into the Strait and you can make a decision about heading out into it at that point. If you decide to enter the Strait, you can pass either side of the two almost-linked islands, **Bath** and **Saturnina.**

Pass either side of the **Tugboat Island Light** or, if the tide is in, you can take a shortcut through the passage between **Sear Island** and Gabriola. The water can get down to 1.2 M. at lower water in there. The sure shot is around **Tugboat Island.** When you turn between Tugboat and **Vance Island,** favor the Vance Island shore as you pass the green light mounted on a mast with a white and green square daymark.

Silva Bay: You may find this protected port chock-a-block with anchored boats. One of the reasons for the popularity of this place is that the offshore waters are good fishing grounds and there is abundant anchorage in the bay.

The extensive docks that you see on the bay side of Tugboat Island are part of an out station of the Royal Vancouver Yacht Club.

There are two marinas in Silva Bay: The Silva Bay Shipyard and the Silva Bay Boatel.

The shipyard has a complete marine facility for repairs, with a railway capable of handling 150 tons and a 12-ton travelift. It has welding service, diesel and gas inboard and outboard service, electrical and electronic shops, hardware, chandlery, surveying, and moorage. There is a small store and gift shop connected with the yard.

Entrance to Silva Bay.

Silva Bay Boatel has a laundromat, a well-stocked grocery store which carries fishing gear and offers late fishing information.

It also has transient moorage.

There is a road from the ferry landing at Descanso Bay at the opposite end of the island to Silva Bay.

There is some anchorage in the small cove between the islet off **Lily Island** and **Law Point.**

West of Gabriola Passage, the shoreline of Gabriola becomes steep and extensive drying and submerged reefs reach out into the end of Pylades Channel.

Gabriola Residents

Gabriola Island's popularity didn't just begin in the 1960's when off-islanders began to enjoy the seclusion and relaxation of island living. In the 1930's there was a factory which produced millstone wheels from the consolidated sandstone east of Descanso Bay. Another factory produced bricks from the shale at False Narrows.

Settlers began farming and logging in the last part of the 19th century, more than 100 years after the Spanish explorers discovered the island.

But the Indians were the first residents of the island, having lived there since the birth of Christ. An anthropologist wrote in the 1880's:

"I still find it incredible that these people, certainly not the savages they're thought to be, pack up their village each year and move it to the mainland and then back here again (Newcastle Island). This village, called 'Saysetsen' by the natives, is occupied from September to April, at which time these people move over to Gabriola Island to fish for cod and to gather clams and the tuber of a blue-flowered lily called 'camass'. In August they move to the mouth of the Fraser River in time for the sockeye and hump-back salmon runs. Once these are finished, they move back here and catch dog salmon." (From 'Ghosts of Newcastle Island.)

False Narrows: There are two schools of thought concerning taking your cruising boat through this passage. One says only a madman would try it. The other says it's a piece of cake.

Well, we went through it up and down in our kayaks and we want to say that we probably could do it—but we ain't gonna!

Sure the currents in there are only about half as strong as they are in Dodd Narrows. But when they are running, it would make the trip something like slaloming down a ski slope in your boat.

If you're dead set on doing it, here's our advice:

Approaching from Pylades Channel at low tide, it looks like the whole danged area is filled with rocks. But there is a course that can get you through except at low minus tides. The shallowest you are likely to encounter is 3 M. at lower water. It will look a lot shallower than that, though. The water is cold and clear in that area, and you can look down and see shell bottom remarkably clearly.

As you enter, you will find depths from 0.6 M. to 3 M. if you stay close to the **Mudge Island** shore. You will see a nice beach on the south shore which has a piling. We know that the chart #3475 says there are 6 pilings there, but we saw only one. Just beyond that is a curved reef which looks like a giant crab's pincer. But you will not get to it if you line up the red beacons on the Gabriola shore, and head towards them. Tip: don't get much off course to the west. You will see a respectable crop of kelp. This beacon system gets you past the first no-no.

Now, you have a long slender reef that parallels the shoreline. It is closer to the Gabriola side than it appears on the chart. You should run quite close to the beach on Gabriola. You will pass a road which leads down to the water and you will see a phone booth next to the road. This is probably put here so you can row ashore and call somebody to haul you off the rocks! Incidentally, you may not see any kelp on this side of the center reef.

False Narrows has kelp-covered reefs.

The next bugaboo is a shoal that comes out from shore and curves right in front of you just beyond the second set of beacons. When you reach them, turn southwest keeping them lined up behind you. It may help to take note that the course aims roughly toward a stairway on the Mudge Island side. Again, there is little or no kelp to guide you around this shoal. Continue on this course until you are fairly close to the Mudge Island side and can see down Percy Anchorage.

Do not be confused by the big red and white boards on the uplands in Percy Anchorage—they signal the power line that flies overhead.

Just at the exit to False Narrows there is a park with an extraordinary beach. It is called locally, 'The Brickyard', because it was once the site of a brick works. The whole beach is strewn with broken pieces of brick, stamped 'Dominion'. There is a public toilet in this park and a couple of picnic tables, and a garbage can. It's too shallow to offer anchorage, though.

Percy Anchorage Public Dock: It's marked on the chart, just a little east of the power lines. We never noticed it before. It's a tiny one. It has about 30 M. of moorage space. There are no amenities offered. In a recent pamphlet put out by the Ministry of Fisheries and Oceans, it is not even listed. It may have been abandoned. We noted that it has not been painted the characteristic red—it's blue.

This dock was in constant use a few years back during a ferry strike. The road down to it is a one-laner, with no turn-outs. Gabriola folks remember the hair-raising encounters and the traffic jams getting down to get on a passenger boat to go to Vancouver Island. There is a private dock right next to the public one. You may see a tiny old rusty yard tug tied up to it.

The Gabriola Island shore of False Narrows has a lot of homes on the beach. They call it 'Clam Beach'. The title is an apt one: we stopped and waited for the current to change before heading back through the passage. While we waited, we dug a bucket of clams with our bare hands.

On the trip east, a number of seals on logs on the Gabriola Island shore plopped into the water and swam out and huffed and puffed at us as if they were annoyed by our interference.

Percy Anchorage: The water depths are ideal for anchorage, but the prevailing winds down Northumberland Channel could make it chancy.

Descanso Bay: The Spanish explorers dubbed this body of water 'La Cala de Descanso', which means 'The Bay of Rest'. It offered a haven for crews who had ridden out storms on the Strait. The name is apt today. It could be called 'The Bay of Retirees'. This is one of the most heavily-populated and prestigious islands of the Gulf, with more than 4,000 residents. A ferryboat makes an all-day series of turn-around runs between Nanaimo and Descanso Bay. It's a Shangri-la for Vancouverites who want an island hideaway. They can cross to Nanaimo and over to Gabriola in several hours and spend most of their weekends in their summer digs.

Some of the scenery from the west and northwest shores is breathtaking.

While Gabriola Island has a large population, the only services for boaters are in the Silva Bay area. In fact, there is only one other grocery store and pub on the island, plus a service station. Although there two provincial parks, at Drumbeg and Gabriola Sands, boats are prohibited in the areas. There is also no public overnight camping.

There is a golf course and country club.

But the things we want to share with you about Gabriola Island have nothing to do with amenities. They are the spectacular and historic **Galiano Galleries** at Malaspina Point; and the fascinating pre-historic petroglyphs at the **Weldwood Site** on the southeast inland side of the island.

In touch with the past.

Galiano Galleries

The area is the site of the famous 'Galiano Galleries', which inspired pictures that hang in the Prado in Madrid. They were named that by the Spanish explorers for the commanding officer of the expedition. Commander Dionisio Alcala Galiano, in 1792, made sketches of them and wrote a report that introduced them to the European art world. They are also called 'The Malaspina Galleries' because they are on Malaspina Point. These natural rock carvings are remarkable for two very diverse reasons.

First of all, the sandstone has been worn away by wave action into a series of grottoes. Like giant shells, they have been sculptured into whorls and scallops. In places the sandstone is as thin and intricate as a Chinese ivory carving. In one of the shallow caves, a thin stalk of rock rises from the floor like the leg of a ballerina and widens as it reaches the ceiling into an abstract form that could be human or bird. The patterns seem to follow no natural rule of order. You could study them for days and find new designs.

But the second aspect of this wonder is one that almost makes you want to break into tears. On almost every plane and curve of this gallery is the handiwork of spray-painting vandals! Strangely, graffiti is not common in the Gulf Islands. We saw very few examples of defacing of the natural beauty. But it's almost as if the full fury of people angry at natural grandeur has been vented on these sculptures.

A woman who lives nearby said, "I never look at the gallery during the day because it makes me so sad to see the mindless desecration of something so beautiful! In the late evening, the surfaces are shrouded in shadow and the paint splotches tend to recede."

"But who would do a thing like that?" we asked.

"It's the kids," she sighed. "Sometimes I think every teenager in Nanaimo has been over here with a spray can or a knife."

She explains that it began decades ago when some island youngsters found that if they painted their initials on the rock, the wave action would not wash away the painted surface and it would become embossed. You can still see some of those old initials; the paint has long ago vanished but the letters stand out sharply, two or three inches in relief. With the passage of time, paints got more wear-resistant and the introduction of the aerosol spray paint made it easy for one kid to write whole sentences on the rock.

Several years ago, interested people hired some youngsters to remove the paint, but the job was too difficult and the results were disappointing. A few months later, the visiting vandals found new fresh surfaces to mar.

We pointed out that there were no signs forbidding graffiti. Our friend said, "It wouldn't do any good. It would only make it more of a challenge for them."

We are happy to say that we found more of these gallery carvings on another shore which is not so accessible to visitors. We do not want to pinpoint the location, however, for fear that they too would be defaced. However, if you cruise in close to shore in that general area, you might be rewarded with a sight of this smaller gallery.

Malaspina/Galiano Galleries.

Across The Centuries

We stepped out of the cool evergreen forest on Gabriola Island into a large rocky clearing. Hot summer sun shimmered over gently sloping sandstone, interspersed with tufts of grass and moss. Only the buzzing of the bees and the raucous cry of crows broke the silence that encompassed us. The tangy scent of dry cedar and fir hung in the air.

Scarcely daring to speak above a whisper, we tiptoed across the sandstone, hunting for the petroglyphs we knew were there—somewhere. We walked slowly, searching the pitted surfaces of the rocks with each step, not wanting to step accidentally on an ancient carving.

"Maybe that's one," Jo said, pointing to strange marks on a stone.

"No," said our kindly island guide. "That's where a bulldozer blade scraped across the rock." How could anyone have dared to run a bulldozer in this hallowed spot, we wondered.

Then we found pock marks on a rock. They seemed to take on a shape, although nothing that we could immediately recognize. We got down on our hands and knees and ran our fingers wonderingly across the ridges and grooves.

"That's one—you've found them," said our friend. "Now you'll see them everywhere". We had discovered what we would later think of as a 'serpent'.

We looked around. He was right. Now that we knew what we were looking for, it was easy to find them. We located a fish, a crab, a bird, a human head and all kinds of other figures. Later we found the 'dancing man'. This stick-figure picture became our favorite of all the carvings. Maybe it was his joyous appearance, with his knees bent and his arms flexed at the elbows—as though he were doing a Highland Fling.

Grandson Kwin, who was with us, was fascinated by him, especially when the guide said that he had a hole in his side where the bad spirits could leave his body. He also had a plume or a crest, which supposedly distinguished supernatural figures from ordinary mortals.

We laid a piece of cotton fabric on the heated rock and held it in place with stones. Then, carefully feeling the carved-out areas, we began rubbing with crayons. Jo hadn't done anything like this since she discovered rubbing crayons over nickels while she sat at her desk in the fourth grade. Neither had Al. But 12-year-old Kwin took to the technique like a natural.

We talked in hushed tones as we worked, still awed by the spirits that filled the clearing. We were caught up in these symbolic carvings carrying messages across the centuries from one culture to another.

We were at the 'Weldwood Site' on Gabriola, the first stop in our search for

Rubbing of "The Dancing Man."

the ancient carvings. The thrill of that initial discovery is still with us.

Our first acquaintance with petroglyphs came from Al Wilding, a charter boat operator in the San Juans, who took passengers to study petroglyphs in Desolation Sound. We were fascinated.

We didn't realize they existed in the Gulf Islands until we met Grant Keddie, of the Archeology Division of the B.C. Provincial Museum in Victoria. We were in the capitol doing historical research for this cruising guide to the Gulf Islands. We had found Grant, buried deep in his office among shelves and trays of primitive artifacts. He is obviously a man who loves his work.

He gave us reams of technical data on middens (prehistoric garbage dumps, actually), and decorative lip plugs called 'labrets', as well as the more familiar items. He used scientific terms to describe glacial periods, most of which we skimmed through but didn't quite fathom.

It was Grant who turned us on to Gulf Islands petroglyphs.

We decided that people who cruise in the area should at least be aware of the legacy of these carvings. Even if they didn't particularly want to go to the trouble of finding them, they should know about them. Those who really want to find them and enjoy them will do so. Others will at least have an awareness of their existence.

An easy place to find them is to visit Petroglyph Park just outside Nanaimo. This exhibit has been established to preserve them. Many original carvings are located here. The park also provides concrete replicas for people to touch and to do rubbings. One of the carvings may have been done as long as 15,000 years ago, according to scientists.

We found a book written by Mary and Ted Bentley, called 'Gabriola: The Petroglyph Island'. We pored over this delightful book and decided we had to find the 'Weldwood Site'. The Bentleys had discovered those wonderful carvings in 1976 and had carefully documented and photographed each one.

A mutual friend introduced us to Mary's parents who live in Degnen Bay. They took us to the site. As grandson Kwin whispered when we saw the carvings, "It's awesome!"

Who were these Indians who had so painstakingly pecked out these symbols in the sandstone? What do they represent? When did they do all of this?

The Bentley book, which you can find in B.C. book stores, says they were undoubtedly carved by the Coast Salish Indian shamans, using various sizes of sharpened hammerstones. They also say that it is almost impossible to accurately date petroglyphs, although there is some evidence that they may go back to 2,000 or 3,000 B.C.

Maybe they were done to record legends or myths. Perhaps they were hammered out near streams to draw spawning schools of salmon. They might even have been done simply as works of art. The Bentleys believe that most petroglyphs came into existence to serve religious functions.

"Probably the most significant purpose petroglyphs achieved was in association with an individual's pursuit of spiritual power and guardian spirits," the Bentleys wrote.

"The ritualist or shaman training-site was an isolated, secret area. The Kulleet Bay pool on Vancouver Island and the Gabriola Weldwood Site suggest such mystical centres where shamans and solitary individuals endured a self-inflicted ordeal of physical torture, praying, fasting, retching and cleansing in an effort to experience hallucinatory visions.

The Weldwood Site is a small clearing.

Perhaps the young carver hoped to acquire the strength of the spirit conjured in his trance by incising it on stone."

Another researcher, Douglas Leechman, said perhaps adolescents may have recorded their mystical visions on stone to exorcise the power of frightening monsters or to retain the forces of guardian spirits.

Although we didn't take time to fully research petroglyphs, we did buy Beth Hill's wonderful book, 'Indian Petroglyphs of the Pacific Northwest', so we could try to locate other glyphs in the Gulf Islands.

A Degnen Bay site is perhaps the easiest to locate. It is near the head of the bay on the beach. It is described as a 'killer whale' by local residents, but we thought it more resembled a porpoise.

It's on sloping sandstone below the high tide line. It was first documented over 100 years ago by a provincial surveyor who used it as a section line marking point on August 18, 1874. There are other sites further inland on Gabriola, and we have visited them.

Those petroglyphs which we found deep in the woods on Gabriola still fill us with a sense of mystery and admiration. They are truly elegant, we think. We hope others will feel the same and help preserve these legacies for future generations to enjoy.

We were struck by a quotation from Wilson Duff's book, 'Images: Stone B.C.'.

"Stone's lastingness makes it a proper medium for man's eternal truths."

12. Vancouver Island Gulf Ports.

After a week or so of ducking into some of the inviting anchorages in the Gulf Islands, boaters often find themselves wanting a few of the urban luxuries and head for the Vancouver Island shoreline marinas. There are a number of government docks and commercial facilities from Sidney to Nanaimo.

By and large, the public facilities in these ports are disappointing. The public docks are often small or crowded with local pleasure boats and fishboats. Many of the dock managers show up only to collect moorage and then disappear. It is seldom that there is anyone around to direct boats into available slips. Usually, moored transients will come to the aid of a skipper coming into a dock. Some of the docks are in poor shape. Some have garbage and discarded gear strewn on them. Often, the dock is quite a distance from the shopping centers, so it becomes a chore to buy groceries and ice and haul them back to the ship.

We have talked to merchants in these towns and they tend to agree that more should be done to make the visiting boater feel welcome. They say that the fishing fleet has been for years the economic mainstay of the area. Mayors, leading citizens and even the Chambers of Commerce think of tourism as being tied to the main highway. We think they are overlooking a good bet in the patronage of the visiting yachting people.

The commercial facilities, on the other hand, are usually very much aware of the value of the boating public, and they do their best to provide for their needs. Almost all of them are faced with two inescapable facts. One, the kind of facilities most needed by visiting boaters require considerable investment: showers, laundromats, fresh-water lines, adequate electrical power and fuel pumps are expensive to install and maintain. Two, boating tourism is growing slowly, and it will be a while at this rate of growth before the improvements are financially feasible.

Possibly one of the reasons the Gulf Islands are slow to adjust to more visitors is the attitude of the governing body, the Islands Trust. This group, which supervises land use planning and meters growth, has apparently not been enthusiastic about newcomers. A resort owner told us that the policy of the Islands Trust is: "tourism without promotion". We couldn't find out whether that was an official policy or a philosophy.

On the other hand, one of the joys of boating in the Gulf Islands is that there are not a lot of transients—compared to the San Juans, for example. Most boaters tend to scoot through the Gulf Islands, missing some of the neatest anchoring and beachcombing spots in the Pacific Northwest, and hurry up to Desolation Sound where they are in a virtual sardine-pack of boats.

However, there are so many little-known hideaways that it may be a decade before you will find your favorite spots crowded.

Okay—enough preamble. Let's start discovering the Vancouver Island ports.

Cowichan Bay: While we are in this area south of the Narrows, we should investigate what the local folks call 'Cow Bay'. **Separation Point** is really a point. It has a white tower 20 feet high and a flashing white light. There is a focusing lens that throws its brightest beam on a bearing of 304 degrees which is toward the entrance to Genoa Bay. It is named Separation Point because it acts as the limit of the Sansum Narrows and Satellite Channel. There is a white rectangular daybeacon on shore just west of the point.

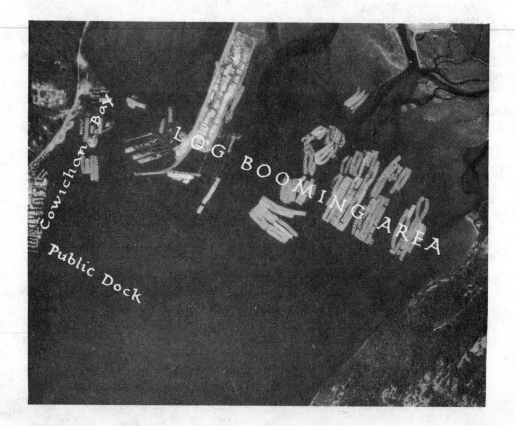

Cowichan has one of the biggest public docks in the Gulf area.

The government wharf at Cowichan Bay has 566 M. of moorage space. It has electric power, 20 amps. There's water on the dock, garbage disposal and a grid. A telephone booth can be found up on the pier.

Pier 66 offers some moorage, a gas dock, ice, and boat rentals. They have a repair shop for outboards and I.O.'s. Their hours during the summer are 8:30 to 8:30, and in the winter 8:30 to 5:00. The Bluenose Marina has very clean and convenient showers and a laundromat. There is transient moorage and free overnight moorage for dinner guests. They sell propane, they have a chandlery, fishing gear, charters and boat rentals. The Bluenose Restaurant is fully licenced and has a tank from which you can select a live lobster to be prepared for your dinner.

A resort called 'The Inn At Cowichan Bay' has a couple of licenced lounges, an indoor pool, a whirlpool and a sauna.

There are four ship repair facilities at Cowichan Bay. Coastal Shipyard has a ways, cleans bottoms, and permits owners to work on their own boats. Covey Marine has a ways and a skilled diesel mechanic. Cowichan Shipyard works on fishboats and occasionally on pleasure boats. Anchor Marine has a coffee shop and a repair facility, and some moorage.

The Masthead Restaurant is just above the Government dock and has a very popular pub called the 'Black Douglas'. It has beer available for 'off sale'.

Cherry Point: This very rounded point, 2½ miles south, off **Boatswain Bank** has a marina. It doesn't look like it on the chart, but it's there. It has primarily leased moorage but they do have some space for transients. There is a ways available. There is no repairman on duty, but they have men on contract. It is possible for owners to work on their own boats. They have space for campers and RV's and there are washrooms, but no showers. There is a launching ramp, too.

Genoa Bay Marina is a homey place.

Proceeding west along the shore of Cowichan Bay, you come to a cove which is not named on the chart, about a half-mile northwest of Separation Point, but which is called **'Antoine Bay'** by local boaters. It has a very attractive beach and there is room for about four boats at anchor. An old-timer who loves to spend the night in this bay says he waits until evening when the lunch-hook sailors depart.

Genoa Bay: This is one of the most protected anchorages in the Gulf Area. It is protected from northwest winds and partly from southeasterlies which sometimes whistle up Satellite Channel. Chart #3470 gives you a blow-up of Genoa Bay. Although there is good detail, the area can be confusing. The chartmaker lists a black buoy at the breakwater. Actually, it is a green buoy (they are all being changed to green now) but we could swear that it was much further out in the channel, almost abeam the red marker.

The square figure you see on the chart is the symbol for an aquaculture installation. It is there. It looks like a series of salmon-pens. We didn't see any names on the houses at the end of the dock.

When you round the pens, you see Genoa Bay Marina.

Entre nous, we keep promising ourselves that we will keep an objective attitude about commercial establishments. This is important in a book that does not solicit advertising. But we were really charmed by Genoa Bay Marina. The people were so friendly and casual that we found ourselves planning to return and spend some time there.

It's run by a very pleasant couple—the Lambrechts, Len and Helga. She has acquired quite a reputation among B.C. and U.S. boaters for her cooking skill. She has written several cookbooks and they have a charming little restaurant at the marina.

There is a lot of moorage for transients. They have a laundromat, showers, a fuel dock, a book-exchange, a store and they carry propane. There is a marine mechanic on the premises, too.

Our next stop will be in the Maple Bay area of the Vancouver Island side of Sansum Narrows. For more information on Sansum Narrows, check the chapter on Saltspring Island where we treat the whole of this waterway.

Paddy Mile Stone is a whopper, about (2 M.) in diameter. It looks like it had been rolled onto the beach by some giant. It's on a point which is the south entry to Maple Bay. Where did that name come from? The only clue we have is a note by Bill Wolferstan that says it may have been named "after Ailsa Cragg near Culzean in Scotland" by some homesick Scot, possibly.

Maple Bay: This is a bay which is screened by tall mountains on Saltspring from nor'westers and is secure to the southeast. Birds Eye Cove, in the southeast head, is even more sheltered. Maple Bay has long been a favorite spot for yacht club rendezvous from both B.C. and the U.S.

As you swing around the points on the east shore of Maple Bay, you will see an impressive home on a point near the entrance to Birds Eye Cove. At the entrance to this cove, you see a big red and white sign on shore reading 'SLOW!' A few hundred yards beyond is a second sign of similar design reading 'SLOWER'! Birds Eye is narrow and there are a lot of boats moored in a small area; wakes from speeding boats could cause problems.

The little bay at the head of Birds Eye Cove, tucked in behind the unnamed island, goes completely dry at low, low tides. It's a fun place to explore by shore boat, and the island is a park reserve so it's okay to let the kids run there.

Maple Bay Marina is at the end of the cove. It has transient moorage and an alluring restaurant at the head of the dock: the 'MAI TAI'. It also has a pub and a store. Showers and propane are available.

Birdseye Cove Marina is just north of Maple Bay Marina. It has an ESSO gas dock. There is a remarkably complete shipyard next to it, which has a railway, a hoist and a straddle-lift.

The next dock belongs to 'Camp Imadene.'

Maple Bay Yacht Club has a large marina. There is a kiosk at the end of the float. Signs on the docks warn that mooring cables extend out 80 M. and boats should not anchor off the floats. That is a necessary imprecation, because there is very limited space to anchor in Birdseye Cove.

Proceeding up the shoreline at the head of Maple Bay, you come to the Public Wharf. It has an H-shaped float with 107 M. of space. There is a boat launching ramp nearby. (You can see the symbol for this on the chart; it is a small black triangle.) Above the government float is a large building with the word 'Store' printed on it.

North of the public dock is an installation of the Royal Canadian Sea Cadets.

Maple Bay is clearly a resort community. There are dozens of homes along the beach.

Leaving Maple Bay, following the northwest shore, you come to **Arbutus Point.** with its gently rising headland. Around the corner, so to speak, you will see the terminus of a complex of overhead power lines. Ten cables vault over the Narrows at

Maple Bay Yacht Club

this point. There are marker boards on both sides of the narrows, calling your attention to them—as if you could overlook them! They are, according to the chart, 61 and 66 M. above the high tide. They look a lot lower when you pass under them, but at those heights, your mast should clear.

Next as you head north is **Grave Point** with its flashing green light.

Crofton: This is a mill town and a ferry terminus for the boat from Vesuvius on Saltspring Island. It is in **Osborn Bay.** It's the site of the Crofton Pulp and Paper Mill. There is a breakwater and a public dock with two long floats which provide 308 M. of moorage. One float is reserved for fish-boats, however. There is a big crane, a boat launch ramp, garbage disposal, power and water on the docks, and a phone booth. There is a grid over near the ferry dock.

On shore, you will find a coin-op laundry, a hotel with a pub, a hardware store, coffee house, beauty salon and a store.

Notice we have not mentioned a liquor store so far in these Vancouver Island ports. We asked a couple of guys who were chatting outside the Brass Bell Restaurant in Crofton where the nearest liquor store was. One of them said, "Duncan." The other offered, "There used to be a great bootlegger here, but he died 7 years ago." The first guy said, "That's the way it goes with cottage industry."

Incidentally, chart #3475 has a good blow-up of Osborn Bay.

Chemainus: (Hold onto #3475. It's good for this port and for Ladysmith, too.) Now this is a town you have to see! It is famous for its murals. Up in the city center many of the walls of the buildings have been used as giant canvases for paintings of the history of the area. There is a tourist information booth made out of an old caboose. The town is on the Island Railroad. There is a picturesque little station which you will want to photograph, especially when the train comes in.

There is a liquor store up in the shopping center. There is not a single pub open to the general public in the town, however.

As far as the waterfront is concerned, the facilities leave much to be desired.

The government wharf has 320 M. of moorage, but no running water and no power. The dock manager does not have an office on the dock, so he parks his pickup on the wharf, with a sign in the window announcing that the dock manager is present—or can be called at a telephone number on the sign. There are sanikans; they are put there for the ferry patrons who travel to Thetis and Kuper Islands.

The floats are in poor condition and much of the space is taken up by local boats, some of which look as if they haven't been used for decades. It's okay for a quick visit, but not very attractive for an overnight stop.

There is a small shopping center near the dock, but it is a long haul up into the main part of town. The Chamber of Commerce has provided stenciled footprints on the sidewalks to show you how to make the half-mile trek.

Some nice folks run a grocery store called the '49th Parallel' which is at the head of the dock. There is a laundromat and dry cleaners about a block away.

"Chee-may—nus!
Chee-may-nus!"

The murals seem to leap out at you.

The British General and the Spanish Virgin

It was named after Lady Smith in Natal, South Africa, which was also a coal mining city. Her maiden name was (get ready for this:) Juana Maria de los Dolores de Leon. She was a descendant of Ponce de Leon.

She met and married her future husband, Major General Sir Harry Smith at the time of the battle of Salamanca, in 1812, when she was 14 years old. Here is a report on the meeting of the Spanish noblewoman and the General.

The diary of Sir Harry says: "After the slaughter at Bajados, a scene of horror I would willingly bury in oblivion, the atrocities committed by our soldiers on the poor and defenseless inhabitants of the city were dreadful. Yet this scene of debauchery, however cruel to many, to me has been the solace and the whole happiness of my life for thirty-three years. A poor defenseless maiden of thirteen years was thrown upon my generous nature through her sister."

A friend of his recounts their meeting. "I was conversing with a friend at the door of his tent, when we observed two ladies coming from the city, who made directly towards us. The elder of the two threw back her mantilla to address us in that confident heroic manner so characteristic of the high-bred Spanish maiden, and told us who they were, the last of an ancient and honourable house. Her house, she said, was a wreck, and to show the indignities to which they had been subjected she pointed to where the blood was still trickling down their necks caused by the wrenching of the ear-rings through the flesh. For herself, she said, she cared not, but for the agitated and almost unconscious maiden by her side—she saw no security for her but the seemingly indelicate one she had adopted—of coming to the camp and throwing themselves upon the protection of any British officer who would afford it, and so great, she said, was her faith in our national character, that she knew the appeal would not be made in vain nor the confidence abused. Nor was it made in vain; nor could it be abused, for she stood by the side of an angel; a being more transcendingly lovely I have never before seen, one more amiable I have never yet known." (From 'British Columbia Coast Names' by Capt. Walbran.)

Ladysmith: This town once was called 'Oyster Harbour'. The origin of the name is a charming story.

Like its neighbor and rival, Chemainus, this town has made little concession to the visiting boater. The public dock is somewhat better than the previous one. It has 450 M. of moorage, 20 amp power (it's called 'hydro' in B.C.) and water. but it's a hike of almost a mile up to the shopping area. Over the years, the visiting boaters have made a path through the woods which is something of a shortcut. Take along a container when the blackberries are ripe.

To find this path, go up to where the parking lot meets the road. You will find a small office building there. It belongs to a nice guy who manufactures concrete floats. He is hoping to build a marina there. He seems to be the only person around who gives a damn about boaters—and he's neat!

Just beyond this office, to the left, you will see where the path begins. Follow it up the hill, across a side road and a railroad and up to another road which parallels the highway. The path takes you to a laundromat, filling station and two restaurants. There is another '49th Parallel' grocery in Ladysmith; it is the nearest the marina. To get there, you go up the hill one block past the fried chicken restaurant and turn right. Then walk about 4 blocks—away from the town, incidentally. Unless you have your own private sherpa on board, your best bet is to call a cab.

Oh, there are a couple of pubs in the town.

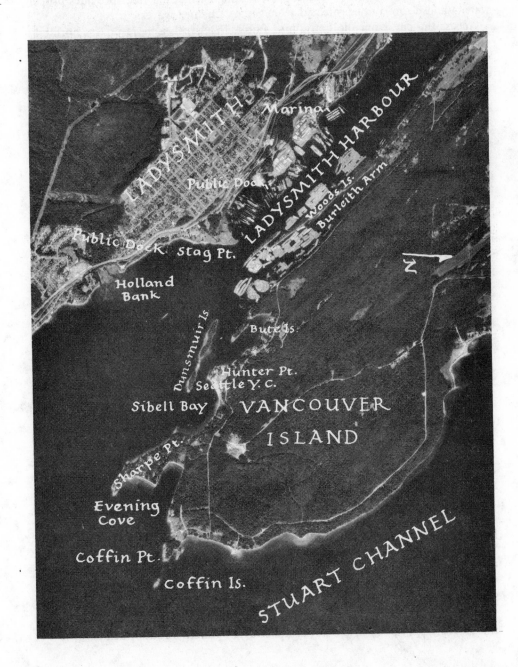

Ladysmith Harbour: Looking at chart #3475, you would think there were a great number of good anchorages in this harbor, but in reality the many log booms and rafts take up much of the space. **Burleith Arm** looks ideal, but it has little free space. The head of the harbor is very shallow and there is a long fetch from Stuart Channel. Some anchorage at high water can be found between **Dunsmuir Island** and **Bute Island,** but the cove is too shallow to provide for many boats. **Sibell Bay** is attractive but only the space adjacent to the small Seattle Yacht Club float provides proper water—and it too is not protected from Stuart Channel waves.

Across the bay from the Ladysmith Public Wharf, in a more or less northerly direction, is the well-known 'Manana Lodge and Marina'. They offer moorage, rooms, bed and breakfast, showers, laundry, licenced restaurant, fuel, power, water and 'gourmet waterfront dining'.

Farther northwest is 'Ivy Green Marina' which offers complete repair facilities and also sells diesel and gas.

Evening Cove is located at the end of Ladysmith Harbour between **Sharpe** and **Coffin Points.** The shore is part of an Indian Reserve. There are some attractive summer cabins just off the sandy beaches; they may be on land leased from the Indians. There are good anchorage depths in this cove except for **Collins Shoal** where it will reach 1.2 M. at datum level. It would be ideal anchorage during the prevailing summer northwest winds; it would be a bad spot if the winds switched to southeast as they often do. One clue is the fact that there were not any private mooring buoys in this cove when we looked. That often means that the area gets hairy.

Coffin Island has a green topped tower on an exposed rock. Between this flashing white marker and **Coffin Point** there is one rock which dries at 0.6 M. If it is not visible, it would be unwise to make a shortcut through there. **Nares Rock,** which is due west of Coffin Point, has no marker and we couldn't see any kelp to warn you. Give the area a wide pass. On the shore you will see a boat launch ramp and a cluster of mobile homes. From this point northward there is no beach and few visible houses.

Kulleet Bay is surrounded by an Indian Reserve; the Kulleets are an ancient and well-respected tribe. Wolferstan has a fascinating story about the origin of the name.

Historians record that there were only 65 Kulleets in the area in 1905. Maybe the white man's drink and diseases fulfilled the prediction of Chief Broken Chest.

Kulleet Bay is a pictorial delight! On a calm day, it is a wide expanse of crystal clear water with only a few homes along its shores, the homes of the tribal members. At the head of the bay is a large building which is called 'The Band House'. It is a tribal headquarters. A small community surrounds it.

The northern shore of the bay is very inviting for anchorage. The water is quite deep up to near the shore. There is a very small cove up near Deer Point, but it has a private mooring buoy in it and there is not enough space for an anchored boat.

On the south shore, you will find a tide flat within two rocky fingers. A reef which dries at 0.9 M. stands out at right angles to the shoreline. Chart #3443 shows a triangular daybeacon with the notation 'not' but it was not in place when we walked that beach. It is probably a harbor limit marker.

There is a very ancient cemetery on high ground above the marsh. Some of the present Kulleet forebears are buried there.

The band house of the Kulleets.

A marker in the Indian graveyard.

Chief Broken Chest

"An interesting story about the origins of the local Indians has been related by Harry Olsen: Apparently an early Shaman interpreted some of the carvings at the pool as a prophecy telling of "the coming of a black-faced man (early coal miners?) who will bring a new drink that drives men mad so they kill one another in their madness. These strangers will also bring new diseases that kill in many terrible ways until our village will be empty and trees will grow where our houses now stand". The villagers were very troubled until one of them had an inspiration.

"Only the magician can read the markings on the rock. If we kill him, perhaps all those terrible things won't happen." Thinking this was a good idea, the tribesmen ambushed the magician and drove a spear through his chest.

Two moons later, the man they believed was dead strode into the village nd threw aside his cedar bark cloak.

"Look at me," he shouted, "I have a hole in my chest and I am still alive. Spears cannot kill me and all the things I told you about will happen."

They called him 'Tsa-meeun-iss', meaning 'broken chest' and he became their chief. They were so proud of having a chief with a hole in his chest, they began to call themselves 'the Tsa-meeun-iss people'.

By the time the first white man arrived, the Tsa-meeun-iss people had spread from Kulleet Bay to beyond Chemainus and had villages on many of the closer Gulf Islands.

('British Columbia Coast Names')

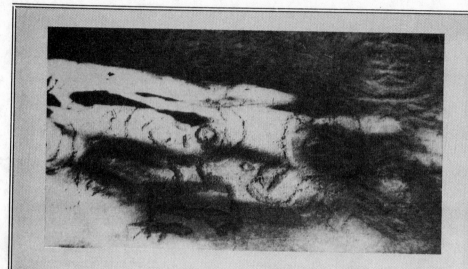

The Shaman's Pool

This is a famous Indian rock carving, and it is relatively easy to find. It is on the Indian Reserve land at Kulleet Bay. The residents of the area are proud of it and they are willing to lead visitors to see it.

We anchored 'Sea Witch' off shore in about 5 M. one sunny afternoon and kayaked to shore to find it. We had a fair idea of its location. The reference in the Beth Hill book, 'Petroglyphs of the Pacific Northwest', says that it is in a stream that empties into the saltwater near the head of the bay. We walked along the shore studying the bank, but couldn't find a trace of a stream. Finally we decided to go up the road to a house and ask the owner if he knew how to find it.

There were two houses on a road which comes down along the shoreline. One of them had a satellite TV antenna in its front yard. The other had a boat-trailer and a nice outboard boat. As we neared the house with the boat, we saw a young man sitting on the front stairs. In the lawn in front of the house, there were two small tow-headed children playing. As we got within speaking distance, we asked him if he knew where the petroglyph was.

The man and the kids all responded immediately. "I'll show you," he said pleasantly. The boys started out ahead. "It's this way! It's this way!" they shouted.

Their father said, "My grandfather used to show people the pool — and I guess his grandfather before him did too. Now my kids are ready to take over."

We asked if he had any idea how long it had been there.

"I seems like it must have been there forever," he said, matter-of-factly.

We went up the road for a few hundred yards and the children took a path that led into the woods away from the shore. We walked for a few yards and then followed the kids on a path that led off to the left. When we came into a small clearing, he pointed to a shallow, rock-lined depression.

"There it is," he said. He and the children left.

We stood looking at it in wonder. It was called 'The Shaman's Pool' because it was a ritual bathing spot for the tribe. It was a very small pool, no larger than a bathtub. Rock faces made up the slanting sides of the pool. On the two long sides, almost every inch of space had been filled with figures.

Most of them were faces, some were human bodies. A few could be recognized as fish or birds or deer. The side nearest the path seemed to have many more faces than the opposite one. It almost looked like some sort of meeting or confrontation—the two groups of faces staring across the opening at each other.

We tried to see if we could find any difference between the two groups of faces. Was one side the white man and the other the Indian? Was one group made up of spirit people and the other mortal beings? The side with the greater number of faces had all of the animal representations. Could that have been significant?

The light under the trees was dim, so attempts to get photographs were not very successful. It seemed wrong somehow to suggest using flash-bulbs.

We went back to the Indian and his children and thanked him. We said that we would return to the site the next morning and see if the light was better. He nodded.

The next morning, the man was not there, but his father, whose name was Edward Seymour, volunteered to accompany us.

He seemed to be as proud of the carvings as the son was. He told us that the pool is still being used by the tribe for a kind of ritual baptism for young people.

Both males and females, we asked? Yes, both. When did the ritual take place? In the winter, he said.

The light was only a little better. We tried to bring out the incisions by pouring water on them, but it didn't help much. We had been told by archeologists that it was considered vandalism to put chalk or any kind of artificial accentuation on the pictures.

We took some rubbings, but they are not among our best. The lines are rather faint and hard to capture on cloth with wax.

Before we left, we dropped off a couple of six-packs of beer as a gift. They were well-received.

Finding the spot is not difficult. Come along the north shore until you see the road which can be seen running along the shore. You will see the two houses. If you want to ask for help, the people in either house will be willing to assist.

If you want to find it by yourself, walk along the shore until you come to a large culvert, possibly 16 inches in diameter which runs under the road and can be seen behind some bushes on the shore. Cross the road and find the other side of the ditch that ends up in the culvert. There you will find a path. Take the left trail at the Y. That's it. We hope you feel some of the wonder we did when you see the Shaman's Pool.

Incidentally, petroglyph sites are protected by the B.C. government.

Look for this culvert, leading to the Shaman's Pool.

The "Inn of the Sea at Yellow Point"

Far out on the **Coffin Point** shoreline, the chart shows a boat launch ramp. This is probably an old logging road incline. There is a petroglyph on a rock on that shore somewhere. The description of the location hints that it may be near a log dump. We couldn't find it, however.

Yellow Point Lodge: One of the most famous resorts on Vancouver Island is this historic and scenic establishment at Yellow Point. It has been a favorite spot for Canadian and American visitors for decades. For a few years recently it was occupied by a film and recording company, but it has now returned to catering to vacationers.

It is not a stop for transient boaters, however. The point has no natural breakwaters and the log dock and small floats are not equipped to moor cruising boats. If you wish to visit or have dinner there, it would be necessary to make arrangements by phone before arriving.

Just west of Yellow Point, near **Nicholson Cove** you will find the **Inn of the Sea at Yellow Point.** It offers moorage, swimming pool, laundromat, garbage disposal, ice and a fine restaurant with a licenced lounge.

There are several more resorts with docks along this coast, but no anchorages until you reach Boat Harbour.

Boat Harbour: Stymied by the currents at Dodd Narrows? Is the wind making up and you want a protected anchorage? Some daring souls drop the hook around behind **Round Island.**

But a much more convenient and safer spot is Boat Harbour.

The entrance is flanked by **Flewett Point** to the southeast and a long and threatening reef to the northwest. This unnamed hazard is marked with a red triangular daybeacon. Just behind the marker you will see a drying rock at most tides.

The approach to Flewett Point has a long reef and a rock that has 1.2 M. over it. The reef becomes an ugly, mossy spine at low tides.

The harbor itself is somewhat shallow in configuration. It consists of two lobes, the northerly one being behind **Reynolds Point.**

The better of the two coves, the southeasterly one, is nearly all taken up by two extensive private docks and a couple of mooring buoys. Some anchorage can be found up near Reynolds Point in about 2 M. The upland has many houses fronting on the beach.

The coves are protected from typical storms from both the northwest and southeast, but there are often gusts and strong breezes from the other quarters.

Incidentally, the older charts indicate a rock off Reynolds Point. More recent editions do not. That makes for uneasiness, doesn't it? What happened to that rock? It wouldn't just disappear. Which chartmaker was making a booboo on his chart?

Well, we looked for that rock and couldn't find it. We didn't see any kelp in the area, but we can't guarantee it isn't there. Remember the adage: "always err on the side of chicken!"

Dodd Narrows: Let's have a 'heart-to-heart' about this 200 M. stretch of water.

We know the boating guides all warn you that the current can run up to 10 knots at the spring tides, and, of course, that's true. They also warn that tugs and small freight boats sometimes hog the pass, that's also true. We also know that before you have made this little trip a few times, it can be a source of frazzled nerves. Some skippers regard it as only slightly less perilous than going over Niagara Falls in a plastic bag.

We suspect that if you goof monumentally and get there at the wrong time, you might have a circus ride. But we have never heard of anyone who got piled up on the rocks. Scuttlebutt has it that there are back eddies along the shore that will keep you out of harm's way. Of course, if you have a conveyor belt of water running at 10 knots under you, you might end up coming out of the chute backwards or sidewise. Unless you can run at about 20 knots, you will not have much steerage in a following current. If you have less than 10 knots you will sit there and spin your prop trying to fight your way into it against the flow.

If this is your first time through, let us offer some easy advice. Figure out (or ask somebody who knows how to do it) when the slack water is. Then get there about a

Tugs and tows often crowd Dodd Narrows.

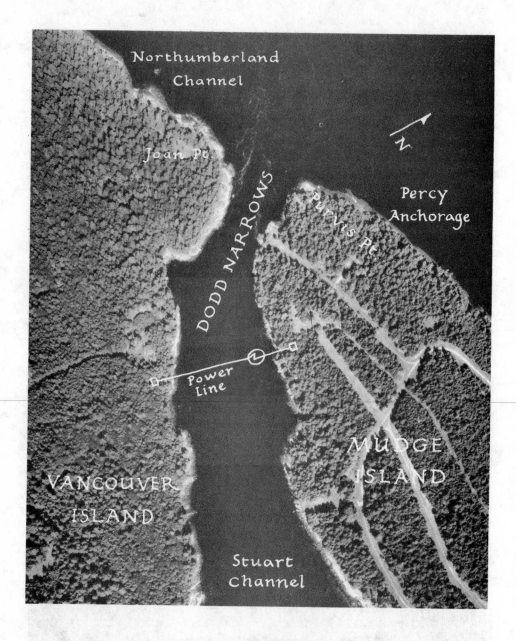

half hour early, if you can. When you arrive, you will find a number of boats which have been stalling around in the wide spot in the channel. Find one or two like yours. When they go in, you follow. Simple, n'est-ce pas?

You're likely to have a much bigger problem than coping with the current if you discover that there's a tug with four sections of logs entering from the opposite side. But don't worry, he'll leave you a clear, if slightly narrow, path.

One more vital bit of information: Dodd Narrows used to be known as 'Nanaimo Rapids'.

And yet another: it was named after Capt. Charles Dodd who worked for the Hudson's Bay Company in the 1830's. He skippered their boats.

Nanaimo: This town's name came from an Indian word: 'sne-ny-mo' which meant 'a whole strong tribe'. Five tribes made their homes there and apparently formed a confederation. When the white man came, he discovered great beds of coal in the earth and the indigenous folks were elbowed out of the way.

Nanaimo Harbour: The public dock in Nanaimo is called 'The Port of Nanaimo Small Craft Basin'. It has 1710 M. of moorage. It is located behind a breakwater and is sheltered from winds and wakes. It has water, 'hydro' (power), a grid, laundromat, showers, bathrooms, garbage disposal, ice and several phone booths. It has a gas dock, too.

Yes, it has all of the amenities you could ask for. But the biggest advantage of this basin is—it's right in the heart of town. There is a world of shopping within a short stroll. The liquor store is an easy walk from the dock. There are plenty of pubs and restaurants and licenced premises and boutiques and bookstores and a big Safeway nearby. You can borrow their grocery carts to take your bags to the dock.

Most American boaters make a beeline to Nanaimo after clearing customs in Bedwell. They ice up, stock the galley, take on beer, maybe buy a few needed charts at the Nanaimo News Store—then it's off for Desolation Sound.

If they happen to be weathered in or are waiting for new crew members who are arriving by ferry from the mainland, they may wander around the town and patronize the watering holes. Those who do, find the place a lively and cosmopolitan small city. The stores offer everything you need.

There are several private fuel docks and moorages in the harbor. Nanaimo Yacht Club offers reciprocal moorage for many visiting yachtspeople.

The historic Bastion at Nanaimo.

Newcastle Island: This whole lovely island is a provincial marine park. It isn't one of the Gulf Islands, of course, but we're including it because we want you to know about it and enjoy it when you get to Nanaimo.

Its area is 306 hectares (that's about a mile wide and 1½ miles long—nautical miles—or 750 acres)—just across the channel from Nanaimo.

There is a public dock facility in **Mark Bay** with about 400 M. of moorage space. There is a fee for overnight stays. About a dozen mooring buoys are also provided, but there is plenty of anchorage space. There is fresh water available at the head of the dock, also a phone booth and washrooms.

In summer, the water in Mark Bay is often warm enough to swim in.

A small passenger ferry provides hourly service from Nanaimo during the summer. There are quite a few campsites and picnic tables.

Close to the ferry dock, there is a concessionaire who rents boats. Just a few dozen meters from the dock you will find a large pavilion which has a lunch counter. There are playfields, cook-out buildings, benches, firepits and an information center. There is even a beached boat for kids to play on. There is a mock-up of a mine shaft entrance.

Probably the most fascinating element in the park is the quarry where giant 'pulpstones' were cut. They are big stone wheels, looking like something out of the TV 'Flintstones' series. They were transported to Vancouver Island and sent to the various pulp mills to grind wood into small fibers.

There are 12 miles of very pleasant trails. Several come to a small lake in the middle of the island—Mallard Lake. It has no beach, so you can't swim in it. It is rimmed with lily pads and dead snags, but it's still very picturesque.

There is a launching ramp for the service boats near the quarry.

How did it get its name? Newcastle is a famous coal mining town in Britain. Remember the saw, 'carrying coals to Newcastle'? Well, this island is honeycombed beneath the surface by mine galleries. At one time it was a big producer of coal. Seems hard to believe now, the only traces of industry are those big circular holes in the rocks. The rest of the island is just a beautiful park land.

You'll really enjoy it!

Petroglyph Rubbings

We think you may become as fascinated with petroglyphs as we were when you see them. If you want to make a record of them, the best way is to make a rubbing. Photographing is difficult because the grooves are often very indistinct and shallow.

When we first started, we knew little about the process. Later, we talked with Harold and Mabel Cliffe of Gabriola. They are the parents of Mary Bentley who wrote the wonderful book, 'Gabriola, Petroglyph Island'. They told us their daughter used crayons and fabric for her rubbings. They said her technique was to study the shape of the picture, then spread fabric over the area. She ran her fingers over the surface of the rock until she felt a groove and then made careful crayon strokes away from the channel as her finger traced it.

We tried her technique and it worked fairly well. Our first ones were made with an old bed-sheet and some kids' crayons. Later, we talked to the owner of an art-supplies store in Ganges and she said that there was a kind of wax that cobblers use that comes in pullet-egg-sized lumps. We went to the cobbler in the Mouat Mall and bought two of them, one dark brown and one black. They set us back $10, but they would make a lot of pictures.

The next series of rubbings we did were with the cobbler's wax, but we found the results were not as good as with the crayons.

One of the problems you will encounter is deciding just how much of the flat surface you want to darken. We found that trying to fill in the spaces didn't improve the picture. It seemed that just outlining the grooves was best. One of the more experienced fans said that she found a flat piece of sandstone on the beach and took it home with her. Then she could take her time and darken in the untouched surfaces to the right degree. We found a good piece of sandstone and brought it home, but we haven't tried to use it. We are afraid we will make a botch of it.

We experimented with several different types of fabrics, but decided we like the results we got with off-white bleached muslin the best. Incidentally, there is no fabric-store in downtown Nanaimo, so you would do well to try to buy a bedsheet at one of the stores if you don't have the right material on board.

We made wall-hangings from the rubbings by hemming the edges and hanging them with dowels at the top and bottom. We were told that it might improve them to try stretching the fabric on frames.

As you're doing the rubbings, don't be discouraged if you can't see the picture. It is always necessary to stand back about ten feet or so to see the outlines come into focus. It is that sort of vague shape that makes them seem so mysterious and challenging.

Petroglyph Park

If you've gone all through the Gulf Islands and not had the opportunity to find one of the petroglyphs, you can stop off in Nanaimo and see an absolute gallery of them. Put on your comfortable walking shoes, take your camera and your cloth and crayons and hike south on the Island Highway. In a mile and a half, you will come to Nanaimo's famous Petroglyph Park.

It is located slightly off the road to the west at the end of a trail through a grove of trees. The park has been created to not only preserve the stone carvings, but also to let you inspect them close up and touch them and make rubbings.

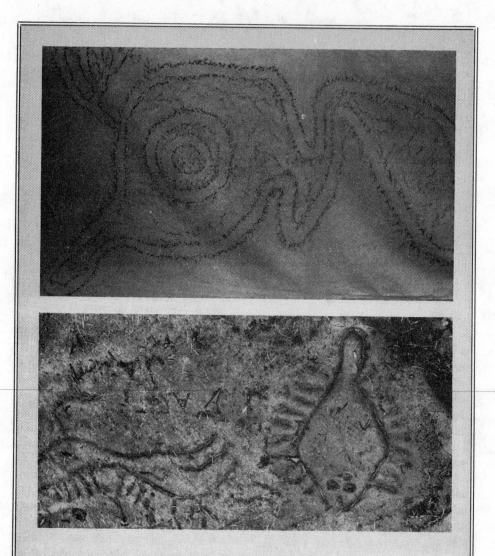

They were first seen by white men in 1860. It is believed the site was used for ancient Indian ceremonials.

The original petroglyphs on a sloping sandstone face are fenced off. They can be viewed, but not touched. Part of the display is an area in which vandals defaced some of the carvings. Concrete castings, exact duplicates of the original, have been made and set in the ground so you can do rubbings to your heart's content.

Even though this is a public park, a sense of awe and mystery still remains, particularly if you find the park on a rainy, misty day with no other visitors present, as we did.

A large information board gives you a complete rundown on the possible uses and meanings of the pictures. It points out that stone cannot be tested by carbon-dating procedures, so no one knows just how old these carvings are. Estimates range from 500 to several thousand years old.. They may well be as old as the Egyptian pyramids.

BIBLIOGRAPHY

Bentley, Mary and Ted. 'Gabriola: The Petroglyph Island'. Sono Nis Press, Victoria, B.C. 1981

Boorstin, Daniel J. 'The Discoverers'. Random House, Vintage Books, N.Y. 1983

Borradaile, John. 'Lady of Culzean', Borradaile, Victoria, 1971

'British Columbia Small Craft Guide, Vol. I, 6th Edition', 1984

'Canada, Government, Ministry of Fisheries and Oceans', 'Canadian Tide and Current Tables, Vol. 5'. Scientific Informations and Publications Branch, Ottawa, 1985

Canada, Ministry of Supply and Services, 'Current Atlas: Juan de Fuca Strait to Strait of Georgia'.

Chettleburgh, Peter. 'An Explorer's Guide: Marine Parks of British Columbia'. Maclean Hunter, Vancouver, B.C. 1985

Cole, Phil and Gwen. 'Northwest Boat Travel' 8th Edition. Northwest Boat Travel, Anacortes, WA. 1985

Conover, David. 'Once Upon an Island'. Paper Jacks

Elliott, Marie 'Mayne Island & the Outer Gulf Islands, a History' Gulf Islands Press, Mayne I., B.C. 1984

(Editor) 'Mayne Island School Centennial, 1883-1983' Mayne I. School Centenary Committee, 1983.

'Plumper Pass Lockup and Mayne Island Museum', Mayne I. Agricultural Society, 1981

Freeman, Beatrice J. S. 'A Gulf Islands Patchwork'. Fleming Printing, Ltd. 1983

Garner, Joe, 'Never Fly Over an Eagle's Nest'. Cinnabar Press, Nanaimo, B.C. 1982

Hill, Beth and Ray. 'Indian Petroglyphs of the Pacific N.W'. Hancock House, Saanichton, B.C. 1974

Hunt-Sowery, W.W., '100th Annniversary Mayne Island Post Office, 1980',

Meade, Edward 'Indian Rock Carvings of the Pacific N.W.' Gray's Publishing, Ltd. Sidney B.C. 1971

Mouat Family, 'Centennial Reunion Booklet', Saltspring I. 1985

Obee, Bruce. 'The Gulf Islands Explorer—the Complete Guide'. Gray's Publishing, Ltd. Sidney, B.C. 1981

Ovanin, Thomas K. 'Island Heritage Buildings', Islands Trust. 1984.

Reimer, Derek (compiler) 'The Gulf Islanders' Provincial Archives of B.C.' Victoria, B.C. 1976

Roberts, Eric A. 'Salt Spring Saga'. Driftwood, Ganges B.C. 1962

Toynbee, Richard Mouat. 'Snapshots of Early Salt Spring and other Favoured Islands'. Mouat's Trading Co, Ltd. Ganges, B.C. 1978.

Walbran, Capt. John T., 'British Columbia Coast Names, 1592-1906' Douglas & McIntyre, Vancouver, B.C. 1971

Washburne, Randel. 'Washburne's Tables 1985'. Weatherly Press, Bellevue, WA. 1985

Wolferstan, Bill. 'Cruising Guide to British Columbia, Vol. 1, Gulf Islands and Vancouver I. from Sooke to Courtenay'. Interpress Publications, Ltd. Vancouver, B.C. 1976

PERIODICALS:

The Province , Victoria, B.C., editions of 1896 and 1897.

INDEX OF GEOGRAPHIC FEATURES
of the people and places of the beautiful Gulf Islands .